THEMES AND VARIATIONS IN
SHAKESPEARE'S SONNETS

£4.95

D0272604

BY THE SAME AUTHOR

The Metaphysical Poets: Donne, Herbert, Vaughan, Traherne
The Three Parnassus Plays (1598–1601)
Translating Horace
The Monarch of Wit
The Art of Marvell's Poetry

TRANSLATIONS FROM RAINER MARIA RILKE
Requiem and Other Poems
Duino Elegies
Sonnets to Orpheus
From the Remains of Count C. W.
Poems (1906–1926)
Selected Works: Poetry
New Poems

TRANSLATIONS FROM HÖLDERLIN
Selected Poems

THEMES AND
VARIATIONS IN
SHAKESPEARE'S SONNETS

J. B. Leishman
late Senior Lecturer in English Literature
in the University of Oxford and
Fellow of St John's College

HUTCHINSON UNIVERSITY LIBRARY

LONDON

822.1
SHA

HUTCHINSON & CO (*Publishers*) LTD

178-202 Great Portland Street, London W1

London Melbourne Sydney
Auckland Bombay Toronto
Johannesburg New York

★

First published 1961
Second edition 1963
Reprinted 1967

WITHDRAWN FROM CIRCULATION

WITHDRAWN FROM CIRCULATION

PUBLIC LIBRARY ★ PONTYPRIDD

The paperback edition of this book is sold subject
to the condition that it shall not, by way of trade or
otherwise, be lent, re-sold, hired out or otherwise
circulated without the publisher's prior consent in
any form of binding or cover other than that in
which it is published and without a similar condition including this condition being imposed on
the subsequent purchaser

231191

© Hugh Robert Leishman and Harold Howie Borland 1967

This book has been set in Bembo, printed in Great Britain
on Smooth Wove paper by Anchor Press, and
bound by Wm. Brendon, both of Tiptree, Essex

TO THE MEMORY OF

RUDOLF KASSNER

Tu duca, tu signore, e tu maestro

Contents

III

'HYPERBOLE' AND 'RELIGIOUSNESS' IN SHAKESPEARE'S EXPRESSIONS OF HIS LOVE

Preface to the second edition

The call for a second edition has enabled me to make various corrections and supplementations, chiefly in the footnotes. The reader's attention may be particularly directed to the note on page 84, where, thanks to an article by Professor C. Schaar, which I unfortunately did not discover until after the first edition had been published, I have been able to explain the presence in one of Daniel's sonnets of a line by which every careful reader must surely have been baffled. The note on pages 145–6 was prompted by the objections of a learned friend, whose judgment I greatly respect, but with whom I cannot here fully agree.

I had supposed that in my introductory chapter I had sufficiently indicated the precise scope of this book and what I was and what I was not proposing to do. It would seem, though, from the complaints of some reviewers, that I did not announce my programme loudly enough or often enough. I will therefore say here (since it would seem to be necessary) that this book is not intended to be either a history of Elizabethan literature, or a history of the Elizabethan sonnet, or even a complete or 'definitive' study of Shakespeare's sonnets, but a study of certain selected sonnets of Shakespeare on certain selected themes, and a comparison and contrast between his treatment of those themes and their treatment by other poets.

Preface to the first edition

Portions of the First Part of this book have already appeared in *Elizabethan and Jacobean Studies presented to Frank Percy Wilson in Honour of his seventieth Birthday* (Clarendon Press, 1959), and I am grateful to the editors and publishers for permission to reprint them. For many years it had been in my mind to write about Shakespeare's Sonnets, and it was the request for this contribution that finally set me to work.

My colleagues Miss Helen Gardner, Fellow of St. Hilda's, and Mr. Donald Russell, Fellow of St. John's, were kind enough to read through the whole of the first draft in typescript and to make many most valuable suggestions for correction and supplementation in matters large and

small. I express here both my deep gratitude to them and my awareness
that by no means everything I have written carries their *imprimatur*.

I cannot omit some mention of the great man to whose memory I
have ventured to dedicate this book. In the course of my work as a
translator of Rilke I had long become familiar with many of the books of
his friend, the Austrian writer, traveller and sage, Rudolf Kassner, but it
was not until 1952 that I paid my first visit to him at Sierre, visits which
I continued almost every summer until his death in 1959. It was only
after our first meeting, when he sent me a copy of *Die Geburt Christi*,
that I discovered the great books he had been publishing in Switzerland
since the end of the war. The combined influence upon me of the man
and his books has been, so far as I am aware, the most powerful single
influence I have experienced since I reached maturity. It has been a great
liberating influence, under which I seem to have acquired a new, more
independent, more fruitful, way of looking at things.

In the course of one of our conversations during my last visit to him in
1958, I mentioned that I was writing on Shakespeare's Sonnets, and he
remarked that the only poetry that seemed to him at all comparable with
some of Shakespeare's sonnets to his friend were Michelangelo's to
Vittoria Colonna. I did not ask him to enlarge upon this remark, but I did
not forget it, and when I returned to England, I re-read Michelangelo's
sonnets. How far Kassner would have approved of what I have written
about the resemblances and differences between them and Shakespeare's,
I do not know: I record the fact, partly because his books, though seldom
about other books, are full of just such profound and penetrating com-
ments on literature, thrown out incidentally and left for the reader to
develop; partly because it is both a particular and personal link between
Kassner and this book and, more importantly, between him and Shakespeare, whom he admired above all other poets. He had a great love of
England, where he spent two long visits, made many distinguished friends
and once thought of residing for several years; his first book, written
during his first visit as a very young man, was a collection of brilliant
essays on English poets, and he later published a translation of Sterne's
Tristram Shandy. In 1911 Rilke wrote to the Princess von Thurn und Taxis:
'Isn't this man, I say to myself, perhaps the most important of all of us
now writing and expressing?' He was certainly one of the most important
both then and at any time from then until his death, and it is deplorable
that not one of his books has been translated into English. May these
few words do something to spread an awareness of this omission and to
arouse a demand that it be supplied!

Introductory

It is commonplace of criticism that there are certain obvious differences between Shakespeare's Sonnets and those of all his predecessors and contemporaries: that for no single one of them has it been possible to produce a recognisable 'source', that most of them are addressed to a man, not to a woman, and that behind the collection as a whole we are aware of situations and relationships which cannot have been invented, if for no other reason than that they have been left so tantalisingly obscure. Unfortunately, the fact of these undeniable differences seems to have been accepted by most writers on the Sonnets as something like a dispensation from the task of literary criticism, and they have either devoted their whole energies to unprofitable speculations about the identity of 'Mr. W.H.', the friend, the rival poet and the 'Dark Lady', or else, assuming, apparently, that because no recognisable 'sources' have been produced, Shakespeare's Sonnets are in the most literal sense incomparable, they have omitted from their attempts at stylistic analysis many possible and illuminating comparisons. And yet nowhere else is comparison so possible and so profitable, in no other portion of his work can Shakespeare be so appropriately 'committed with his peers'; for very many of the sonnets—perhaps, indeed, nearly all the most memorable—are concerned with a few large general topics, of which Shakespeare's treatment, both in its resemblances and in its characteristic differences, may be illuminatingly compared with that of various poets from the beginnings of European literature until his own day.

Although I am not here attempting a comprehensive survey of all Shakespeare's sonnets, and shall be mainly, if not exclusively, concerned with those which may be most profitably compared and contrasted with the sonnets and love-poems of others, it seems desirable to begin with a brief summary of my attitude to various chronological, factual and biographical matters to which, in the following study, I shall only incidentally refer.

The collection consists of two clearly distinguishable series of sonnets. The first series (1–126) is addressed to a youth, or to a very young man, of great beauty (in 108 he is called 'sweet boy' and in 126, not a sonnet but a poem of twelve lines in couplets, which may or may not have been written after the sonnets which precede it, he is described as 'my lovely boy'), and the poet frequently insists both on their great difference in age and their great difference in social position (36, 87, 111, 117, etc.), which he laments as a barrier between them. The first seventeen sonnets urge the youth to marry and perpetuate his charms through offspring, a theme which thereafter disappears and is not resumed. In sonnets 40-2 the youth is forgiven for having stolen, or been stolen by, the poet's mistress: this may or may not be the 'sensual fault' mentioned in sonnet 35 (l. 9) and adumbrated in sonnets 33-4. Sonnet 95, beginning:

> How sweet and lovely dost thou make the shame
> Which, like a canker in the fragrant rose,
> Doth spot the beauty of thy budding name!
> O, in what sweets dost thou thy sins enclose!

and sonnet 96, beginning:

> Some say thy fault is youth, some wantonness;
> Some say thy grace is youth and gentle sport,

seem to refer, not to the affair with the poet's mistress, but to some other example, or examples, of the friend's 'wantonness' and womanising. These, I think, are the only external 'facts' which the sonnets of the first series tell us about Shakespeare's friend, and trivial and irrelevant they are in comparison with the great internal fact of what he 'meant' to Shakespeare.

With the exception of 145, an octosyllabic sonnet, and 153-4, two epigrams on Cupid, which have no discernible connection with the rest, the second series (127-54) consists of sonnets to or about a certain 'dark' mistress, whom the poet in some sense loves, or has loved, but whom he also despises, and despises himself for loving. Since in sonnet 152 she is reminded that she broke her bed-vow for the poet's sake, she was presumably a married woman; and since in sonnet 133 she is said to have enslaved the poet's friend, and since in sonnet 144 ('Two loves I have, of comfort and despair') she appears as the bad angel who has tempted away from the poet that good angel his friend, she is presumably the same woman who is alluded to in sonnets 40-2 of the first series.

The Quarto of 1609 seems to have been printed from an authoritative manuscript, but it contains so many corruptions and misprints that it is impossible to suppose that Shakespeare, even if he in some way authorised the publication, troubled to correct the proofs. Indeed, so much correction is necessary that I have followed the general practice of printing, in my quotations, a modernised text. I agree with Sir Edmund Chambers[1] that it is hard to see how the whole collection could have been, not merely put together, but kept together, by anyone but Shakespeare himself, and I also agree both with him and with Beeching[2] that the arrangement of the sonnets, especially in the first series, is probably Shakespeare's own, perhaps with a few misplacings and a few deliberate departures from the chronological order of composition. Many of them fall naturally into groups, and, as Beeching has said, in the main the arrangement 'justifies itself to an attentive reader'. There have been many attempts to rearrange them, but none of them has seemed to me at all satisfactory, and I have found most of the arguments used in defence of such rearrangements both tedious and unconvincing. There is some resemblance between these attempts and that of the American scholar G. H. Palmer to rearrange the poems in George Herbert's *The Temple* in such a manner as to reveal a steady progress from conflict to settled faith—an attempt that betrays a too imperfect understanding both of the poems themselves and of the words with which Herbert, on his death-bed, placed the manuscript in the hands of Nicholas Ferrar's cousin, Arthur Woodnoth:

> Sir, I pray deliver this little Book to my dear brother *Farrer*, and tell him, he shall find in it a picture of the many spiritual Conflicts that have past betwixt God and my Soul, before I could subject mine to the will of *Jesus my Master*: in whose service I have now found perfect freedom.[3]

In the Third Part of this study I shall consider the 'religiousness' of many of Shakespeare's sonnets and shall suggest that with these the only real parallels are to be found in certain kinds of religious poetry: here I will merely remark that we should be content to regard the whole collection, especially those addressed to the friend, as being, like Herbert's *The Temple*, 'a picture of many spiritual conflicts', of many trials and testings of Shakespeare's love and faith, and as a reflection of his 'inner weather' (to borrow a phrase which Mr. Aldous Huxley[4] once applied to Herbert's poetry) over a period of perhaps as much as ten years.

---

[1] *William Shakespeare: A Study of Facts and Problems*, 1930, Vol. I, p. 562.
[2] *The Sonnets of Shakespeare*, 1904, pp. xv–vi.
[3] Walton's *Lives*, World's Classics ed., p. 314.
[4] *Texts and Pretexts*, 1932, p. 12.

The earliest mention of Shakespeare as a sonneteer is by Francis Meres in his *Palladis Tamia*, 1598, but whether what Meres there described as Shakespeare's 'sugred Sonnets among his private friends' included any of the sonnets we now know must remain a matter of conjecture.[1] Versions of two sonnets from the second series, 138, beginning:

> When my love swears that she is made of truth
> I do believe her, though I know she lies,

and the key-sonnet 144, 'Two loves I have, of comfort and despair', were printed at the beginning of Jaggard's miscellany *The Passionate Pilgrim* in 1599. The one certain allusion to a definite and datable public event is in 107, the famous 'mortal moon' sonnet: I say 'certain', because, despite all that has been written on the subject during the last thirty years or so, I have found no reason to change my conviction that Shakespeare is here alluding to the death of Queen Elizabeth I in 1603 and to the unexpectedly peaceful transition to her successor.[2] The mention, in sonnet 25, of the dishonour and oblivion that overwhelm

> The painful warrior, famoused for fight,
> After a thousand victories once foil'd

is a possible (some would say, a probable) allusion to the disgrace of the Earl of Essex after his return from the unsuccessful Irish expedition in 1599.[3] The mention, in sonnet 124, of

> the fools of Time,
> Which die for goodness, who have liv'd for crime

[1] Perhaps the one really strong piece of evidence for believing that, before they were printed in 1609, Shakespeare had allowed at least some of the sonnets we now possess to be read by his 'private friends' is what seems to be the gradually increasing Shakespearean influence upon the sonnets which Drayton, who had begun by imitating first Daniel and then Sidney, added to the 1599, 1602 and 1605 editions of his *Idea* (see Beeching's edition of Shakespeare's Sonnets, pp. 137 ff.). In sonnet 122 Shakespeare offers as an apology for having either given away or lent a table-book given to him by his friend the declaration that the book's capacity to retain his friend's perfections was so feeble in comparison with that of his own memory: had Shakespeare copied into the book sonnets addressed to his friend, and had it been given to him for this purpose? Sonnet 77 had accompanied the gift of such a blank table-book from Shakespeare to his friend, and had exhorted the friend to write in it.

[2] Donne, who so often glorifies the peaceful government of James I, at least twice dwells upon what seemed the miraculously peaceful transition from Queen Elizabeth to her successor: *Sermons*, ed. Potter and Simpson, I, 217, ll. 1245 ff., 227, ll. 170 ff. See also a letter of Bacon's, quoted by Millar MacLure (*The Paul's Cross Sermons*, 1958, p. 88) from J. R. Tanner's *Constitutional Documents of the Reign of James I*, 1930, p. 4.

[3] See pp. 110–11 below.

is a probable allusion to the Jesuit conspiracies at the beginning of James I's reign, and 'the blow of thralled discontent' in the same sonnet is a possible allusion to the Gunpowder Plot of 1605. All, then, that we can say with absolute certainty is that two of the sonnets in the 1609 Quarto must have been written by 1599 and one not earlier than James I's succession in 1603. The actual period of composition almost certainly extended from some date before 1599 until some date after 1603, but attempts to establish these anterior and posterior dates with any plausibility must depend on a careful use of internal evidence, that is to say, of 'parallels' with plays whose dates are either definitely known or generally accepted. If attention is paid only to really significant 'parallels',[1] that is to say, to repetitions, or near-repetitions, of phrases and unusual words, to similarities in syntax and construction, and not merely to superficial resemblances in 'thought', this internal evidence will suggest that the writing of the Sonnets coincided with the period of play-writing which extended from *I Henry IV* (1597) to *Antony and Cleopatra* (1606–7), but that probably more sonnets were written between 1597 and the completion of *Hamlet* in 1601 than between 1601 and 1606–7.

Only after due consideration has been given to the external and internal evidence I have been summarising is it permissible to begin searching among Shakespeare's contemporaries for a suitable candidate for the position of 'Mr. W.H.', to whom, as 'the onlie begetter of these insuing sonnets', the publisher, Thomas Thorpe, wished 'all happinesse and that eternitie promised by our ever-living poet'. Of those who have been proposed by far the likeliest seems to me William Herbert, eldest son of the second Earl of Pembroke by his third wife Mary Sidney, sister of Sir Philip, who was born in 1586, who succeeded his father as third Earl of Pembroke in January 1601 (New Style), and to whom, along with his younger brother Philip, Earl of Montgomery, Heminge and Condell dedicated the First Folio in 1623—approaching, it is true, that 'incomparable paire of brethren' with an almost prostrate humility:

For, when we valew the places your H.H. sustaine, we cannot but know their dignity greater, then to descend to the reading of these trifles . . . But

[1] Beeching, whose edition of the Sonnets (1904) seems to me by far the most sensible and satisfactory that has yet appeared, has some excellent remarks on this subject: Introd., pp. xxiv–xxvii, I–Iii. At least twice in the following study (see footnotes on pp. 196 and 201) I shall have occasion to insist that apparent inferiority, immaturity or conventionality of style ought not in itself to be regarded as proof of earlier composition; that Shakespeare, when languid or uninspired, was at any time liable to fall into a style indistinguishable from that of the average level of the average Elizabethan sonneteer; and that the arrangement of the sonnets in Thorpe's edition need not be suspected merely because of the great variations of style we often find within groups of sonnets on the same or similar themes.

since your L.L. haue beene pleas'd to thinke these trifles some-thing, heereto-
fore; and haue prosequuted both them, and their Authour liuing, with so
much fauour: we hope . . .

Lord Herbert (to give him the courtesy title which, until his succession
to the earldom, he was invariably accorded) possessed all the external
characteristics which are incidentally mentioned in the Sonnets: he was
far above Shakespeare in social position; he was of great personal beauty,
and in 1596 or 1597, when Shakespeare probably began to write the
sonnets, he was sixteen or seventeen years of age and might then, and
perhaps for some time afterwards, have been appropriately addressed as
'sweet boy' and 'lovely boy'; he was (and remained until the end of his
life) a womaniser, and until 1604, when he married the daughter of the
Earl of Shrewsbury (for her fortune, as Clarendon suggests, rather than
for her person), he revealed a strong disinclination to marry. It is this
last characteristic that completes the series of resemblances and seems
(for me, at any rate) to make them more than accidental; for the one
thing about Shakespeare's sonnets that is really puzzling and that requires
some special explanation is the fact that they begin by urging the young
friend to marry, a subject which, after the first seventeen sonnets, is
dropped and never resumed. I cannot imagine how this subject could
have occurred to Shakespeare spontaneously, or why he should have
begun with it (and there is every reason to suppose that it was with these
sonnets that the series began) unless it had been suggested to him by
persons deeply concerned about the young man's future. Now we
happen to possess a number of letters from Rowland Whyte, the London
agent of Sir Robert Sidney (brother of Sir Philip Sidney and of the
Countess of Pembroke, Lord Herbert's mother), to his Master, Sir
Robert, then at Flushing, which record various unsuccessful attempts to
betroth Herbert between the autumn of 1595 and August 1600.[1] On
22 November 1595 Whyte reported that a proposed match between
Herbert, then aged fifteen, and the daughter of Sir George Carey had
been broken off 'by his not liking'. In 1599 Whyte was trying to arrange
a marriage between Herbert and a niece of the Earl of Nottingham,
but on 16 August 1600 he had to admit that he did not 'find any disposition in this gallant young lord to marry'. Herbert seems first to have
come to London in the Spring of 1598, but Shakespeare might well

---

[1] Extracts from these letters were printed by Arthur Collins in his *Letters and Memorials
of State*, 1746, but the full story was not revealed until C. L. Kingsford made further extracts,
which were printed in the second volume of the *Report on the Penshurst MSS* in 1934. See
E. K. Chambers, 'The "Youth" of the Sonnets', in *Shakespearean Gleanings*, 1944, pp. 125 ff.

have addressed the first sonnets to him while he was still at Wilton—perhaps at the suggestion of Samuel Daniel, who had been Herbert's tutor and whom Shakespeare must surely have known, or even at the suggestion of Herbert's father, the second Earl of Pembroke, to whose company of players Shakespeare may have belonged before he joined the reconstituted Lord Chamberlain's Men in 1594. Herbert was, or eventually became, something of a poet himself,[1] and was to be a generous patron of poets, and it may well have occurred to his by now desperate parents that he might perhaps be persuaded to listen to a poet even though he refused to listen to them. It was in August 1600 that Rowland Whyte reported that he could not 'find any disposition in this gallant young lord to marry': it must have been precisely at this time that he was seducing the Queen's Maid of Honour, Mary Fitton, for in March 1601 she gave birth to a child, which, fortunately perhaps, soon died. On 5 February, less than three weeks after Herbert's succession to the earldom, Sir Robert Cecil wrote to Sir George Carew,[2] then in Ireland as Lord President of Munster:

We have no news but that there is a misfortune befallen Mistress Fitton, for she is proved with child, and the Earl of Pembroke, being examined, confesseth a fact, but utterly renounceth all marriage. I fear, they will both dwell in the Tower awhile, for the Queen hath vowed to send them thither.[3]

Whether it was 'all marriage' in general, or merely all thought of marriage to Mary Fitton, that Pembroke renounced we can only guess: if the former, he proved a martyr to his convictions, for he was imprisoned for a month in the Fleet and banished from Court for the rest of the Queen's lifetime. The attempt of Bernard Shaw's old acquaintance[4] Thomas Tyler to identify Mary Fitton with the 'Dark Lady' has tended to discredit other attempts to identify the friend with Pembroke: the 'Dark Lady', who had broken her bed-vow (sonnet 152), was a married woman, and Mary Fitton was both unmarried and, unless the portrait at Arbury grossly flatters her, not dark but fair. Nevertheless, there is

[1] In 1660 the younger Donne published *Poems written by the Right Honourable William Earl of Pembroke . . . whereof many of which are answered by way of Repartee by Sr Benjamin Ruddier, Knight. With several distinct poems, written by them occasionally, and apart.* Many even of the poems signed 'P' are demonstrably by other poets, but some of them are presumably by Pembroke. Norman Ault included two of them in his *Elizabethan Lyrics,* 1928, pp. 422–3.

[2] Not to be confused with Sir George Carey, later the second Lord Hunsdon, to whose daughter an unsuccessful attempt had been made to betroth the young Herbert in 1595.

[3] *Calendar of the Carew Manuscripts, 1601–3,* p. 20.

[4] See Shaw's Preface to *The Dark Lady of the Sonnets.* Tyler's edition of the Sonnets was published in 1890.

a possible allusion to her, or, more specifically, to the disgrace which
Pembroke incurred through his seduction of her, at the beginning of
sonnet 95:

> How sweet and lovely dost thou make the shame
> Which, like a canker in the fragrant rose,
> Doth spot the beauty of thy budding name!
> O, in what sweets dost thou thy sins enclose!

Since Pembroke's disgrace followed almost immediately upon his
succession to the earldom, Shakespeare could have appropriately spoken
of his 'budding name'. And lines 9–10 of the 'mortal moon' sonnet (107),

> Now with the drops of this most balmy time
> My love looks fresh,

could well allude to Pembroke's return to Court on the accession of
James I. And in a presumably earlier sonnet (3) the lines

> Thou art thy mother's glass, and she in thee
> Calls back the lovely April of her prime

would acquire a deeper significance if we knew that the mother was
indeed 'Sidney's sister, Pembroke's mother'. In fact, there is nothing in
the Sonnets inconsistent with the supposition that they were addressed to
Pembroke, and there are several phrases which seem less vaguely and
conventionally 'poetical' if that supposition is accepted. But to return to
poor Mary Fitton, there is no reason to suppose that she was the first of
this young marriage-hating nobleman's conquests; on the contrary, if we
assume that all the sonnets in the first series were addressed to one man
and that all those in the second series are either to or about one woman,
the fact that the key-sonnet 144 ('Two loves I have, of comfort and
despair') was printed in 1599 makes it necessary to suppose that Herbert
(if he was the man), since his coming to London in the Spring of 1598,
had already seduced, or been seduced by, Shakespeare's 'Dark Lady'.
Indeed, Shakespeare may well have lost all interest in the 'Dark Lady'
by the time he came to write many of the sonnets in the first series. If it
was with her that the youthful Herbert began, he never, as one might
say, looked back, for Clarendon's admirable description of him, from
which I will quote mainly because of other qualities which he may

already, in some measure, have possessed, and which may have endeared him to Shakespeare, reveals that he remained until the end of his life an inveterate womaniser. In his account of the principal personages at the Court of Charles I after the assassination of Buckingham, Clarendon contrasts the detested and detestable Earl of Arundel with William, Earl of Pembroke, 'the most universally loved and esteemed of any man of that age':

> He was a man very well bred, and of excellent parts, and a graceful speaker upon any subject, having a good proportion of learning, and a ready wit to apply it and enlarge upon it; of a pleasant and facetious humour, and a disposition affable, generous, and magnificent ... And as his conversation was most with men of the most pregnant parts and understanding, so towards any who needed support or encouragement, though unknown, if fairly recommended to him, he was very liberal.

Clarendon admits, though, that he had 'great infirmities':

> He indulged to himself the pleasures of all kinds, almost in all excesses. Whether out of his natural constitution, or for want of his domestic content and delight, (in which he was most unhappy, for he paid much too dear for his wife's fortune by taking her person into the bargain,) he was immoderately given up to women. But therein he likewise retained such a power and juris-diction over his very appetite, that he was not so much transported with beauty and outward allurements, as with those advantages of the mind as manifested an extraordinary wit and spirit and knowledge, and administered great pleasure in the conversation. To these he sacrificed himself, his precious time, and much of his fortune. And some who were nearest to his trust and friendship were not without apprehension that his natural vivacity and vigour of mind began to lessen and decline by those excessive indulgences.[1]

Many have asked, and no doubt will continue to ask, why, if Pembroke was the man to whom the Sonnets were addressed, did Thorpe in 1609, many years after his succession to the earldom, dedicate them to him as 'Mr. W.H.'; and why, if Thorpe wanted to give him the title that was his at the time when Shakespeare first addressed him, did he not refer to him as 'the Lord W.H.' or 'the Lord H.', since the young Herbert was always addressed and referred to as 'the Lord Herbert'? These objections appear less formidable when one considers the only possible alternatives. The Earl of Pembroke in 1609 was perhaps not quite so

[1] *History of the Rebellion*, ed. Macray, 1888, Vol. I, pp. 71-3.

great a figure as he was in 1623, but he was already a very great figure indeed, and, when one recalls the trembling servility with which Heminge and Condell thought fit to dedicate to him and to his brother 'Mr. William Shakespeares Comedies, Histories, & Tragedies' as 'these trifles', one will not be inclined to waste words on demonstrating the utter impossibility of printing:

TO . THE . ONLIE . BEGETTER . OF.

THESE . INSVING . SONNETS.

THE RIGHT . HONOVRABLE . WILLIAM . EARL . OF . PEMBROKE.

KNIGHT . OF . THE . MOST . NOBLE . ORDER . OF . THE . GARTER.

AND . GENTLEMAN . OF . HIS . MAIESTIES . CHAMBER.

ALL . HAPPINESSE . AND . THAT . ETERNITIE.

PROMISED.

BY.

OVR . EVER-LIVING . POET.

Even 'The Lord W.H.' or 'The Lord H.' could have come too near, whereas the initials 'Mr. W.H.' would have been, in Pindar's phrase, $\phi\omega\nu\hat{\alpha}\nu\tau\alpha\ \sigma\upsilon\nu\epsilon\tauo\hat{\iota}\sigma\iota\nu$, 'vocal to those that have understanding', and to them alone. Did Thorpe find the initials 'W.H.' in his manuscript? Was it as 'Mr. W.H.' that the young Herbert used to visit Shakespeare and was known among his friends? And how did Thorpe acquire that manuscript? For it seems inconceivable that either Shakespeare or the person to whom they were addressed should have scattered among their friends copies of *all* these sonnets. May, in fact, the publication, with its superficial appearance of piracy, have been in some gentlemanly fashion arranged, as the result of a perhaps mutual desire to see Shakespeare's name, his all too 'branded' name, prefixed to something less trifling, less ungentlemanly, than a play—as it had once been prefixed to *Venus and Adonis* and *The Rape of Lucrece*, those wholly impersonal poems dedicated to an earlier and less intimate friend, whose patronage could be openly acknowledged?

For the sake of brevity, I have stated the case for Pembroke as the Friend as convincingly as possible and as though I accepted the identification. I admit that anything like certainty is unattainable. All that seems to me desirable and, to some extent, necessary is to try to form some impression of the *sort of man* it was to whom Shakespeare addressed these sonnets, the sort of man to whom all their so often tantalisingly obscure allusions would consistently apply. And here I encounter an obstacle that seems to me far more serious than the one I have just tried to dispose

of—perhaps the only really serious obstacle to the identification of the
friend with Pembroke. In several of the sonnets, some of which I
consider in the last pages of this study, Shakespeare writes as a man who
has been deeply wounded by his friend—not by his theft of the 'Dark
Lady', which seems to have been soon forgiven, and may have been
soon forgotten, but by his having, perhaps rather too often, allowed the
difference in rank between them to become more of a barrier to genuine
reciprocity than it need have been; by his having, at least sometimes,
made Shakespeare feel that he was, after all, if no longer a player, at any
rate an ex-player and one who still wrote 'trifles' for players; one who
had no right to take any liberties with a man of such rank as his friend,
or to presume in any way upon former intimacy and former kindness.
Was Pembroke, despite his weaknesses, the sort of man who would have
treated Shakespeare with this aristocratic insolence? Would it not have
been altogether too inconsistent with the traditions of Wilton and of
Penshurst? One would like to think so. And yet, despite the abundant
testimony to his munificent patronage of poets and writers, is it not
clear from Clarendon's portrait that this man who 'indulged to himself
the pleasures of all kinds, almost in all excesses', this man who was incapable of denying himself anything, was also, despite his easy generosity,
a selfish and perhaps rather superficial man, only very limitedly capable
of giving what Shakespeare could give so prodigally and, it may be, so
terrifyingly—himself?

So much for matters with which, in the pages that follow, I shall
only be occasionally and incidentally concerned. As a kind of preliminary
conspectus of the course I intend to pursue, I offer the following list of
sonnets on large general topics, together with a few brief and provisional
indications of various resemblances and differences between Shakespeare's
treatment of these topics and that of earlier poets.

(a) Twenty-eight sonnets about his own poetry

(i) As that which will preserve his friend's perfections from Time (15, 18,
19, 54, 55, 60, 63, 65—with which 64, though entirely on the theme of
Devouring Time, is closely connected—81, 100, 101, 107, 122). This, as
every reader must be aware, is a topic which, from Pindar onwards,
has made various significant or insignificant appearances in European
poetry; but with most of the variations upon this topic, or with the
kindred topics, which I shall proceed to list, it would, I think, be difficult
to produce really significant parallels from other poets. I should add that

by no means every one of the sonnets in these lists is wholly confined to
the topic under which I have listed it. (ii) As that which his friend should
not alone trust to for perpetuation (16, 17); (iii) as that in which the
better part of him will remain with his friend (74, with which 73, though
entirely on the theme of his own transience, is closely connected); (iv) as
that which, if his surviving friend looks upon, he should forget the hand
that writ it (71, and perhaps 72); (v) as that which owes any merit it
possesses entirely to his friend (38, 78, 100); (vi) as that which is immeasurably inferior to what it celebrates (83, 103); (vii) as that which, though
its style be surpassed by others, his surviving friend should continue to
read for the love it expresses (32); (viii) as that whose style remains
recognisably the same because its subject does not change (76); (ix) as
that which others may surpass in rhetoric but not in truthfulness (82).

In some of these sonnets (and it is possible that there may be more
than twenty-eight of them and that there are allusions to his poetry in
others which I have overlooked) Shakespeare refers only passingly or
unarrestingly to his own poetry, but many of them are among his very
finest, and, so far as I am aware, no writer on the Sonnets has remarked
upon the fact that this poet, who is commonly supposed to have been
indifferent to literary fame and perhaps only dimly aware of the mag-
nitude of his own poetic genius, has written both more copiously and
more memorably on this topic than any other sonneteer. It seems to be
generally assumed, in a vague sort of way, that most, perhaps all, sonneteers, English, French and Italian, perhaps even from Petrarch onwards,
had written a great deal about their own poetry, and that Shakespeare
was merely saying the sort of things they had said, but saying them
better: this, though, as I shall attempt to demonstrate, is far from the
truth.

(b) *Sonnets containing personifications or metaphorical descriptions of Time,
    Youth, Beauty, etc.*

These, which it seems scarcely worth while to attempt to list, recur
continually in the sonnets where Shakespeare urges his friend to perpetuate himself through offspring, speaks of the perpetuating power of
his own poetry, or declares that his love is not Time's fool. They may be
compared, on the one hand, with various passages in Horace, Ovid,
Propertius, etc. on the theme that poetry is *aere perennius*, and, on the
other hand, and perhaps above all, with various metaphorical descriptions
or personifications in Horace's Odes. Here, though, the differences in

spirit are more significant than the occasional resemblances in style, for with Shakespeare's characteristic defiances of Time there is nothing comparable in ancient love-poetry, while the ancient love-poets' characteristic invitations and exhortations to make the best use of time, their variations on the themes of *carpe florem* and 'ingrateful beauty threatened', are entirely absent from Shakespeare's sonnets.

(c) Twenty-five sonnets containing 'hyperbolical' or 'religious' expressions of Shakespeare's love for his friend

(i) All other beauties but shadows or imperfect copies of his friend's (53, 97, 98, 99, 113, 114). Here, at first sight, Shakespeare seems to be saying something very like what Petrarch and his imitators are so often saying, although the more closely one pursues the comparison, the more aware one becomes of certain characteristic and significant differences. (ii) All truth and beauty are incarnated in his friend and will perish with him (14, 104). Here Shakespeare seems to be saying what, for the true Platonist, or even for the popular Platonist, would amount almost to blasphemy. For the remaining topics it is very difficult to find anything like parallels except in specifically religious poetry, or in some of Donne's *Songs and Sonets.* (iii) All beauty described by earlier poets was a prophecy of his friend's (59, 106). (iv) In a declining age his friend is a reminder of what beauty once was (67, 68). (v) His friend is a compensation for all his own deficiencies of talent and fortune and for all his failures and disappointments (25, 29, 37, 90, 91). (vi) His friend is a compensation for the evils of life in general (66). (vii) All he had supposed lost live again in his friend (30, 31). (viii) His life is dependent on the continuance of his friend's love (92). (ix) His friend is a perpetual subject of recollection or anticipation (52, 57). (x) All else is nothing to him in comparison with his friend (109, 112).

The *thisness* of the sonnets I have listed, among which are many, if not most, of the finest in the collection, can be far better, as the French would say, *approfounded* and *precised* by some attempt at comparison and contrast than by anything we are ever likely to learn about the identity of their recipient.

I

POETRY AS IMMORTALISATION FROM PINDAR TO SHAKESPEARE

I must make it clear that I am not here attempting to write a history of the idea of literary fame, or to unload an exhaustive card-index catalogue of allusions to it in poetry (let alone in prose), but simply indicating certain characteristic handlings of the topic in ancient poetry (other than epic), in passages either memorable in themselves or extensively imitated by Renaissance poets; and that, from Petrarch onwards, I am almost exclusively concerned (a) with the appearance of the topic in love-poetry and, more particularly, in sonnets, and (b) with the contrast between the merely incidental and seldom very serious treatments of it in ancient love-poetry and the importance and centrality it eventually assumes in Shakespeare's Sonnets, and that I am almost as much concerned with the profound religious, moral and cultural changes which this contrast reflects as with the topic itself.

The best general treatment of the topic of literary fame with which I am familiar is an essay by Oliver Elton, 'Literary Fame: a Renaissance Study' in *Otia Merseiana*, Vol. IV, published for the University of Liverpool by Williams and Norgate in 1904, pp. 24 ff.

1

Shakespeare and the Roman poets

In the poetry of Augustan Rome it is possible to distinguish between passages in which the poet speaks of the immortality he will achieve for himself and those in which he speaks of the immortality he will confer upon others, but in the great public odes of Pindar, celebrating victors in the Panhellenic Games, these two themes are really inseparable, and indeed we sometimes seem to catch sight of the poet holding out what, as one might say in Miltonic language, *seems* his hat and insinuating, with decent obscurity and periphrasis, that the man who is wise as well as wealthy will not omit to pay a poet to immortalise him. These passages on the immortalising power of poetry are very frequent in Pindar's odes and often very splendid.[1] Here it must suffice to quote (in Sandy's translation) two representative examples. From the tenth Olympian (ll. 91–6):

> Whensoever a man, who hath done noble deeds, descendeth to the abode of Hades, without the meed of song, he hath spent his strength and his breath in vain, and winneth but a little pleasure by his toil; whereas thou hast glory shed upon thee by the soft-tongued lyre and by the sweet flute, and thy fame waxeth widely by favour of the Pierid daughters of Zeus.

From the sixth Pythian, for Xenocrates of Acragas, where Pindar declares (ll. 1–18) that he is once more approaching the Delphic temple, where a treasure-house of song has been built up for Acragas, for Xenocrates and for his ancestors:

> Which neither wintry rain with its invading onset, the pitiless host launched from deep-thundering clouds, nor the storm-wind with its swirl of shingle, shall buffet and sweep away into the recesses of the sea.

There are similar passages among the surviving fragments of Bacchylides and Simonides, and, to descend to the Alexandrian period, there is a

[1] I think the following list contains most of the really significant ones: Olympian odes, X, 91–6, XI, 1–10; Pythian odes, III, 110–15, VI, 1–18; Nemean odes, IV, 81–6, VII, 11–21, VIII, 44–8, IX, 6–8; Isthmian odes, IV, 35–42, VII, 16–19.

very notable *locus* (magnificently improved upon by Horace in the
Lollius ode) in the sixteenth Idyll of Theocritus, addressed to Hieron of
Syracuse, where the poet mentions the names of many who would have
been forgotten had they not been celebrated by Homer and Simonides.
So far as we know, the first Roman poet to make really memorable use
of this familiar Greek *topos* was Horace. He was certainly the first Roman
poet to declare that lyrical, as distinct from epic, poetry could secure
lasting fame both for its author and for those he deigned to celebrate,
and Professor Fraenkel has noticed[1] that although, in the magnificent
epilogue to the Third and last Book of his first published Odes, beginning

Exegi monumentum aere perennius

('I have completed a monument more enduring than bronze'), he
confidently prophesied his own immortality, it was only, among the
odes in those three books, upon the Bandusian Spring (III, xiii) that he
actually ventured to confer it, and that it was not until the later Fourth
Book, after he had been selected to compose the *Carmen Saeculare* and
been publicly recognised as the Roman laureate, that he seems to have
felt entitled to follow the example of his Greek lyric masters and to
promise immortality to some of his contemporaries. In the Censorinus
ode (IV, viii), *Donarem pateras*, Horace begins, with a kind of safeguarding
modesty, by declaring that, were he a wealthy man, he would give
bronzes and tripods, statues and paintings to his friends, but that, being
what he is, all he can offer them are poems—the superior value of which
he proceeds to imply by declaring that the fame of Scipio Africanus owes
more to the poetry of Ennius than to all the public records of his achievements, and that Romulus and Aeacus would have been forgotten had
they not been celebrated in verse (by, respectively, Ennius and Pindar).
Here the only poet to whom (or rather to whose Muses, his *Calabrae
Pierides*) Horace specifically refers is Ennius, author of the *Annales*,
and even in Rome there was nothing presumptuous or unusual in the
notion that an epic poet could confer immortality; but in the immediately
following ode to Lollius (IV, ix), *Ne forte credas*, after proclaiming, in
the very first stanza and in verse even more resonantly impressive than
that of the epilogue to the Third Book (*Exegi monumentum*), the im-
perishability of his lyric achievement, Horace proceeds to justify this
conviction by reminding his friend that, although Homer is supreme,
the great Greek lyric poets (*Pindarus novemque lyrici*), whom he either

[1] Eduard Fraenkel, *Horace*, 1957, p. 423.

names or alludes to, are no less remembered. Then come three stanzas
(doubtless suggested by Theocritus, whom Horace immeasurably surpasses) declaring that the deeds both of Helen and of many who fought
on either side at Troy were far from unexampled, leading to the superb
climax:

> vixere fortes ante Agamemnona
> multi; sed omnes inlacrimabiles
>   urgentur ignotique longa
> nocte, carent quia vate sacro.

> ('Heroic souls before Agamemnon's day
> were not infrequent; all unlamented, though,
>   are whelmed unknown in everlasting
> darkness for want of a sacred minstrel.')

Without pausing to insist upon the now sufficiently obvious implication
that, since lyric poetry can be as enduring as Homer's, it can confer a no
less enduring fame upon those it celebrates, Horace now reaches what
one is almost tempted to regard as his ostensible rather than his real
subject, and declares that he will not allow the great public virtues of
Lollius to fall into oblivion. Thus concludes the most impressive single
treatment of the theme of poetic immortality in the whole of European
poetry.

Although in the Censorinus ode Horace may seem to intimate that
he is in a position to confer immortality upon any of the friends whom he
condescends to mention, it is only in the Lollius ode that he ventures to
promise it to a particular person, and then only for the sake of that
person's public virtues. Promises of immortality without reference to
public virtues and achievements, promises of it to persons whom the
poet merely happens to love or like, are not common to ancient poetry
and are perhaps inconsistent with what might be called the civicism of
the ancient world. They do, as we shall see, occur occasionally in the
Roman elegiac poets, but there they seldom seem very seriously intended.
In fact, the only memorable and weighty utterance of this kind which I
have met with in Greek poetry is in the collection of elegiac verses
ascribed to Theognis of Megara, who flourished round about 520 B.C.
In the middle of this collection of what seem to be short separate poems,
giving, sometimes a bit flatly and platitudinously, moral, social and
political advice to his young friend and protégé Kyrnos, Theognis

suddenly breaks out into a resonant promise of immortality—or, rather'
into a poem reproaching with ingratitude one upon whom immortality
has already been conferred:

> I have given you wings, with which you shall fly with ease, high over the
> boundless sea and the whole earth: at all banquets and parties you shall be
> present, upstored in the mouths of many, and with shrill-voiced pipes youths
> of graceful loveliness shall beautifully and clearly sing you; and when beneath
> the depths of dusky earth you step into the wailful dwellings of Hades, not
> then, not in death, shall you lose glory, but shall be for ever in the thoughts of
> men, having an imperishable name, Kyrnos, and going up and down upon
> the mainland of Hellas and among the islands, crossing the fishy and un-
> harvestable sea—not mounted on the backs of horses, but the glad gifts of the
> violet-crowned Muses shall be your convoy: for to all who care for it, even
> to those yet to come, you shall be song, so long as earth and sun endure. But
> as for me, I do not get the least respect from you, but you deceive me, as
> though I were a little child, with words (ll. 237–54).

In the few fragments of her poetry that have survived there are suggestions that Sappho, a still earlier poetess, may have occasionally promised immortality to her friends and lovers; but Sappho wrote a kind
of poetry wholly lacking in that publicness and impersonality which
characterise almost all Greek poetry of the classical period. Plato, had
he possessed the word, might well have accused her of 'personalism'.
Horace, strongly tainted with 'personalism', may almost be said to have
rediscovered her, but all surviving copies of her books were eventually
sought out and destroyed in the eleventh century by the Roman and
Byzantine theocracies—presumably because they seemed permeated with
a kind of idolatry which no attempts at allegorical interpretation could
Christianise.

But to return to Horace: since there seems no reason why I should
withhold all mention of my main subject until I chronologically reach
it, I will here permit myself a few parenthetical remarks on certain of
Shakespeare's sonnets. The two odes we have been considering are
immediately preceded by what Housman regarded as the most beautiful
of all Latin poems, *Diffugere nives* (IV, vii), that ode to Torquatus on the
return of spring and on the sad contrast between the returning seasons
and the unreturning lives of men; and Professor Fraenkel has expressed the
(so far as I am aware) original conviction[1] that these three odes were
deliberately intended to form a kind of central triad, and that between

[1] *Horace*, 1957, pp. 419, 421, 426.

Diffugere nives, declaring that we shall all end as no more than *pulvis et umbra*, and the two following odes there is, as it were, an implied, but thereby all the more impressive, 'nevertheless': upon what would else be but *pulvis et umbra* poetry, and poetry alone, can confer immortality. Professor Fraenkel has noticed a similar transition of thought, more explicitly though far more faintly expressed, in an epinikion of Bacchylides:

> Deep Aether is undefilable, water of the sea does not dry up, gold is a gladness; but to man it is not permitted, once gray age has come, to regain flourishing youth. Nevertheless the brightness of virtue does not fade with the body, but the Muse nourishes it.

Professor Fraenkel's contention seems to me to be supported by the interesting fact that a relationship similar to that between *Diffugere nives* and the Censorinus and Lollius odes exists between two pairs (64 and 65, 73 and 74) of Shakespeare's finest sonnets, although in each case the transition is far more explicit than with Horace and the four sonnets in question form two almost inseparable pairs. Sonnet 64 begins:

> When I have seen by Time's fell hand defaced
> The rich proud cost of outworn buried age,

and leads to the conclusion:

> When I have seen such interchange of state,
> Or state itself confounded to decay,
> Ruin hath taught me thus to ruminate,
> That Time will come and take my love away.
>   This thought is as a death, which cannot choose
>   But weep to have that which it fears to lose.

Sonnet 65, where Shakespeare explicitly asks and explicitly answers the questions which Horace (even if Professor Fraenkel is right) only implicitly raises and implicitly replies to, must, familiar though it is, be quoted in full, partly because it is impossible to summarise and partly because it contains some of the very finest of those metaphorical personifications with which, as it seems to me, the only real parallels are those in some of Horace's odes:

> Since brass, nor stone, nor earth, nor boundless sea,
> But sad mortality o'er sways their power,
> How with this rage shall beauty hold a plea,
> Whose action is no stronger than a flower?
> O, how shall summer's honey breath hold out
> Against the wreckful siege of battering days,
> When rocks impregnable are not so stout,
> Nor gates of steel so strong, but Time decays?
> O fearful meditation! Where, alack,
> Shall Time's best jewel from Time's chest lie hid?
> Or what strong hand can hold his swift foot back?
> Or who his spoil of beauty can forbid?
>   O, none, unless this miracle have might,
>   That in black ink my love may still shine bright.

Sonnets 73 and 74 contain profoundly beautiful and original variations on this ancient topic, for in 73, beginning

> That time of year thou mayst in me behold
> When yellow leaves, or none, or few, do hang
> Upon those boughs which shake against the cold,
> Bare ruin'd choirs where late the sweet birds sang,

and concluding

> This thou perceiv'st, which makes thy love more strong,
> To love that well which thou must leave ere long,

Shakespeare is contemplating, not human transience in general, nor even, as in so many of his other sonnets, the time-threatened loveliness of his friend, but his own transience; and in 74, perhaps the most beautiful of all his sonnets, he is content to regard his own poetry as no more (and no less) than that in which his friend, should he survive the poet, will continue to possess the 'better part' of him:

> But be contented: when that fell arrest
> Without all bail shall carry me away,
> My life hath in this line some interest,
> Which for memorial still with thee shall stay.
> When thou reviewest this, thou dost review

The very part was consecrate to thee:
The earth can have but earth, which is his due;
My spirit is thine, the better part of me:
So then thou hast but lost the dregs of life,
The prey of worms, my body being dead,
The coward conquest of a wretch's knife,
Too base of thee to be remembered.
    The worth of that is that which it contains,
    And that is this, and this with thee remains.

I find it hard not to believe that not only the phrase 'the better part of me'[1] but the whole thought (or, since he thought in metaphors, all the metaphors) of this sonnet were suggested to Shakespeare by the proud boast of his favourite Ovid, at the end of the *Metamorphoses*, that he is ready for that day which can claim only his body to end when it will the uncertain course of his life, since by the better part of him he will be carried up in immortality above the stars on high and his name shall be indestructible and his fame as lasting as the power of Rome:

> Cum volet, illa dies, quae nil nisi corporis huius
> ius habet, incerti spatium mihi finiat aevi:
> parte tamen meliore mei super alta perennis
> astra ferar nomenque erit indelebile nostrum;
> quaque patet domitis Romana potentia terris
> ore legar populi, perque omnia saecula fama,
> siquid habent veri vatum praesagia, vivam.

Among the many notable examples of imitation and transformation in Renaissance poetry I can think of nothing quite comparable with Shakespeare's appropriation and transformation of Ovid's proud and

---

[1] Shakespeare had already used this phrase at the beginning of sonnet 39:

> O, how thy worth with manners may I sing,
> When thou art all the better part of me?

This is the earliest example of the phrase 'better part' quoted by *O.E.D.* (*better*, sense 3c), which I cannot but think is wrong in supposing it to mean the same as the phrase 'better half', i.e. 'greater half'. *O.E.D.* may well be right in supposing that Statius's *animae partem . . . nostrae majorem*, in a passage (*Sylvae*, III, ii, 6–8) declaring that his young friend Metius Celer **is** being entrusted to a ship of perilous alder and is preparing to transport the greater part (or major portion) of Statius's soul across the sea, is the origin of the phrase 'better half', but while in 'better half' the word *better* = 'greater' (Statius's *pars major*), in Shakespeare's (and, as we shall see, in Drayton's) 'better part' *better* is undoubtedly the comparative of *good* (Ovid's *pars melior*). An earlier example of the phrase is in Peele's *Arraignment of Paris*, II, i, where Pallas speaks of 'the mind, the better part'.

public boast into this so humble and private and personal reassurance.[1]

I will conclude these parenthetical remarks upon the affinity between these four sonnets and the great Horatian triad by quoting two stanzas from *Diffugere nives*, where that affinity in metaphor to which I have already referred is especially striking:

> Frigora mitescunt zephyris, ver proterit aestas
>   interitura simul
> pomifer Autumnus fruges effuderit, et mox
>   bruma recurrit iners.
>
> damna tamen celeres reparant caelestia lunae:
>   nos, ubi decidimus
> quo pius Aeneas, quo Tullus dives et Ancus,
>   pulvis et umbra sumus.

Partly because of a problem of interpretation in the second of these stanzas (it concerns the exact meaning of *caelestia damna*) which, after much badgering of more learned friends, I have settled to my own satisfaction, I append a very inadequate but perhaps useful translation:

> Chillness yields to the western wind, Spring's victim of Summer,
>   destined to perish as well
> soon as Autumn unloads her ripe-grown fruits; and, with sudden
>   numbingness, Winter returns.
>
> While, though, swiftly the moons upbuild those seasonal ruins,
>   we, when we've fallen to where
> pious Aeneas and richest Tullus and Ancus have fallen,
>   linger as shadow and dust.

Perhaps the passage which, in mere content, the first of these stanzas most obviously resembles, a passage, though, where Shakespeare is somewhat below his best, is one in sonnet 5 (ll. 5–8):

> For never-resting Time leads summer on
> To hideous winter, and confounds him there;
> Sap check'd with frost and lusty leaves quite gone,
> Beauty o'ersnow'd and bareness every where.

[1] It seems possible that, together with this recollection of Ovid, there may also be a recollection of the *Book of Job* (xix, 26): 'And though . . . worms destroy this body, yet in my flesh shall I see God.'

But for something more like an equivalent of the compressed and dynamic image in *ver proterit aestas*, the image of Summer, like a pursuing horseman, riding down and trampling upon fugitive Spring, one would have to turn to such things as the 'fell arrest without all bail', or the 'coward conquest of a wretch's knife'. In translating some of Horace's odes and attempting to convey to readers ignorant of Latin something of their *thisness*, I was often compelled, sometimes consciously, sometimes unconsciously, to make him sound just a little like Shakespeare. For example, in the Soracte ode (I, ix) Horace exhorts the young Thaliarchus not to worry too much, but to enjoy himself

> donec virenti canities abest
> morosa,

a passage which seems to mean (that is, poetically mean) something like 'While yet from your spring-green flourishing winter-white hoariness with its morosity is absent.' I translated it

> While yet from Youth's green flourish the snowy touch
> of gloomy Age hangs distant—

an attempt which doubtless invites an all-too-unsustainable comparison with

> Time doth transfix the flourish set on youth

in sonnet 60. Be that as it may, the only metaphors that seem to me really like these and similar metaphors in Horace's Odes are those in Shakespeare's Sonnets, and the only metaphors that seem to me really like the most characteristic ones in Shakespeare's Sonnets are some in Horace's Odes. Only the necessity of keeping this digression within reasonable limits prevents me from attempting some description of what seem to me fundamental differences between Horace's metaphors and those of Pindar and Aeschylus, and from suggesting that Shakespeare, in some of his later tragedies (and occasionally even in his sonnets), is the only poet who has written at all like Aeschylus: who else but the author of the *Prometheus Vinctus* could have written some of the great outbursts of Lear, and where but in Aeschylus do we find such metaphors as those in Macbeth's speech about

> pity, like a naked new-born babe
> Striding the blast, or heaven's cherubin hors'd
> Upon the sightless couriers of the air?

But that is 'matter for another tale'. Was Shakespeare familiar with Horace's Odes? I can see no way of proving that he was, but, on the other hand, it seems to me almost incredible that he should not have been. Almost all other great poets have learnt from their predecessors, either by way of a progressively unimitative imitation, or simply through an ever-renewed awareness of the infinite possibilities of expression and of what great poetry could and ought to be; but it seems to be generally assumed that, except for a few translations, Shakespeare, when he read at all, read chiefly almanacks, Fat Stock Prices, and whatever may have been the Elizabethan equivalent of a financial weekly. What I find so incredible about this is the lack of curiosity it presupposes. I can well understand that Shakespeare should never have wanted to read Homer in Greek, for, after all, very few even of his most learned contemporaries knew any Greek at all, but did it never occur to him to brush up what Ben Jonson called his 'small Latin' sufficiently to enable him to perceive in the Latin poets some of those things which no translation could reveal? Or must we suppose that the world's greatest poet never attempted to establish any direct contact with any of the world's greatest poetry, that he remained but vaguely and intermittently aware of its existence, as of a thing that did not immediately concern him, and was content, as it were, with travellers' tales? No doubt the fact that he could write like Aeschylus without ever, perhaps, having even heard the name of Aeschylus, makes it not impossible to suppose that he could write like Horace without ever having read him. On the other hand, we cannot assume that Shakespeare had not read him simply because we cannot produce from his poems and plays such immediately recognisable imitations or variations of Horatian phrases and passages as we can produce from Petrarch or Ronsard or Ben Jonson. As has been obvious ever since it was first pointed out by Lessing, Macbeth's words about that blood on his hand which not all great Neptune's ocean could wash away were suggested to Shakespeare by either or both of two passages in Seneca's *Hippolytus* and *Hercules Furens*. This is far from being the only passage in his plays where Shakespeare is indebted to Seneca, but, here no less than elsewhere, though here most astonishingly, he has, to a far greater degree than any other Elizabethan dramatist, transformed what he has borrowed from Seneca, has, as one might say, Shakespeareanised it.[1] We cannot therefore assume that Shakespeare's knowledge of the Latin poets was small and superficial simply because it is so hard to trace, or to exhibit in such a manner as would satisfy a jury in a case of breach of copyright.

The contrast between what I can best describe as the *publicness* of Horace, whose eye, in *Diffugere nives*, is not so much upon his friend Torquatus as upon that spectacle of human transcience from which he exhorts him to draw the appropriate moral, and who, after, as it were, preparing the ground in the Censorinus ode, almost openly appears in its companion as the publicly acknowledged successor of the great public celebrators of public virtues and public deeds—the contrast between this and the privateness of Shakespeare, for whom the humanity threatened by Time seems to exist only in the person of his nameless and unidentifiable friend, and who, though he elsewhere speaks at times with an Horatian resonance of his poetry

> (Not marble, nor the gilded monuments
> Of princes, shall outlive this powerful rhyme.
>
> 55
>
> So long as men can breathe, or eyes can see,
> So long lives this, and this gives life to thee.
>
> 18),

mentions it in 65 only with a kind of tremulous questioning ('Unless this miracle have might'), and who in 74, the most beautiful of all his sayings about it, professes to regard it as no more than a 'memorial' of him which his friend can never lose—this contrast, to which I shall have to return, is sufficiently great and sufficiently obvious. Nevertheless, Horace and Shakespeare 'have shook hands as over a vast and embraced as from the ends of opposed winds'. On this topic of poetry as the Defier of Time each of them has written more great and more memorable poetry than any other European poet. Pindar is the only other ancient poet who has written something approaching as many *lines* on this topic as Horace, but the merely incidental treatments of it in Pindar's odes, magnificent as they often are, cannot, in weight and total impressiveness, compare with the epilogue to the Third Book of the Odes and the great

[1] On the difference between Shakespeare and other Elizabethan dramatists in this respect see an excellent article by Francis R. Johnson, 'Shakespearian Imagery and Senecan Imitation', in *Joseph Quincy Adams Memorial Studies*, 1948, pp. 33 ff. See also F. P. Wilson, 'Shakespeare's Reading', in *Shakespeare Survey 3*, 1950, p. 19 (on the difference between Shakespeare and Webster, who kept and used a common-place book).

triad (as Professor Fraenkel would have us regard it) in the Fourth. The only modern poet who has written as much as (perhaps even more than) Shakespeare on this topic is the youthful Ronsard, but those many passages in his odes where Ronsard has imitated almost everything on this topic in the ancient poets (above all in Pindar and Horace) and applied it to himself and to his own (shall we say?) not yet quite comparable achievements, these, when weighed on even the most primitive of critical balances against Shakespeare's sonnets, fly up and kick the beam. On this topic Horace is only really comparable with Shakespeare and Shakespeare only really comparable with Horace.

The various brief and incidental treatments of this topic by those whom Milton called 'the smooth Elegiac Poets' of Augustan Rome were probably both suggested and justified by the example and authority of Horace. They are worth recalling, because, although few of them would be likely to arrest the attention and remain in the memory of a modern reader, they were nearly all frequently imitated by the vernacular poets of modern Europe from Petrarch onwards. By far the most splendid and memorable of them are the concluding lines of the last book of the *Metamorphoses*, which I have already quoted as the possible 'source' of Shakespeare's 74th sonnet. It is an epilogue which, as its opening lines reveal, was almost certainly suggested by Horace's epilogue to the Third Book of his Odes, and in which Ovid seems to be almost deliberately placing his own *opus* beside Horace's *monumentum*:

> Iamque opus exegi quod nec Iovis ira nec ignis
> nec poterit ferrum nec edax abolere vetustas.

('I have now completed a work which neither the wrath of Jove nor fire nor iron nor devouring age shall be able to abolish.') The phrase *edax vetustas* recalls, and was perhaps intended to recall, the phrase *tempus edax rerum* (which almost certainly gave Shakespeare his 'Devouring Time' in sonnet 19) in the apostrophe to Time earlier in this last book (ll. 234–6):

> Tempus edax rerum, tuque, invidiosa vetustas,
> omnia destruitis vitiataque dentibus aevi
> paulatim lenta consumitis omnia morte.

('Time, devourer of things, and you, jealous Age, you destroy all, and, when they have once been impaired by the teeth of transience, gradually consume all with lingering death.') In the latter part of the

Fourteenth, and in the Fifteenth and last, Book of the *Metamorphoses* Ovid relates legends connected with various Roman heroes from Aeneas to Augustus. The Fifteenth Book begins with Numa, and Ovid accepts the tradition that he visited Croton and there became a pupil of Pythagoras. This provides an opportunity to introduce Pythagoras and make him give something like a summary of his philosophy: how, although the eternal substance of things persists and nothing utterly perishes, the appearance of things is being perpetually altered by *tempus edax rerum.* Was this impressive discourse on mutability (ll. 179–236 are the most important), which meant so much to Spenser and other Elizabethans, introduced mainly in order to display Ovid's learning, or was it intended, despite much intervening matter, to recur to the reader's memory when he reached the epilogue and to add weight to that final exaltation of poetry as the only conqueror of Time? Whatever be the right answer to this question, there can be no doubt that both passages were very much in Shakespeare's memory and imagination when he was writing these sonnets about poetry as the defier of Time.

More sadly, but no less triumphantly, Ovid was to repeat this boast at the conclusion of a verse epistle (*Tristia*, III, vii, 43–54), written during his exile at Tomis, to the young poetess Perilla, who may have been his step-daughter, wishing that her own practice of the art of poetry might prove happier than his, which (in the offence given to the reforming Augustus by the *Ars amatoria*) had been the ultimate, if not the immediate, cause of his banishment:

> Singula ne referam, nil non mortale tenemus
>   pectoris exceptis ingeniique bonis.
> en ego, cum caream patria vobisque domoque,
>   raptaque sint, adimi quae potuere mihi,
> ingenio tamen ipse meo comitorque fruorque:
>   Caesar in hoc potuit iuris habere nihil.
> quilibet hanc saevo vitam mihi finiat ense,
>   me tamen extincto fama superstes erit,
> dumque suis victrix omnem de montibus orbem
>   prospiciet domitum Martia Roma, legar.
> tu quoque, quam studii maneat felicior usus,
>   effuge venturos, qua potes, usque rogos!

('In a word, we possess nothing that is not mortal except the blessings of heart and genius. Look at me: though I lack my country and you and my home and have been deprived of all that could be taken from me,

I still have the companionship and enjoyment of my genius; over that Caesar was unable to exert his jurisdiction. Let who will end my life with cruel sword, my fame shall none the less survive my extinction. As long as Martian Rome shall gaze victoriously from her hills upon the whole conquered world, I shall be read. You too (may your practice of the art prove happier than mine!) keep on eluding to the best of your ability those approaching funeral fires.')

The remaining *loci* may be more summarily treated. In Ovid's *Amores* there are two passages concerned with the immortality which the poet himself can achieve, as distinct from that which he can confer: in I, xv, in reply to those who accuse him of idleness, he gives a long list of poets who have achieved eternal fame, and concludes

> Ergo etiam cum me supremus adederit ignis,
> vivam, parsque mei multa superstes erit

('Hence, even when the final fire has consumed me, I shall live and a great part of me will survive')—lines which contain an audacious and obvious imitation of a passage in Horace's epilogue to the Third Book:

> Non omnis moriar multaque pars mei
> vitabit Libitinam.

('I shall not wholly die and a great part of me will escape the funeral goddess.') In III, ix, the beautiful funeral elegy on Tibullus, the two themes are in some sort combined in the lines (27–30) declaring that, although Homer too has perished, his fame, and the fame of those he has celebrated, have survived:

> Hunc quoque summa dies nigro submersit Averno.
> defugiunt avidos carmina sola rogos.
> durat, opus vatum, Troiani fama laboris
> tardaque nocturno tela retexta dolo.

('Him too a final day submerged in black Avernus. Songs alone escape greedy funeral pyres. It endures, thanks to poets, the fame of the Trojan labour and the slow web unwoven [by Penelope] with nocturnal guile.') And then come two lines (39–40) memorably imitated by Herrick:

> Carminibus confide bonis; iacet, ecce, Tibullus,
> vix manet e toto parva quod urna capit.

('Trust to good songs. Here, look, lies Tibullus: there scarcely remains of the whole of him what a small urn will hold.')

In those passages where the elegiac poets promise, if not eternal, at least contemporary, fame to their mistresses and their 'lovely boys' the emphasis is mainly upon the enduringness of poetry in general, for a Roman poet could not publicly exalt the object of a purely personal affection with the weight and resonance with which Horace could celebrate the public virtues of Lollius and the achievements of Augustus. Great revolutions had to take place in European civilisation and sensibility before a Petrarch could speak as he did of his Laura or a Shakespeare of his friend. The theme of Horace's Censorinus ode, *Donarem pateras*, often reappears: the mistress or the boy may indeed find many lovers able to bestow more costly gifts, but the gifts bestowed by the poet will endure for ever. Thus in *Amores* I, x (59–62) Ovid declares that, while garments will get torn and gold and gems get broken, the fame conferred by his songs will be everlasting, and in II, xvii (27–8) that his *carmina* supply the place of a large fortune and that many women long to be celebrated by him. This theme reappears rather more impressively in the Third Book of the *Ars amatoria* (529–54), where Ovid tells women to be content with such gifts as their lovers are capable of giving: what poets have to give are songs, which can confer fame such as Tibullus's Nemesis, Propertius's Cynthia and Gallus's Lycoris enjoy, not to mention his own Corinna (in the *Amores*), about whose identity so many have enquired:

> Vatibus Aoniis faciles estote, puellae;
>   numen inest illis Pieridesque favent;
> est deus in nobis et sunt commercia caeli;[1]
>   sedibus aetheriis spiritus ille venit.

---

[1] Cf. *Fasti*, VI, 5 ff., where Ovid anticipates the objection that he is inventing and that no divinities have ever appeared to mortals:

> Est deus in nobis: agitante calescimus illo.
>   impetus hic sacrae semina mentis habet.
> fas mihi praecipue vultus vidisse deorum;
>   vel quia sum vates, vel quia sacra cano.

('There is a god within us: through his upstirring we grow warm. This impulse has in it seeds of the sacred mind. It was lawful for me above all to have beheld countenances of gods, both because I am a poet and because I sing of sacred things.') It may well have been from these passages rather than from unironical Renaissance commentaries on Plato's ironical treatment of it in the *Ion* that, as distinct from conventional allusions to the Muses, something like a theory of, or belief in, the divine inspiration of poets reached Spenser and others. Spenser quotes the half-line *agitante calescimus illo* as 'Cuddies Embleme' at the end of the October eclogue in *The Shepheardes Calender*.

('Be compliant, girls, with the Aonian bards; there is a divinity in them
and the Muses favour them. There is a god within us and commerce
with heaven; from the aetherial seats comes that inspiring breath.') In
the fourth elegy of Tibullus's First Book (61 ff.) Priapus, having
declared, in reply to the poet's question, that kindness and compliance
are the best ways to win a boy's affection, recollects that in these bad
days boys expect presents, and urges them to love poets and the Muses
and to disdain golden gifts:

> Quem referent Musae, vivet, dum robura tellus,
>   dum caelum stellas, dum vehet amnis aquas.

('He whom the Muses tell of shall live while earth bears oaks, sky stars,
stream waters.') Only Propertius, I think, and he only in a single passage,
has achieved something of an Horatian, almost, one might say, of a
Shakespearean, resonance on this topic of the contrast between the
poverty of the poet and the uniqueness of what he can bestow, when,
at the end of the second elegy of his Third Book (17 ff.), he declares that
his *carmina* shall be so many monuments to Cynthia's beauty and that,
while pyramids and temples and costly tombs are destroyed by fire or
weather or time, the fame his *ingenium* has achieved shall endure for ever:

> Fortunata, meo si qua est celebrata libello!
>   carmina erunt formae tot monumenta tuae.
> nam neque Pyramidum sumptus ad sidera ducti,
>   nec Iovis Elei caelum imitata domus,
> nec Mausolei dives fortuna sepulcri
>   mortis ab extrema condicione vacant.
> aut illis flamma aut imber subducet honores,
>   annorum aut ictu pondere victa ruent.
> at non ingenio quaesitum nomen ab aevo
>   excidet: ingenio stat sine morte decus.

('Happy you who have been celebrated in my book! My songs shall be
so many monuments of your beauty. For neither the starward-raised
costliness of the Pyramids, nor the heaven-imitating house of Jove at Elis,
nor the rich abundance of Mausolus's tomb are exempt from Death's
ultimate condition. Fire or rain will steal away their glories or, stricken
by the years, they will collapse under their own weight. But the name
acquired by genius shall not fall from memory through lapse of time:

for genius there abides undying its renown.') In *Amores* III, xii, Ovid professes to regret having celebrated Corinna's beauty, since by so doing he has turned her into a prostitute, made himself her bawd and pandar, and himself opened the door to other lovers, but Propertius, so far as I know, and again only in a single passage (III, xxiv, 1–8), is the only ancient poet who has declared, in a fit of anger, that his mistress's reputation for beauty is an illusion that has been created entirely by himself:

> Falsa est ista tuae, mulier, fiducia formae,
>   olim oculis nimium facta superba meis.
> noster amor tales tribuit tibi, Cynthia, laudes.
>   versibus insignem te pudet esse meis.
> mixtam te varia laudavi saepe figura,
>   ut, quod non esses, esse putaret amor;
> et color est totiens roseo collatus Eoo,
>   cum tibi quaesitus candor in ore foret.

('False is that confidence of yours in your beauty, woman long since made too proud by my [admiring] eyes. It was my love, Cynthia, that bestowed such praises on you. I am ashamed of the eminence you have acquired through my verses. Often did I praise the mingling in you of varied beauty, so that my love came to believe you to be that which you were not, and time and again your complexion was compared to rosy Dawn, although the brightness in your face had been acquired [by art].') It was no doubt this passage which suggested to Thomas Carew his famous

> Know *Celia*, (since thou art so proud,)
>   'Twas I that gave thee thy renowne,

where (again, so far as I know) the topic makes its first reappearance in modern vernacular poetry. On its absolute incompatibility with Petrarch's sonnets to Laura and Shakespeare's sonnets to his friend it is unnecessary to insist; although it is not, perhaps, so utterly remote from the mood of some of Shakespeare's sonnets to or about the 'Dark Lady'. It also sufficiently illustrates the contrast between the general light-heartedness, lack of reverence, and comparative superficiality in the promises, or proffers, of immortality which the elegiac poets make to their 'flames' and the *gravitas* with which Horace declares that he will not allow the public virtues of Lollius to be lost in oblivion. Indeed, except for some of the things which they are sometimes led on to say about poetry in general, the love-poets' verses on this topic of the poor but powerful poet seem, at least to a modern reader, to be continually approaching the territory of comic opera, or even of the music-hall joke ('You stick to me, Dolores— immortality's worth more than a mink coat').

2

Shakespeare and Petrarch

Leaving to others, if they think it worth while, to investigate the use of this topic in various ephemeral panegyrics by late Latin and medieval Latin poets, I will now turn to Petrarch, whose influence, direct or indirect, upon all Renaissance sonneteers was so inescapable and, to a considerable extent, determining. I cannot claim to have noticed every passage in his sonnets and canzoni where he speaks of the fame which his poetry has achieved, or may achieve, for Laura and for himself, but those which I have noticed among the 366 poems of the *Canzoniere*, and which I will briefly mention, are remarkably few and, for the most part, so modest and tremulous and muted that they might easily escape attention, and perhaps few students of Petrarch who had not been attentively looking for them would be able to remember that they were there. Shakespeare's treatments of this topic form an unforgettable and inseparable portion of our total impression of his sonnets, but Petrarch's require to be pointed out and do not significantly modify our total impression of the *Canzoniere*. Since few poets have thought more about posthumous fame than did Petrarch, 'the laureat poetë', as Chaucer called him, this might at first sight seem surprising, but there are, I think, two convincing explanations. In the first place, Petrarch's hopes of poetic immortality were based, not upon his vernacular, but upon his Latin poetry; and, in the second place (and perhaps far more importantly), the whole tradition, the whole manner of thinking and feeling, behind his poetry to and about Laura was absolutely incompatible with anything like resonant self-confidence or boastfulness. For Petrarch may be regarded as the first great populariser of that characteristic combination of Courtly Love and partly philosophic, partly Christian, idealism, unworldliness, and 'spirituality' which had been more reconditely expressed by Dante and some of his early Italian predecessors.

It is significant that in none of the Laura poems does Petrarch venture to speak of poetry as he does in 104,[1] *L'aspettata vertú, che'n voi fioriva*, a sonnet addressed to Pandolfo Malatesta, Lord of Rimini, who had already begun his distinguished military career, and for whom Petrarch declares that he wishes to write something that will make his name mount into esteem, since not even marble statues can be as permanent as writings. In the sestet the influence of Horace's Censorinus ode and Ovid's *Amores*, I, x (59–62), is sufficiently obvious:

> Credete voi che Cesare o Marcello
> O Paolo od Affrican fossin cotali
> Per incude già mai né per martello?
> Pandolfo mio, quest'opere son frali
> Al lungo andar; ma'l nostro studio è quello
> Che fa per fama gli uomini immortali.

('Do you believe that Caesar or Marcellus or Aemilius Paulus or Scipio Africanus could ever have become what they are for us through anvilled bronze or hammered marble? My Pandolf, these works are frail for long continuance, but the art we study is that which, through fame, makes men immortal.') In nearly all the Laura poems his allusions to *fama* are far more muted and humble than this, and are often, as it were, merely slipped in. Thus, in 61, *Benedetto sia 'l giorno e'l mese e l'anno*, after blessing the time and place of his first sight of her and all the sweet pain that followed, he concludes:

> E benedette sian tutte le carte[2]
> Ov'io fama le acquisto e 'l pensier mio
> Ch'è sol di lei sí ch'altra non v'ha parte.

[1] In my references to the *Canzoniere* I give the numbering in the edition by Carducci and Ferrari, which is that of most of the best modern editions, and I discard the cumbrous use of Roman numerals. I also give, in each case, the first line.

[2] Was Petrarch's habitual use of the word *carte*, in which he was followed by other poets, including Tasso, a Latinism imitated from Horace's declarations that he would not keep an unadorning silence about Lollius in his *chartae*:

> Non ego te meis
> chartis inornatum silebo (IV, ix, 30–1),

and that Censorinus's well-doing would not receive its due reward if *chartae* remained silent about it:

> Neque
> si chartae sileant quod bene feceris,
> mercedem tuleris (IV, viii, 20–2)?

('And blessed be all those parchments where I acquire fame for her, and [blessed be] my thought which is so entirely of her that no other woman has any part therein.') In 71, *Perché la vita è breve*, the first of three canzoni on Laura's eyes, he attributes to their power whatever merit his verse may possess (ll. 7–13):

> Occhi leggiadri dov' Amor fa nido,
> A voi rivolgo il mio debile stile
> Pigro di sé, ma 'l gran piacer lo sprona:
> E chi de voi ragiona
> Tien dal suggetto un abito gentile,
> Che con l'ale amorose
> Levando il parte d'ogni pensier vile.

('Charming eyes where Love makes his nest, to you I apply my feeble style, inert in itself, but great delight spurs it; and he who discourses of you draws from the subject a gentle habit which, with amorous wings exalting, withdraws him from all ignoble thought.') In 146, *O d'ardente vertute ornata e calda*, he seems to make a definite distinction between what he might have achieved in Latin and what he must be content with achieving in the vernacular. After apostrophising, in the octave, Laura's spiritual and physical beauty, he declares that, if his rhymes could be understood so far away, he would fill the remotest corners of the world with her praise, but that, since he cannot reach so far, he will make sure that Italy hears it,

> udrallo il bel paese
> Ch'Appennin parte e 'l mar circonda e l'Alpe.

In 186, *Se Virgilio et Omero avessin visto*, he declares that if Virgil and Homer had seen Laura they would have devoted all their powers to her celebration, to the discomfiture of Aeneas, Achilles, Ulysses, Augustus and Agamemnon. Scipio Africanus, 'that ancient flower of virtues and of arms, what a resembling star he would have had in this new flower of honesties and beauties. Ennius of him sang a rugged song, of this other I: and, oh, if only my wit be not tiresome to her and she do not disdain my praise!' In 187, *Giunto Alessandro a la famosa tomba*, Petrarch alludes to what was to become for Renaissance writers perhaps the most memorable of all *loci* on poetic immortality, the description by Plutarch in his *Life* and by Cicero in the *Pro Archia* of Alexander's visit to the tomb of Achilles, where he exclaimed, according to Cicero, *O fortunate adolescens, qui tuae virtutis Homerum praeconem inveneris!*[1] Petrarch regrets that the incomparable Laura

> Nel mio stil frale assai poco rimbomba,

'achieves so little resonance in my feeble style'. Worthy of Homer, Orpheus or Virgil, fate has committed her to one who adores her but whose telling of her perhaps diminishes her praise. In 194, *L'aura gentil che rasserena i poggi*, returning from Tuscany to the neighbourhood of Laura's Avignon and, it would seem, punning (in a manner often imitated by Tasso) upon *l'aura*, the breeze, and *Laura*, he declares that by its sweet breathing he recognises the gentle breeze which is unclouding the hills and awakening the flowers as that through which it is decreed that he should mount into torment and into fame,

> Per cui conven che 'n pena e'n fama poggi.

203, *Lasso, ch'i' ardo, et altri non me'l crede*, contains the nearest approach to something like an Horatian or Shakespearean proclamation. He reproaches her for pretending not to be aware of his love for her, which is so apparent to all others:

> Quest'arder mio, di che vi cal sí poco,
> E i vostri onori in mie rime diffusi
> Ne porian infiammar fors'ancor mille;
> Ch'io veggio nel pensier, dolce mio foco,
> Fredda una lingua e duo belli occhi chiusi
> Rimaner dopo noi pien di faville.

('This ardour of mine, for which you care so little, and your glories promulgated in my rhymes may yet perhaps be able to inflame thousands; for I behold in thought, sweet my fire, one cold tongue and two fair closed eyes remaining behind us full of sparks.') Here it seems probable that Petrarch had in mind Horace's beautiful lines about Sappho in the great roll-call of Greek lyric poets in the Lollius ode:

> Spirat adhuc amor
> vivuntque commissi calores
> Aeoliae fidibus puellae.

[1] Imitated by Spenser in *The Teares of the Muses*, 433–4. Petrarch's lines were quoted by E.K. at l. 65 of the October eclogue of the *Shepheardes Calender*. The story was retold by Amyot in the Preface to his translation of Plutarch's *Lives* and by Du Bellay in his *Deffense et Illustration de la langue française*, II, v.

('The love still breathes and the ardours still live that were confided to the Lesbian maiden's lyre'.) In 205, *Dolci ire, dolci sdegni e dolci paci*, after having comforted his soul, in the preceding sonnet, with the thought that Laura is leading it to God and the bliss of heaven, he now declares that she is also leading it to fame on earth: 'Do not repine, but endure and be silent, and temper the sweet bitterness which has distressed us with the sweet honour which you have received through the loving of her to whom I said: You alone delight me.' Some of the utterances we have already considered might be regarded as variations upon that familiar topic of panegyrical poetry and oratory, the author's apology for his inability to do justice to his subject, although on the lips of a courtly lover such professions can vibrate with a meaningfulness and a genuine humility that widely separate them from the tones of a courtly flatterer. Thus in 261, *Qual donna attende a gloriosa fama*, after declaring that other ladies can learn from Laura what true virtue is, Petrarch continues:

> Ivi 'l parlar che nullo stile aguaglia,
> E 'l bel tacere, e quei cari costumi
> Che 'ngegno uman non po spiegar in carte.

('Here is the speech which no style equals, and the lovely silence, and those dear manners which human wit cannot display in parchments.') And in what he says of 'fame' in the *Canzoniere* Petrarch often conveys the impression (perhaps, indeed, it is the total impression left by these passages) that to acquire it for Laura is a kind of religious duty, and that any fame he himself may acquire thereby is to be regarded as something more or less incidental, or at best as a kind of reward conceded to human frailty rather than as a personal achievement. Thus at the conclusion (ll. 73–6) of 268, *Che debb'io far? che mi consigli, Amore?*, a canzone written after the death of Laura, Love commands him not to be transported by his grief to suicide and thus lose Heaven where Laura is, sighing only for him:

> E sua fama, che spira
> In molte parti ancor per la tua lingua,
> Prega che non estingua,
> Anzi la voce al suo nome rischiari,
> Se gli occhi suoi ti fûr dolci né cari.

('And for her fame, which still breathes in many places through your speech [Horace's *spirat adhuc amor* yet again], she prays that it may not be extinguished, but rather that your voice may brighten at her name, if to you her eyes were sweet or dear.') It would seem that it was only gradually that Petrarch came to perceive that his poetry about Laura was achieving fame both for her and for himself. In 293, *S'io avesse pensato che sí care*, one of the sonnets written after her death, he declares that had he known that his 'rhymed sighings' (*le voci de' sospir miei in rima*) would become so cherished, he would have written more of them and in a better style:

> E certo ogni mio studio in quel tempo era
>   Pur di sfogare il doloroso core
>   In qualche modo, non d'acquistar fama.
> Pianger cercai, non già del pianto onore.

('And truly all my study at that time was to find some means of discharging my sad heart, not to win fame. Weeping I sought, in no wise honour through weeping.') Indeed, in the *Canzoniere* Petrarch seldom professes to regard his own fame (as distinct from any he may have won for Laura) as more than a consolation. In what I think is the last allusion to it, in 360, *Quell'antiquo mio dolce empio signore*, a canzone in which the poet cites Love before the tribunal of Reason, Love declares in his defence that it has been solely through him, who raised his intellect to where it would never have been raised by itself, that the poet has risen into some degree of fame (ll. 88–90):

> Salito in qualche fama
> Solo per me, che 'l suo intelletto alzai
> Ov' alzato per sé non fôra mai.

It is fascinating and illuminating to attempt, as the French say, to 'approfound' and 'precise' certain resemblances and differences between, on the one hand, Shakespeare and Petrarch and, on the other hand, between each of them and the ancients, in their treatment of this topic of poetic fame. To me, at any rate, it seems that from such an examination the almost uniquely mediatorial position of Shakespeare between the ancient and the modern, the Pagan and the Christian, worlds becomes most strikingly apparent. While the emphasis of Horace and Ovid and the rest is almost wholly upon the monumental and monumentalising quality of poetry in general and of their own poetry in particular, as an individual achievement that will be inseparably associated with themselves, and only secondarily, and in their love-poetry, one might almost say, only trivially, upon those whom they condescend to honour, Shakespeare and Petrarch alike never speak of their own poetry other than as a thing wholly dedicated, wholly subordinated, to the person it professes to honour. Shakespeare, like Petrarch, sometimes declares (though not, it must be admitted, in his very finest sonnets), and perhaps always implies, that his friend has been the sole inspirer of his verse, and only once, I think (in 107, the 'mortal moon' sonnet), does he use the pronoun 'I' in such a context and speak of the perpetuation of himself and of his friend on, as it were, equal terms:

> Now with the drops of this most balmy time
> My love looks fresh, and Death to me subscribes,
> Since, spite of him, I'll live in this poor rime,
> While he insults o'er dull and speechless tribes:
>   And thou in this shalt find thy monument
>   When tyrants' crests and tombs of brass are spent.

Some, no doubt, would say that even Shakespeare, when he wrote sonnets, was compelled, perhaps almost unconsciously, to conform to what might be called the sonnet tradition, which Petrarch himself had done so much to establish, and in which what was most central and unalterable was the tone and attitude, which must remain predominantly, despite any temporary back-slidings and rebelliousnesses, one of humility and adoration. Shakespeare, though, was writing these sonnets over a period during which not only was the vogue of the English sonnet declining, but during which the young men of the Inns of Court, stimulated no doubt by the example of brilliant Jack Donne of Lincoln's Inn, together with some of the young disciples of Ben Jonson, were rejecting and satirising all that Petrarch represented, and were attempting to revive, sometimes agreeably enough, but often, in what they doubtless regarded as achievements of the true Roman *sal* and *facetia*, with an embarrassing mixture of crudeness and caddishness, all those specifically pagan elements in ancient love-poetry which find no echo in either Petrarch or in Shakespeare. If Shakespeare remained, to a considerable extent, within the tradition of Petrarch, it was because of a certain spiritual affinity. 'Spirituality', indeed, a quality almost completely absent from ancient love-poetry, is perhaps the best single word to describe what the sonnets of Petrarch and of Shakespeare have in common. In a certain sense, perhaps, Shakespeare's sonnets to his friend are even more 'spiritual' than Petrarch's about Laura; for, while Petrarch, after all, has told us quite a lot about Laura, and all his contemporary readers knew, and were intended to know, who she was, how wholly inward and invisible in Shakespeare's sonnets is that 'life' which he promises to perpetuate! What was it in his friend that 'lives' there? We do not even know his name, and, if he was in any sense a public man, we have not a single allusion to any of his public acts, whether as courtier, soldier, statesman, or ruler of a great house or great estate. All we know of him is what he 'meant' to Shakespeare, which amounts to no more (and no less) than knowing something of what love and friendship meant to Shakespeare. How little here remains of the ancient conception of fame, of κλέος, or, if anything of it remains, what a strange metamorphosis it has undergone! That generalisation of the particular and particularisation of the general which becomes so increasingly characteristic of Shakespeare's dramatic verse is here, perhaps, most recognisably and persistently at work. All those qualities which make a person lovable, all those, perhaps, which for Shakespeare made life itself lovable and livable, are particularised, incarnated, in an individual, and that individual is generalised into their unique but alas! so transient incarnation. It is as though Shakespeare could only apprehend the meaningfulness of life when it was, for him, incarnated in a person, and as though he could only really love a person as the incarnation of that meaningfulness. (How enormous is the gulf between the most characteristic, that is to say, the most wholehearted, of Shakespeare's sonnets to his friend and those to or about the 'Dark Lady', with their continual admissions of recognised and hated self-deception, of the degradation of love into lust, and of the enslavement of the spirit to the flesh!) *Et incarnatus est*: whatever may have been Shakespeare's intellectual attitude towards that mystery, whether he 'died a Papist' or remained no more than a kind of half-believer, it inescapably and unconsciously influenced all his thinking and feeling. The 'inwardness' of his sonnets, in comparison with the 'outwardness' of the odes of Pindar and Horace, reflects not merely a difference in genius and temperament, but also certain characteristic differences between the Pagan and the Christian worlds. For Shakespeare, no less than Petrarch, is celebrating, not a doing, but a being, and is treating something inward and private and personal with a largeness and seriousness and solemnity such as an ancient poet could have extended only to something outward and public and impersonal. Such a reversal of ancient values would have been impossible but for Christianity, with its wholly new conceptions of incarnation and personality and inwardness and with its new and paradoxical conception of greatness. The reason why ancient love-poetry, and Renaissance imitations of ancient love-poetry, seem shallow in comparison with the love-poetry of Dante and Petrarch and Shakespeare is partly because Christianity, as Rudolf Kassner has finely said, gave a new depth-dimension to the human consciousness.

And yet, despite their affinity in spirituality and inwardness and in their dedication of their verse to the service of the beloved, whom both declare to have inspired it, how different are the manners in which Petrarch and Shakespeare speak of their poetry and of its purpose! Why does Petrarch habitually speak of it so humbly, mutedly and, as it were, inconspicuously, while Shakespeare so often speaks with an unforgettable and Horatian resonance of his 'powerful rime'? The reason is, I think, that Shakespeare is undertaking a larger, a more tremendous, a more desperate task. Petrarch conceives, or professes to conceive, it his duty to proclaim what one might almost call the gospel of Laura in order that her 'fame', her good fame, may increase among mankind at large the love of goodness and of gentleness; but, although he must try to ensure that her terrestrial life lives on in his verse as an 'example', he never suggests that her whole life is dependent upon him for its continuance, or that he alone stands between it and devouring Time. During her life-time he is fully convinced that her soul will find a place in Heaven, and, after her death, he conceives himself to be pleasing her soul in Heaven by continuing to spread the fame of what was heavenly in her among men on earth. Whether Shakespeare in any sense, if at all, 'believed' in the Christian doctrine of immortality I find impossible to decide; nevertheless, and although I should hesitate to pronounce with any confidence what non-metaphorical meanings may or may not be implicit in the utterances of one who so habitually thought in metaphors, I can only record my impression that from Shakespeare's Sonnets no less than from Horace's Odes there breathes the conviction that it is only in his poetry that anything of his friend and of himself beyond *pulvis et umbra* will survive. Survive in this world, survive among men? The distinction and the implication *may* be present, but they are not, I am inclined to say, meaningfully and poetically present. Shakespeare's sonnets, like Petrarch's, are unworldly, but not, like Petrarch's, other-worldly, and they are filled with a sadness different from Petrarch's and resembling that which breathes from so much of the great poetry of the ancient world: an almost overwhelming sadness at the fact of human transience.

3

Shakespeare and Tasso

Of Italian poetry and, more particularly, of the Italian sonnet from Petrarch to Tasso, I cannot claim more than a slight and superficial knowledge. The quantity, published and unpublished, must be so vast that there is probably no scholar who has read it all, and certainly no scholar able to remember even what he has read well enough to enable him to make confident generalisations about the presence or absence of significant treatments of particular topics. On this topic of poetic immortality the only really memorable utterances that I have been able to discover are in three sonnets of Tasso. There may well be many more in many other poets, and although some might say that, if they were really memorable, we should have heard of them by now, I do not myself feel able to anticipate their possible production with such easy assurance—true though it be that I strongly doubt whether the most diligent investigator would be able to produce enough memorable poetry to disprove my assertion about the joint pre-eminence, on this topic, of Horace and Shakespeare.

Of the three sonnets of Tasso, one is addressed to Alfonso II, Duke of Ferrara, declaring, as the title has it, 'that there is on earth no truer image of eternity than the glory obtained through writers'. The latter part of it may well have owed something to Du Bellay's *Antiquitez de Rome*, which had been published in 1558, but it is perhaps the most memorable of all Renaissance poems on the 'outlastingness' of poetry and by far the finest of those all-too-numerous sonnets in which the unhappy poet appealed from his confinement to the various grandees of Italy. In the Miltonic manner in which the sense is 'variously drawn out from one verse into another', it is a superb example of that new style introduced into the writing of Italian sonnets by Bembo and carried further by Della Casa, whom Tasso admired and imitated.[1]

Quando nel ciel tra mille aurate sedi
Che piene son de'tuoi grandi avi illustri,

[1] On this subject see F. T. Prince, *The Italian Element in Milton's Verse*, 1954.

T'innalzerà dopo girar di lustri
Chi comparte le pene e le mercedi,
Sorger vedrai sotto gl'invitti piedi
Gl'imperi e poi cader quasi ligustri[1]
Frali, e capanne ti parran palustri
Gli eccelsi tetti de' tuoi regi eredi;
Di Menfi e di Babel cadute e sparte
Le meraviglie barbare e sepolta
Roma fra le ruine onde s'ammira:
Solo in terra vedrai farsi le carte
Del cielo imago, e'n lor tua gloria accolta
Qual vivo sol se tua pietà m'aspira.

('When into Heaven amidst thousand gilded seats which are filled with your great illustrious ancestors shall exalt you after revolving of lustres He who allots the penalties and the rewards, you shall see rising beneath your invincible feet the empires and then falling like frail privets, and marsh cabins shall appear to you the lofty roofs of your royal heirs; of Memphis and of Babylon fallen and scattered the barbarian marvels and Rome buried among the ruins whence she is admired: on earth you shall see parchments alone acting as an image of Heaven, and in them your glory welcomed like a living sun, if your pity lift me up.')[2]

The two sonnets from the *Rime d'Amore* were much imitated, either in whole or in part, and sometimes with, sometimes without, allusions to the faithful poet's verse as a mirror in which the once scornful but now penitent mistress shall behold her vanished beauty, by later poets—by Desportes, for example, and by Daniel in at least three of his *Delia* sonnets;[3] and it seems not impossible (for poetry written on the other side of the Alps seems to have reached him with surprising rapidity) that they may have contributed, together with much else, to the inspiration of Ronsard's most famous sonnet, *Quand vous serez bien vieille*. They were printed consecutively and are among the later sonnets to Lucrezia

---

[1] A reminiscence of Virgil, *Eclogues*, II, 17–18:

O formose puer, nimium ne crede colori:
alba ligustra cadunt, vaccinia nigra leguntur.

('O lovely boy, do not trust too much to your complexion: white privets fall, dark hyacinths are gathered.')

[2] *Rime*, ed. Solerti, III, p. 235. The sonnet *S'egli averrà ch'alta memoria antica* (*op. cit.*, p. 135), telling Lucrezia d'Este, Duchess of Urbino, that if ever he is able to complete the *Gerusalemme Liberata* it will have been due to her encouragement, and that her fame will be coeval with the poem, is perhaps too occasional to be included among poems on this topic.

[3] 36, 39 and 40 in Esdaile's ed. (text of 1623).

Bendidio, for whom Tasso's long passion was now drawing to a close. In the first of them there enters for the first time into what has hitherto been a predominantly Petrarchan world the specifically classical and pagan topic, alien both to Petrarch and to Shakespeare, of 'ingrateful beauty threatened'.

> Vedrò da gli anni in mia vendetta ancora
>   Far di queste bellezze alte rapine,
>   Vedrò starsi negletto e bianco il crine
>   Che la natura e l'arte increspa e dora;
> E su le rose, ond'ella il viso infiora,
>   Spargere il verno poi nevi e pruine:
>   Cosí il fasto e l'orgoglio avrà pur fine
>   Di costei, ch'odia piú chi piú l'onora.
> Sol penitenza allor di sua bellezza
>   Le rimarrà, vedendo ogni alma sciolta
>   De gli aspri nodi suoi ch'ordía per gioco;
> E, se pur tanto or mi disdegna e sprezza,
>   Poi bramerà, ne le mie rime accolta,
>   Rinnovellarsi qual fenice in foco.

('I shall yet see in my requital rapine made by the years of these lofty beauties, shall see standing neglected and white the hair that nature and art curl and gild; and upon the roses with which Nature beflowers that face, winter then scattering snows and frosts: thus shall they too have end, the pomp and pride of her who hates most him who most honours her. Then only repentance of her beauty shall remain with her, beholding every soul loosed from those hard knots of hers she wove for sport; and, even though now she so disdains and despises me, she then shall long, received into my rhymes, to be renewed like phoenix in fire.')

> Quando avran queste luci e queste chiome
>   Perduto l'oro e le faville ardenti,
>   E l'arme de'begli occhi or sí pungenti
>   Saran dal tempo rintuzzate e dome,
> Fresche vedrai le piaghe mie, né, come
>   In te le fiamme, in me gli ardori spenti;
>   E rinnovando gli amorosi accenti
>   Alzerò questa voce al tuo bel nome.
> E'n guisa di pittor che il vizio emende

Del tempo, mostrerò ne gli alti carmi
Le tue bellezze in nulla parte offese:
Fia noto allor ch'a lo spuntar de l'armi
Piaga non sana e l'esca un foco apprende
Che vive quando spento è chi l'accese.

('When these eyes and this hair shall have lost the gold and the glowing sparks, and the weapons of the fair eyes now so piercing shall be by time blunted and tamed, fresh shall you see my wounds, nor, as in you the flames, extinguished in me the ardours, and, renewing the amorous accents, I shall uplift this voice at your fair name. And, like painter who emends the blemish of time, I shall show in lofty songs your beauties in no part harmed: then shall be manifest that at the unpointing of the weapons [sc. that caused it] wound does not heal and the fuel is seized by a fire that lives when extinct is what kindled it.')[1]

Even in the second of these two sonnets there is a certain Roman *superbia*, a certain self-exaltation on the part of the poet and a certain condescension towards the object of his affection, which reveals, I think, the influence of ancient love-poetry (although I cannot recall any ancient love-poet's having declared that his love would outlast his mistress's beauty),[2] and which is alien to the Petrarchan tradition. The tone and spirit of it is also subtly but profoundly different from Shakespeare's greatest and, so far as I know, both literally and metaphorically *incomparable*, utterance on the topic of 'eternity in love protested', an utterance in which even the greatest of poets seems to have become completely merged into something greater, and in which we seem to hear, no longer merely the poet, but love itself defying Time:

Let me not to the marriage of true minds
Admit impediments. Love is not love
Which alters when it alteration finds,
Or bends with the remover to remove:
O, no! it is an ever-fixed mark,
That looks on tempests and is never shaken;

---

[1] *Rime*, ed. Solerti, II, pp. 109–11. These two sonnets, together with thirty-five other sonnets by Tasso, were first printed in *Rime degli Academici Eterei*, dedicated to Marguerite de Valois, in 1567, a copy of which must very soon have come into the hands of Ronsard.

[2] The nearest approach to an example that I have been able to find is an epigram by Strato in the Greek Anthology (xii, 10), addressed not to a mistress but to a boy: 'Even though hair-onbringing down has leapt upon you and delicate auburn curls around the temples, not even so will I forsake my beloved, but his beauty, even with beard, even with hairs, is mine.'

It is the star to every wandering bark,[1]
Whose worth's unknown, although his height be taken.
Love's not Time's fool, though rosy lips and cheeks
Within his bending sickle's compass come;
Love alters not with his brief hours and weeks,
But bears it out even to the edge of doom.
    If this be error and upon me proved,
    I never writ, nor no man ever loved.

(116)

Perhaps, though, it is not quite fair to Tasso, perhaps it would not be quite fair to any poet, to make him stand the push of this comparison.

4

Shakespeare and Ronsard

The young Ronsard, as I have already remarked, in the course of his truly Stakanovitish labours in the service of that great Five Year Plan to raise what I suppose would now be called the 'productivity' of French poetry to a level with that of the ancients, not only imitated almost everything that any ancient poet had ever said about the enduringness of poetry, but also, and often in a quite breath-taking manner, spoke of his own poetry and his own immortality much as Pindar, Horace and the rest had spoken of theirs. Thus, at the end of the Fourth Book of his Odes, published in 1550 when he was twenty-five, he inserted a kind of epilogue *A sa Muse* (later transferred to the end of the Fifth Book when, by the addition of that, he had overtopped Horace's four-book monument), beginning 'Plus dur que fer, j'ai fini mon ouvrage;'[2]

---

[1] From Petrarch onwards (canzone 73, *Poi che per mio destino*, ll. 46–57) this metaphor, which may have been suggested by the first line of a hymn to the Virgin, *Ave maris stella*, appears frequently in love-poetry.

[2] Laumonier, II, 152. I shall quote Ronsard's poetry partly from the still uncompleted edition begun by the late Paul Laumonier for the Société des Textes Français Modernes (1924–), in which the poems, with the later variants, are given in the text and chronological sequence of their first printing, and partly from the complete edition by Hugues Vaganay (1923), in which the text, except for poems printed after that date, is Ronsard's own 1578 edition of his *Œuvres*.

and in the ode *De l'Election de son Sepulchre* he declared that the shepherds would visit every year his tomb on an island in the Loire and would exclaim:

> Que tu es renommée
> D'estre tumbeau nommée
> D'un de qui l'univers
> Ouira [*later:* chante] les vers[1]—

one of those passages where, for an English reader, the short lines become irresistibly reminiscent of eighteenth-century opera libretto and emphasise the difference between the vastness of the claim and the triviality of its expression. Not that I begrudge the 'Prince of Poets' any portion of the fame that has at last been restored to him for his real and imperishable achievements: my intention is merely to point the contrast between the youthful *hybris* of the odes and the comparatively sober and infrequent appearances of this topic in his love-sonnets, of which he must have written upwards of five hundred. It is a contrast which seems to me strong evidence for the restraining and prescribing influence of what I have called the sonnet tradition. Nevertheless, even in his sonnets Ronsard's utterances on this topic are restrained only in comparison with those in his odes; and although, in proportion to the number of his sonnets, they are comparatively infrequent, they produce, when placed together, a total impression of self-exaltation that would have shocked Petrarch, and which is quite different from that exaltation of poetry as the defier of Time and eternaliser of transient beauty that we find in Shakespeare. Of Petrarch's worshipping and evangelising and of Shakespeare's selfless devotion and sadness over human transience, and of what I have called the 'spirituality' of both these poets, there is little trace in Ronsard;[2] and the general impression conveyed by his own utterances about it is that even in his love-poetry he was primarily concerned with building yet further monuments to his own glory—by which I do not mean to imply that the monuments are not often splendid or the glory unachieved.

To the first collection of his *Amours* (1552), celebrating mainly his 'Cassandre', he prefixed a sonnet dedicated to the Muses, which, like so

---

[1] Laumonier, II, 99.

[2] Ronsard was a devout, and even fanatical, Catholic, while Shakespeare, for all we know, may have been about as much of a 'believer' as Montaigne; nevertheless, in a profound sense, Shakespeare is far more Christian. Indeed, greatly as I admire Ronsard's finest poetry, I am sometimes tempted to wonder whether there does not remain, after all, a certain superficiality that excludes him from what Matthew Arnold used to call 'the glorious class of the best'.

many of his poems, underwent much alteration in later editions, and of which the sestet (printed in capitals which it does not seem necessary to reproduce) reads as follows in the text of 1578:

> Ronsard, afin que le siècle avenir
> Maugré le temps en puisse souvenir
> Que sa jeunesse à l'amour fist homage:
> De la main dextre apand à vostre autel
> L'humble present de son livre immortel,
> Son cœur de l'autre aux pieds de ceste image.

There are indeed a few professions of humility in Ronsard's sonnets, but, like the use of the word *humble* in the penultimate line of this dedication, they have a hollow ring and the appearance of mere concessions to a convention he is only pretending to accept. In two of the Cassandre sonnets where he is partly imitating some of Petrarch's professions of poetic insufficiency there are characteristic and significant differences. In 72,

> Amour, que n'ay-je en escrivant, la grace
> Divine autant que j'ay la volonté,[1]

he declares that if only he could achieve the height of style he longs for he would surpass Orpheus. Loftier even than Pindar and Horace, he would dedicate to her divinity a book so weighty that even Du Bellay would give place. Not even Laura would fly so alive through the world in Tuscan verse as she would in French. This was clearly suggested by Petrarch's 146th, *O d'ardente vertute ornata e calda*, but while Petrarch is merely saying (in so many words) that, since he is writing in the vernacular and not in Latin, he must be content with an Italian audience, Ronsard has no doubt either about the universality of the French language or about his own ultimate ability to surpass Pindar and Horace—as his friend Du Bellay already has done! His 87th,

> Si l'escrivain de la Gregeoise armée
> Eust vu tes yeux, qui serf me tiennent pris,

[1] Ronsard continued to add to, rearrange and revise his Cassandre and Marie sonnets and eventually entitled them, respectively, the first and the second *Livres des amours*. To them, in the edition of 1578, he added for the first time the *Sonets pour Helene*. They are all contained in the first two volumes of Vaganay's edition, to which, giving the number and the first line, I shall henceforth refer, and from which (in the text of 1578) I shall quote.

was clearly suggested by Petrarch's 186th, *Se Virgilio et Omero avessin visto*, and 187th, *Giunto Alessandro a la famosa tomba*, but while Petrarch professes to regret that his style, unlike those of Homer and Virgil, is unworthy of his subject, Ronsard declares that if only he is able to celebrate Cassandre worthily,

> Il n'y aura ny myrthe ny laurier
> Digne de toy, ny digne de ma teste.

In 199,

> Pille, Garçon, d'une main larronnesse
> Le bel esmail de la verte saison,

he tells his page to gather flowers for his room, to fetch him his 'lyre', so that he may soothe his torment, and also to give him ink and paper:

> En cent papiers tesmoins de mon souci,
> Je veux tracer la peine que j'endure:
> En cent papiers plus durs que diamant,
> Afin qu'un jour nostre race future
> Juge du mal que je souffre en aimant.

Ronsard, I think, was the first poet to introduce, often with splendid effectiveness, such pieces of self-dramatisation into his sonnets, and I am inclined to think that Sidney learnt the device from him and that Ronsard himself learnt it from some of Horace's odes. I have no doubt whatever that the 'Garçon' in this sonnet is the equivalent of that *puer* whom Horace tells not to spend time searching for some last rose for a chaplet, or to cool some Falernian, or to run and fetch Lyde with her lyre or Neaera with her chestnut hair.

In the sonnets and poems inspired by simple Marie of Bourgueil the immortality theme occurs only in a sonnet, first printed in the *Bocage* of 1554, which, in the editions from 1560 onwards, served as an epilogue to the second *Livre des amours*, where it was preceded by an *Elegie à Marie*, a charming poem, with some notable imitations of ancient poets. The passage, in this *Elegie*, about the temple which, if he were a great king, Ronsard would build on the banks of the Loire, with statues of Marie and of himself, is imitated and elaborated from Theocritus's twelfth Idyll, and the concluding lines, expressing the wish that after their deaths a spirit may descend to him in the Shades, and tell him that his songs about their love are still on the lips of men, are imitated from the tenth Idyll; while the opening lines bring Ronsard, for once at any rate, into the company of Shakespeare, for they were certainly, as I think Shakespeare's 74th sonnet was almost certainly, inspired by Ovid's epilogue to the *Metamorphoses*, and for Ovid's

> Parte tamen meliore mei super alta perennis
> astra ferar

Ronsard has found an equivalent not less memorable than Shakespeare's

> My spirit in thine, the better part of me.

> Marie, à celle fin que le siecle advenir
> De noz jeunes amours se puisse souvenir,
> Et que vostre beauté que j'ay long temps aimée,
> Ne se perde au tombeau par les ans consumée,
> Sans laisser quelque marque apres elle de soy:
> Je vous consacre icy le plus gaillard de moy,
> L'esprit de mon esprit, qui vous fera revivre
> Ou long temps, ou jamais, par l'âge de ce livre.[1]

That in lines inspired, or partly inspired, by the same passage in Ovid both Ronsard and Shakespeare should have used, respectively, the words *consacre* and *consecrate* ('The very part was consecrate to thee') is surely a rather remarkable coincidence, even though not, perhaps, in itself sufficient to prove that Shakespeare had read Ronsard, who, partly, it may be, because of his violent anti-Protestantism, seems (except by Sidney, Spenser and the all too imitative Lodge) to have been less widely read in England than either Du Bellay or Desportes. Ronsard imitated the Ovidian *locus* again in an elegy *Au Roy* (Henri III), beginning *Je resemble, mon Prince, au Prestre d'Apollon*, first printed in the 1584 edition of his *Œuvres*, in a passage concluding with a line which (as we shall see) had already concluded one of the Hélène sonnets:

> Ne vous arrestez point à la vieille prison
> Qui enferme mon corps, ny à mon poil grison,
> A mon menton fleuri: mon corps n'est que l'escorce.
> Servez-vous de l'esprit, mon esprit est ma force.
> Le corps doit bien tost rendre en un tombeau poudreux

[1] Vaganay, II, 145.

> Aux premiers Elements cela qu'il a pris d'eux.
> L'esprit vivra tousjours qui vous doit faire vivre,
> Au moins tant que vivront les plumes et le livre.[1]

Here again the Shakespearean resemblances are striking:

> The earth can have but earth, which is his due;
> My spirit is thine, the better part of me.
>
> (74)

> So long as men can breathe or eyes can see,
> So long lives this and this gives life to thee.
>
> (18)

I find it hard not to give at least serious consideration to the possibility that Ronsard may have helped Shakespeare to find a new meaningfulness in Ovid's lines, and even that it may have been mainly a reading of Ronsard which suggested to him, as a main topic, the theme of poetic immortality, true though it be that Shakespeare treated that topic in his own far less egotistical fashion. The absence, except perhaps in the passages I have just quoted, of any striking resemblances in phraseology is not in itself against this possibility, since, as I have already remarked, Shakespeare transfigured and Shakespeareanised his reading to a far greater extent than any other Renaissance poet. In the main, therefore, we must be content with suggesting possibilities and attempting to estimate degrees of probability. All that we can be really certain about is that he had read far more poetry than we shall ever be able to demonstrate.

In the sonnet (74) which eventually came to serve as epilogue to the second *Livre des amours*, and which begins

> Cesse tes pleurs, mon livre: il n'est pas ordonné
> Du destin, que moy vif tu sois riche de gloire,

Ronsard promises immortality, not to Marie, but to his book, and imitates, with a characteristic piece of outdoing, a passage at the conclusion of the *Amores* (III, xv, 11–14), where Ovid imagines a stranger in days to come contemplating the walls of little Sulmo (now Sulmona), his birthplace:

[1] Vaganay, V, 233.

Atque aliquis spectans hospes Sulmonis aquosi
  moenia, quae campi iugera pauca tenent,
'Quae tantum', dicet, 'potuistis ferre poetam,
  quantulacumque estis, vos ego magna voco'.

('And some stranger, beholding the walls of well-watered Sulmo, which enclose but few acres of plain, "You," he will say, "who were able to give birth to such a poet, however small you are, I call you great." ') Horace and Virgil and Ovid, with a local patriotism that still survives in Italy, all proudly referred to their humble birthplaces as places where they would be for ever remembered, but it was more than problems of scansion that prevented them from introducing into these and similar contexts their own names.[1] Ronsard, I think, was the first, and perhaps the last, great poet to commit this final arrogance:

Quelqu'un apres mille ans de mes vers estonné
Viendra dedans mon Loir, comme en Permesse,[2] boire:
Et voyant mon pays, à peine pourra croire
Que d'un si petit champ Ronsard se vante né.

[1] Only once in his Odes does Horace insert his own name: in IV, vi, where, after celebrating Apollo, first as the preserver, together with Venus, of Aeneas and the destiny of Rome from what would have been the consequences of the wrath of a still living Achilles, and then as his own inspirer, he addresses the choir of boys and girls who are to sing that Carmen Saeculare which he, Apollo's vates, has been commissioned to write by the city which Apollo helped to found:

Nupta iam dices 'ego dis amicum,
saeculo festas referente luces,
reddidi carmen docilis modorum
vatis Horati'.

('Long after being made a wife you will say: "I, in that song pleasing to the gods, when the cycle brought round again the festal days—I took part in singing it, trained in the measures of bard Horatius." ') This single mention in his Odes of Horace's own name is not accompanied by any confident prediction of his own poetic immortality, but has affinity with the simple σφραγίς (seal) in which, at the conclusion of poems or collections of poems, various Hellenistic poets had, as it were, signed their own names, following, it may be, the example of Hesiod at the beginning of his Theogony. Similarly, Virgil's wonderful σφραγίς at the end of the Georgics is not accompanied by any prophecy of his own immortality: he merely says that, while Octavian was triumphing in the East,

Illo Vergilium me tempore dulcis alebat
Parthenope, studiis florentem ignobilis oti.

('At that time I, Virgil, was being nursed by sweet Parthenope and was flourishing in the arts of inglorious leisure.') About most of Ronsard's introductions of his own name into prophecies of his own immortality one feels a want of tact and sensitivity akin to that in certain passages in his sonnets where he has adapted to his own glorification passages where Petrarch is professing his inability to celebrate Laura worthily.

[2] The doubtfully identifiable river Permessus rose on Mount Helicon, and references to it in Virgil (Eclogues, vi, 64) and Propertius (II, xi, 26) suggest that it was an accepted literary symbol for love-elegy, in contrast to the actual summit of Helicon, which stood for heroic poetry: see a letter from P. O. R. Smiley, T.L.S., 17 April 1959.

In the *Sonets pour Helene*, written in late middle age and containing some of Ronsard's finest verse, the immortality theme makes three notable appearances, although in each case, it must be admitted, in a manner and with an emphasis strongly suggesting that Hélène de Surgères was but the occasion for the erection of further monuments to the glory of Pierre Ronsard. In II, 2, beginning

> Afin qu'à tout jamais de siecle en siecle vive
> La parfaite amitié que Ronsard vous portoit,

he sends her a 'sempervive', or sengreen:

> Elle vit longuement en sa jeune verdeur.
> Long temps apres la mort je vous feray revivre,
> Tant peut le docte soin d'un gentil serviteur,
>   Qui veut, en vous servant, toutes vertus ensuivre.
> Vous vivrez (croyez-moy) comme Laure en grandeur,
> Au moins tant que vivront les plumes et le livre.

II, 49, beginning

> Ceste fleur de Vertu, pour qui cent mille larmes
> Je verse nuict et jour sans m'en pouvoir souler,

was clearly suggested by those two sonnets of Petrarch, already referred to, in which he professes to regret that Laura did not live in the days of Homer and Virgil; but while Petrarch dares not hope to do more for Laura, that 'new flower of honesties and beauties', than what Ennius, in his rugged song, was able to do for that 'ancient flower of virtues and of arms' Scipio Africanus, Ronsard not only has no hesitation in declaring that he will do for Hélène what Homer did for Achilles, but even implies, in his concluding lines, that she ought to be very grateful to him for doing it, since, whatever he may have condescended to say in praise of her, 'this creature', in the words of Shakespeare's Cleopatra, 'is no such *thing*':

> Il eut pour sa prouësse un excellent sonneur:
> Tu as pour tes vertuz en mes vers un honneur,
> Qui malgré le tombeau suivra ta renommée.
>   Les Dames de ce temps n'envient ta beauté,
> Mais ton nom tant de fois par les Muses chanté,
> Qui languiroit d'oubly, si je ne t'eusse aimée.

The implication in the concluding lines is quite unambiguously expressed in the fifth of the eight Hélène sonnets first published in 1609, long after Ronsard's death, a sonnet in which he reproaches her with her ingratitude towards him, who has raised her from comparative obscurity to a fame equal to that of Marguerite de Valois, Queen of Navarre, whom the young but up-and-coming Desportes had celebrated in his *Hippolyte* sonnets:

> Quand au commencement j'admiré ton merite,
> Tu vivois à la Court sans louange et sans bruit:
> Maintenant un renom par la France te suit,
> Egallant en grandeur la Royalle Hypolite.
> Liberal j'envoyay les Muses à ta suite,
> Je fis loin de ton chef evanouïr la nuit,
> Je fis flamber ton nom comme un astre qui luit,
> J'ay dans l'azur du Ciel ta loüange décrite.[1]

Ronsard, here and elsewhere, comes very close to that original variation on the theme of 'ingrateful beauty threatened' which, as I have already remarked, seems to have been first fully developed by Carew. Ronsard does not, indeed, go so far as to declare (though he very often seems to imply) that, as Propertius had declared in one of his elegies, his mistress's reputation for beauty is an illusion created by himself, nor does he, like Carew, threaten to 'uncreate' what he has created; nevertheless, the mixture of condescension and self-exaltation, the insolence, that is present in almost every one of the utterances on poetic fame in his love-poetry is far closer to the second stanza of Carew's famous poem than to anything in Petrarch or in Shakespeare:

> That killing power is none of thine,
>   I gave it to thy voyce and eyes:
> Thy sweets, thy graces, all are mine;
>   Thou art my starre, shin'st in my skies;
> Then dart not from thy borrowed sphere
> Lightenings on him, that fixt thee there.

While there is a certain spiritual affinity between Petrarch and Shakespeare, there is scarcely, I am sometimes inclined to think, any more real spiritual affinity between Petrarch and Ronsard than there is between Petrarch and Carew.

[1] Vaganay, I, 473.

T.A.V.I.S.S.—C

I have deferred until now my consideration of II, 24. Ronsard wrote many fine sonnets besides *Quand vous serez bien vieille*, just as Gluck wrote many fine arias besides *Che farò senza Euridice*, but the public at large will probably continue to think of them as, first and foremost, the authors of those two compositions.[1] This sonnet is perhaps the most wonderful single result of the Renaissance theory and practice of 'imitation'; for although, except for the characteristic insolence and dramatisation and introduction, not merely once but twice, of the poet's own name, there is literary precedent for almost every detail, precedent without which the sonnet could not have been what it is, it yet remains in the truest sense original and such as no other poet but Ronsard could have written. The central 'idea', if one may so call it, that of an ageing mistress reviewing in the poet's verses, as in a mirror, her former beauty and reproaching herself with her unresponsiveness to his love, was, I think, first expressed, or first memorably expressed, and in such a manner as to excite many imitations, by Tasso in the two sonnets which I have already quoted; although, while Tasso imagines himself as still living and 'serving', Ronsard imagines himself as dead. The subsidiary ideas or topics, with which this central idea is combined, those of 'ingrateful beauty threatened' and what might be called *carpe florem*, had been frequently handled by the poets of the *Greek Anthology* and by Horace and the Roman elegiac poets, when they threatened an unresponsive mistress or 'lovely boy' with the loneliness and the regret for lost opportunities of pleasure that would come with the all too swift disappearance of transient beauty. Perhaps the most elaborate, most famous, and, by Renaissance poets, most imitated of all ancient treatments of the topic *carpe florem* was the fourteenth Idyll, *Rosae*, of Ausonius, with an imitation of whose concluding lines Ronsard himself concludes his sonnet:

> Collige, virgo, rosas, dum flos novus et nova pubes:
> et memor esto aevum sic properare tuum.

('Gather, virgin, roses, while the flower is new and new its youngness, and remember that just so are hasting the days that are your own.') There remains the setting, the dramatically and almost realistically imagined situation of the ageing mistress, *au soir à la chandelle*, unwinding and spinning flax with her women and murmuring Ronsard's poems about her, mention of whose name rouses them all from their half-somnolent

---

[1] It would, of course, be as impossible to associate Shakespeare with one particular sonnet (or comedy, or tragedy) as it would be to associate Mozart with one particular aria (or symphony, or concerto, or quartet).

labours. Even this was suggested to Ronsard by one of the most memorable things of its kind in Latin poetry, the concluding portion of an elegy of Tibullus (I, iii), which contains two other passages (of a more conventional kind) often imitated by Renaissance poets. Tibullus addresses the elegy to his friend Messalla from a sick-bed in Phaeacia, and, professing to fear that he may die in this foreign land without proper funeral rites, curses sea-faring and introduces an elaborate description of the Golden Age, when sea-faring was unknown. Then he declares that, even if he is doomed to perish here, Venus will conduct him to the Lovers' Elysium, with which he contrasts the place of punishment to which he prays that all interrupters and profaners of his love may come. In the concluding lines (83 ff.) he addresses his mistress Delia:

> But for you, I pray that you may remain chaste, and that, as guardian of holy honour, the old woman may ever sit sedulously at your side. Let her tell you stories when the lamp has been set in its place and draw the long skeins from the full distaff, while around you the maids, bending over their toilsome tasks, gradually grow heavy with sleep and drop their work. Then may I suddenly come, all unannounced, so that I may seem to have been sent from heaven into your presence.

This passage of almost Homeric simplicity, so different from the social backgrounds and scenes which Ovid so often evokes in the *Amores* and *Ars amatoria*, must suddenly have suggested to Ronsard one of those dramatic situations he was peculiarly able to exploit, and it is above all his brilliant transposition and modification of it that makes the familiar topics it enshrines appear as things almost wholly new.

> Quand vous serez bien vieille, au soir à la chandelle,
> Assise aupres du feu, devidant[1] et filant,
> Direz, chantant mes vers, en vous esmerveillant,
> Ronsard me celebroit du temps que j'estois belle.
> Lors vous n'aurez servante oyant telle nouvelle,

---

[1] *Devidant*, 'winding or unwinding from a reel or distaff', is the reading of the editions both of 1578 and 1584, and I think it must stand, although many modern scholars and anthologists seem to prefer *devisant*, 'chatting', which appeared for the first time in some of the posthumous editions. The corresponding lines of Tibullus are

> Haec tibi fabellas referat positaque lucerna
> deducat plena stamina longa colu.

Devisant, it is true, is nearer to *fabellas referat*, but what corresponds to that in Ronsard is *chantant mes vers*, and Hélène could not be both *chantant* and *devisant* at the same time. *Devidant*, on the other hand, exactly corresponds to *deducat*, 'unwinding (flax from the distaff) and spinning'.

Desja sous le labeur à demi sommeillant,
Qui au bruit de Ronsard ne s'aille resveillant,
Benissant vostre nom de louange immortelle.
 Je seray sous la terre, et fantaume sans os:
Par les ombres Myrtheux je prendray mon repos:
Vous serez au fouyer une vieille accroupie,
 Regrettant mon amour, et vostre fier desdain.
Vivez, si m'en croyez, n'attendez à demain:
Cueillez dés aujourd'huy les roses de la vie.

As a love-poem, this great sonnet is in some ways nearer to the ancients and in some ways nearer to the moderns than to either Petrarch or Shakespeare. That splendid *superbia*, sometimes amounting almost to insolence, and that exaltation of the poet, which elsewhere often blends so incongruously with passages that Ronsard has imitated from Petrarch, is an ancient, and, above all, a Roman thing; although in ancient love-poetry such exaltation of the poet is never *integrated* in this way. It is not in love-poetry, but in poetry celebrating public achievements—certain passages in Pindar and Horace's Lollius ode—that we find a similar integration, and even there, although poetry is exalted, the poet does not venture to exalt himself above his subject or to transpose, as it were, from love-poetry the topic of 'ingrateful beauty threatened' and introduce it as 'ingrateful eminence threatened'. In their numerous passages on the topic of 'ingrateful beauty threatened' the ancient love-poets spoke in the main merely as men, not specifically as poets: an ancient poet might declare that the day would come when his mistress would look in her glass and be sorry, but Tasso, so far as I know, was the first poet to declare that the day would come when she would look in his verses and be sorry; and, as I have already remarked, I think it was probably Tasso who suggested the possibilities of this topic to Ronsard. And in this sonnet of Ronsard's not only is there no trace of that humble and religious adoration, that spirituality, and even, at times, 'metaphysicality', that we find both in Petrarch and in Shakespeare: even that profound sadness at the fact of human transience which is so strong both in the ancients and in Shakespeare seems in Ronsard to have been completely swallowed up in his contemplation of the glory of poetry and his own glory as a poet. When I said that this sonnet was in some ways nearer, not only to the ancients, but also to the moderns, than to either Petrarch or Shakespeare, it was chiefly one modern poet I had in mind, W. B. Yeats. The comparatively early

When you are old and grey and full of sleep,
And nodding by the fire, take down this book,

one of his first really great poems, was clearly inspired by Ronsard's sonnet. There are indeed obvious differences: there is far less self-exaltation, far more sadness, tenderness and adoration in Yeats's poem, as there is also, for that matter, in the later and greater *The Folly of being comforted*; but they are both magnificent examples of that 'dramatic lyrical expression' which Yeats so admired in Ronsard, who, he declared, like Villon, had made splendid drama out of his own life. In the sonnets of our greatest dramatist, no less than in the sonnets of Petrarch, there is nothing that can properly be called 'self-dramatisation'—not, at any rate, in the sense in which we so often have it in Ronsard, in Yeats, and in Donne.

5

Shakespeare and his English predecessors

To turn from the great European poets we have been considering to the sonnets of Shakespeare's English contemporaries is to enter a region of comparative provinciality and amateurishness. There are indeed a few sonnets, more of them by Sidney than by any other poet, which may be 'let alone for the comparison', but both in sheer genius and sheer craftsmanship the general level is far below that of the Italians and the French. Indeed, despite his immense genius and immense achievement, Shakespeare's own craftsmanship, sometimes even in his finest sonnets, is too often slovenly and very far from Coleridge's *desideratum* of 'the best words in the best order': there are too many inversions merely for the sake of rhyme, too many syllable-supplying expletives such as 'do', 'did', and 'doth', and too many rhymes on the final syllable of weak past participles, such as 'remember-ed'. Perfection still remains perfection, even though it be Shakespeare himself who sometimes falls short of it.

In the sonnets of Shakespeare's English predecessors the theme of poetic immortality had only been treated at all extensively, if seldom very memorably, by Spenser, whose *Amoretti* were published in 1595, and by Daniel, whose *Delia* sonnets, after some of them had appeared in the piratical edition of Sidney's *Astrophel and Stella* in 1591, were first printed as an independent collection in 1592 and continued to reappear, with various revisions and small 'augmentations', in volumes containing other poems by Daniel between 1594 and 1623. The only other previous appearances of the theme that I have been able to discover were in one sonnet in Constable's *Diana* (1592 and 1594) and one sonnet in Drayton's *Ideas Mirrour* (1594).

Although Spenser's sonnets, the *Amoretti*, were published later than the first collections of Daniel and Drayton, I will begin with him, not merely because of his seniority, but because in *The Ruines of Time*, written probably in 1590 and published in 1591 in the volume he entitled *Complaints*, he was the first English poet to treat memorably the topic with which we are concerned. *The Ruines of Time* was largely inspired by one of the sonnet sequences of Du Bellay, about which, before proceeding, it will be desirable to say a word or two. The thirty-two sonnets which Du Bellay entitled *Antiquitez de Rome* (1558), though Renaissance in form and style, may almost be called medieval in tone and content, for his reflections on the fall of this illustrious city have much affinity with numerous medieval reflections on the Falls of Illustrious Men and on the 'brittleness' of Fortune. And Du Bellay appended to it a thoroughly medieval *Songe*, consisting of fifteen emblematical sonnets inspired by Petrarch's canzone *Standomi un giorno solo a la fenestra*, an allegorical meditation on the death of Laura which Marot had translated as *Des Visions de Petrarque*. Spenser also included in the *Complaints* a mediocre translation of Du Bellay's sequence, entitled *Ruines of Rome*, together with considerably revised versions of two translations which had appeared anonymously in Van der Noodt's *Theatre for Worldlings* in 1569, the year in which Spenser, at the age of about seventeen, left the Merchant Taylors' School for Cambridge: a translation of Du Bellay's *Songe*, entitled *The Visions of Bellay*, and a translation of Marot's poem, entitled *The Visions of Petrarch*. It was no doubt out of Spenser's long preoccupation with these in many ways thoroughly medieval meditations on the Triumph of Time that the much more notable *Ruines of Time* emerged. It is a confused and unequal poem, but embedded in it is some of the finest verse he ever wrote. Just as Du Bellay, in his *Songe*, had professed to see the genius of the fallen city of Rome on the banks of the Tiber, Spenser professes to see on the banks of Thames the genius of the fallen city of Verulam, who, after lamenting first her own fall and then the death of the Earl of Leicester, whose already forgotten glory no poet has revived, felicitates the more fortunate Sidney, whose terrestrial immortality has been ensured by his own verse, and declares that poetry alone can make great men and great deeds remembered (ll. 344–455). The poem concludes with a series of visions,

> Like tragicke Pageants seeming to appeare,

illustrating the Triumph of Time over some of the most famous monuments of the ancient world, and with a series of sometimes obscure emblems celebrating the entrance into immortality of Sir Philip Sidney. The theme of poetic immortality, or rather, of literary immortality in general, only appears once in Du Bellay's *Antiquitez de Rome*, in the fifth sonnet, declaring that, although ancient Rome has perished, her writings remain: it may have been suggested to Spenser as a main topic either by his independent reading of the Roman poets, whom he occasionally imitates, or by certain passages in other poems by Du Bellay, or by his eventual discovery of Ronsard. In the later *Amoretti* there is, as we shall see, a good deal of Ronsardian bragging, but there is nothing on this topic poetically equal to certain passages in *The Ruines of Time*. Shakespeare's demonstrable indebtedness to Ovid and possible indebtedness to Ronsard, together with the example offered him by Daniel, make it unnecessary to suppose that the topic of poetic immortality and its possibilities was first suggested to him by Spenser. Nevertheless, in many of his sonnets on the Triumph of Time over Beauty and on the Triumph of Poetry, and later of Love, over Time there is an element of 'tragicke Pageant' and of medieval, or near-medieval, allegory and emblem which suggests to me that his imagination may have been kindled, or at least coloured, by *The Ruines of Time* and perhaps by some other things in Spenser's *Complaints*.

In persuading, or in being persuaded to allow, his friend 'E.K.' to write a commentary to accompany the first publication of his *Shepheardes Calender* in 1579 Spenser was probably following, rather precipitately, perhaps, the example of Ronsard, who had allowed the second edition (1553) of his first *Amours* to appear with a commentary by his friend Marc-Antoine de Muret, exhibiting, for the benefit of the less learned, Ronsard's many traces of what Du Bellay called 'rare and authentic erudition', and who in the first collected edition of his *Œuvres* (1560) had allowed what he there entitled his second *Livre des amours* to appear with a similar commentary by his friend and fellow-poet, Remy Belleau.

There is much else in Spenser's shorter poems that reveals him as an emulator of Ronsard and of the Pléiade. In *The Teares of the Muses* and *The Ruines of Time*, published in the *Complaints* of 1591, he had already claimed immortality both for his own poetry and for those it celebrated, and probably there and certainly in no less than thirteen of the *Amoretti* he is, I feel sure, consciously following the example of Ronsard and making for his own poetry claims similar to those which Ronsard had made for his. In several of the *Amoretti* there is an incongruity, similar to that which we have noticed in some of Ronsard's sonnets, between the loudness (sometimes, one might say, the shrillness) of these claims and boasts and the predominantly Petrarchan tone and 'keepings', and Spenser sometimes introduces them into imitations of sonnets by other poets where they neither appear nor properly belong. In his 215th sonnet, *In nobil sangue vita umile e queta*, Petrarch describes the union of loftiness and lowliness and of other opposites in Laura, and concludes:

> E non so che ne li occhi, che'n un punto
> Po far chiara la notte, oscuro il giorno,
> E'l mèl amaro et adolcir l'assenzio.

('And an-I-know-not-what in her eyes that in an instant can make bright the night, dark the day, and [make] honey bitter and sweeten wormwood.') Spenser's 13th, an imitation of this sonnet of Petrarch's in a style whose remoteness from that of its original may be sufficiently suggested by quoting the first two lines,

> In that proud port, which her so goodly graceth,
> whiles her faire face she reares vp to the skie,

concludes with a couplet whose thought and sentiment are as un-Petrarchan as their expression:

> Yet lowly still vouchsafe to looke on me,
> Such lowlinesse shall make you lofty be.[1]

In sonnet 28 Spenser declares that the laurel he gave his beloved and which she is wearing gives him grounds for hope, since it is the badge of his

---

[1] I quote the *Amoretti* from the text (based on the British Museum copy of 1595) given by W. L. Renwick in his edition of *Daphnaïda and Other Poems* (1929). I have made certain necessary or desirable alterations in the often irrational punctuation.

profession, and in 29 he imagines her as declaring that laurel is given by the vanquished to the victors and by them used to crown poets who glorify their deeds: let her then accept him as her 'faithfull thrall',

> that her great triumph which my skill exceeds,
> I may in trump of fame blaze ouer all.
> Then would I decke her head with glorious bayes,
> and fill the world with her victorious prayse.

These two sonnets were almost certainly suggested to Spenser by the tenth of Ronsard's *Sonets pour Astrée*, which begins:

> Quand tu portois l'autre jour sur ta teste
> Un verd Laurier, estoit-ce pour monstrer
> Qu'amant si fort ne se peut recontrer,
> Dont la victoire en tes mains ne soit preste?[1]

Nevertheless, despite the opportunity which might seem to be offered, and which Spenser found irresistible, Ronsard, in this sonnet, was content to leave his poetry and poetic powers unmentioned and to use the laurel simply in order to pay a hyperbolical compliment to Astrée's irresistible charms. Spenser has again out-Ronsarded Ronsard in his partial imitation, in sonnet 85, of *Sonets pour Helene*, I, 10, *Ce siecle, où tu naquis, ne te cognoist, Heleine*: while Ronsard had been content to declare that Hélène's divinity, invisible to all the rest of her sordid and ignorant contemporaries, had been revealed to him alone, Spenser has introduced into his sestet the whole paraphernalia of the inspired poet:

> Deepe in the closet of my parts entyre,
>   her worth is written with a golden quill:
>   that me with heauenly fury doth inspire,
>   and my glad mouth with her sweet prayses fill:
> Which when as fame in her shrill trump shal thunder,
>   let the world chose to enuy or to wonder.

Similarly, into his partial imitation of the thirty-fourth sonnet of Du Bellay's *L'Olive* in sonnet 69 he has been unable to resist the temptation of introducing a promise of poetic immortality which, although it may

[1] Vaganay, II, p. 208.

possibly be implied, is not obviously present in his original. It is worth while to place these two sonnets side by side, for it then becomes immediately apparent that, while Du Bellay's primary intention is to pay a hyperbolical and, in spirit, thoroughly Petrarchan compliment to his mistress, Spenser's primary intention (like that of Ronsard in some of his sonnets and all too frequently in his odes) is to exalt himself.

> Apres avoir d'un bras victorieux
>   Domté l'effort des superbes courages,
>   Aucuns jadis bastirent haulx ouvrages,
>   Pour se venger du temps injurieux:
> Autres craignans leurs actes glorieux
>   Assujetir à flammes et orages,
>   Firent ecriz qui malgré telz outrages
>   Ont faict leurs noms voler jusques aux cieulx.
> Maintz au jourdhuy en signe de victoire
>   Pendent au temple armes bien etophées:
>   Mais je ne veulx acquerir telle gloire:
> Avoir esté par vous vaincu et pris,
>   C'est mon laurier, mon triomphe, et mon prix,
>   Qui ma depouille egale à leurs trophées.[1]

> The famous warriors of the anticke world
>   vsed trophees to erect in stately wize,
>   in which they would the records haue enrold
>   of theyr great deeds and valarous emprize.
> What trophee then shall I most fit deuize,
>   in which I may record the memory
>   of my loues conquest, peerelesse beauties prise,
>   adorn'd with honour, loue, and chastity?
> Euen this verse, vowd to eternity,
>   shall be thereof immortall moniment,
>   and tell her prayse to all posterity,
>   that may admire such worlds rare wonderment:
> The happy purchase of my glorious spoile,
>   gotten at last with labour and long toyle.

Here Spenser's 'trump' is less of a tin trumpet than in many similar utterances in the *Amoretti* and, despite a certain verbosity, may perhaps

---

[1] *Poésies Françaises et Latines de Joachim du Bellay*, ed. E. Courbet, 1918, I, p. 28.

recall the bronze and Horatian resonance of Shakespeare's sonnet 55:

> Not marble, nor the gilded monuments
> Of princes shall outlive this powerful rime . . .
> 'Gainst death and all oblivious enmity
> Shall you pace forth; your praise shall still find room
> Even in the eyes of all posterity
> That wear this world out to the ending doom.

While, though, Shakespeare in this and similar passages is defying time and death and oblivion on behalf of his friend, Spenser is here professing to erect a monument to what he calls 'my loues conquest'. Temperamentally and spiritually Spenser was, I think, nearer to Petrarch and to the poets of the *dolce stil nuovo* and the *cor gentil* than to Ronsard; nevertheless, although one can scarcely imagine him telling his mistress, like Ronsard, that she would have remained unnoticed had he not condescended to celebrate her, he often—largely, I think, under the influence of Ronsard and of what I am tempted to call 'the Movement'—falls into that not merely un-Petrarchan but also somewhat vulgar, pushing and parvenuish manner, with occasional suggestions of one who has accumulated a large wardrobe he does not quite know how to wear, which too often disturbs our admiration for the 'Prince of Poets'. Of this particular kind of impropriety and incongruity there is scarcely any trace, despite their inequalities of style and achievement, in Shakespeare's sonnets. As a last example of this introduction of the Ronsardian and un-Petrarchan promise, though here without obvious incongruity or impropriety, into a thoroughly Petrarchan context, I will quote sonnet 73, which may perhaps have been partly suggested by two sonnets of Tasso, the second of which Spenser had already imitated in the preceding sonnet (72): in the first of these, *Donna, crudel fortuna a me ben vieta*,[1] Tasso declares that his thought will follow his mistress wherever she goes, even though he himself is prevented from doing so; and in the second, *L'alma vaga di luce e di bellezza*,[2] he declares that his soul that would soar to Heaven is drawn down by earthly delight, like a bird descending to where another may feed it and submitting to voluntary imprisonment.

> Being my selfe captyued here in care,
> my hart, whom none with seruile bands can tye

---

[1] *Rime*, ed. Solerti, 1898, II, p. 33.
[2] *Op. cit.*, p. 98.

but the fayre tresses of your golden hayre,
 breaking his prison forth to you doth fly.
Like as a byrd that in ones hand doth spy
 desired food, to it doth make his flight:
 euen so my hart, that wont on your fayre eye
 to feed his fill, flyes back vnto your sight.
Doe you him take, and in your bosome bright
 gently encage, that he may be your thrall:
 perhaps he there may learne with rare delight
 to sing your name and prayses ouer all:
That it hereafter may you not repent
 him lodging in your bosome to haue lent.[1]

Of Spenser's remaining sonnets where this theme appears, and which contain no recognisable imitations of other poets, there is perhaps only one that deserves to be remembered. In most of them the contrast between the all too obvious mortality of the verse and the immortality it promises produces a slightly ludicrous effect, like that often produced by similar passages in Ronsard's youthful odes. When, in the manner of Petrarch, if seldom in a style equal to his, Spenser and other Renaissance poets are occasionally content merely to dedicate their poetic gifts to the service of the beloved and to wish, for her sake, that these gifts were greater,—when, in fact, they at least assume a certain humility, we are not impelled to laugh at them; but they too often reproduce the Horatian and Ovidian boasts in lines that are altogether lacking in Horatian and Ovidian 'indelibility'. Among English poets only Shakespeare was able to achieve it, and Shakespeare, even in his most resonant utterances on this theme, never conveys an impression of self-exaltation, since he always speaks as the champion and defender of a cause and affirms the quality of his verse in a spirit similar to that in which an epic hero or knight of romance might affirm the quality of his sword. In sonnet 27, following, perhaps, the example of Tasso, though with a crudity of which Tasso would have been incapable, Spenser introduces the un-Petrarchan and un-Shakespearean theme of 'ingrateful beauty threatened', declaring that the beauty of which she is proud will perish:

Ne any then shall after it inquire,
 ne any mention shall thereof remaine:

---

[1] Having got his rhyme, Spenser has simply juggled into metre the first words that occurred to him. I doubt whether it would be possible to produce a worse example of such inversion and 'make it yourself' technique from any poet.

> but what this verse, that neuer shall expyre,
>   shall to you purchas with her thankles paine.
> Faire be no lenger proud of that shall perish,
>   but that which shal you make immortall, cherish.

There are a few sonnets where, after either protesting against his beloved's 'cruelty' or marvelling at her condescension, he proffers his poetic services in a comparatively humble and unobtrusive manner, although usually, it must be admitted, in a style as humble as the humility he is professing and which altogether lacks that occasional impressiveness he is able to achieve in his Ronsardian bragging. In fact, we almost never feel, as we so often do with Petrarch on the one hand and with Shakespeare on the other, that he has said exactly the right thing in the right place in the right way. In 36 he begs her not to 'slay' one

>   whose lyfe though ye despyse,
>   mote haue your lyfe in honour long maintayned.

In 48 he apostrophises the 'innocent paper' which her 'cruell hand . . . did sacrifize vnto the greedy fyre', and concludes, with perhaps too little regard for sense and logic:

>   Yet liue for euer, though against her will,
>   and speake her good, though she requite it ill.

In 49 he begs her to be 'merciful':

>   Such mercy shal you make admyred to be,
>   so shall you liue by giuing life to me.

In 66, after expressing wonder that such a paragon as she should have condescended to love one so mean as himself, he declares that her light appears all the greater in his darkness, and concludes:

>   Yet since your light hath once enlumind me,
>   with my reflex yours shall encreased be—

his 'reflex' being, presumably, his reflection of her in his poetry, just as Drayton declared that his own poetry was 'Ideas mirrour'. In 82 he declares that she deserved as her lover 'som heuenly wit' able to have enchased her glorious name on a golden monument:

> But since ye deignd so goodly to relent
>   to me your thrall, in whom is little worth,
>   that little that I am shall all be spent
>   in setting your immortall prayses forth:
> Whose lofty argument, vplifting me,
>   shall lift you vp vnto an high degree.

Spenser's one really memorable sonnet on this theme, though far below the best, not only of Shakespeare but of Drayton and even, perhaps, of Daniel, is 75, where he uses a kind of emblem or allegory which, so far as I know, is original:

> One day I wrote her name vpon the strand,
>   but came the waues and washed it away:
>   agayne I wrote it with a second hand,
>   but came the tyde, and made my paynes his pray.
> Vayne man, sayd she, that doest in vaine assay
>   a mortall thing so to immortalize:
>   for I my selue shall lyke to this decay,
>   and eek my name be wyped out lykewize.
> Not so, (quod I) let baser things deuize
>   to dy in dust, but you shall liue by fame:
>   my verse your vertues rare shall eternize,
>   and in the heuens wryte your glorious name,
> Where, whenas death shall all the world subdew,
>   our loue shall liue, and later life renew.

This, although perhaps a more confident and resonant declaration than Petrarch would have ventured to make in a sonnet to Laura, is closer to the proud humility (as one might almost call it) of Shakespeare than to the condescension and self-exaltation of Ronsard.

While Spenser is writing mainly as a disciple of Ronsard, Daniel, in his seven sonnets on this theme, is writing mainly as a disciple of Tasso—the Tasso of those two famous sonnets which, as I have suggested, may partly have inspired Ronsard's *Quand vous serez bien vieille*. In the general tone and spirit of his love-sonnets Tasso is far nearer to Petrarch than Ronsard usually is, and even in the first of these two sonnets, *Vedrò da gli anni in mia vendetta ancora*, where the pagan and un-Petrarchan theme of 'ingrateful beauty threatened' predominates, Tasso avoids any suggestion of self-exaltation and only in the last two lines declares, as though he were merely stating a fact, that his time-ravaged mistress will then long to be renewed in his verses like the phoenix in fire; while in the second of them his un-Petrarchan foretelling of the loss of his mistress's beauty is combined with a thoroughly Petrarchan profession of eternal fidelity and unextinguishable passion. Despite their frequent feeblenesses and inequalities of style, there is a propriety and unity of tone about these seven sonnets of Daniel's, an absence of stridency and bragging, an ability to affirm the power of his verse without seeming to praise himself, that is far nearer than are most of the *Amoretti* to Shakespeare's sonnets on this topic. They would have been sufficient in themselves to direct Shakespeare's attention to it—if, indeed, his attention required directing, and if the topic had not already been suggested to him by his own reading of the Latin poets and, perhaps, of Ronsard. They are all, it is true, what Shakespeare's never are, poems of courtship, with allusions to his 'wrong' and her 'pride', but they could have suggested to Shakespeare (had he required the suggestion) more clearly, perhaps, than anything in any previous poet, the possibility of speaking with Horatian and Ovidian resonance of his verse, not as a personal achievement and source of pride, but as a weapon for the defence of the beloved's beauty against Devouring Time. Three of them, 36, 39 and 40,[1] are imitations of the two famous and already quoted[2] sonnets of Tasso, a poet whom Daniel greatly admired and whom he has often imitated elsewhere; but it is significant and characteristic that in the first of them Daniel is closer to Desportes's imitation of Tasso, in the 62nd sonnet of his *Cléonice*, than to the Italian original. Desportes, whose sonnet I will place side by side with Daniel's, has considerably toned down what I have called the Roman *superbia* of Tasso's sonnet, the triumphant and, as so often in the Roman poets, rather cruel and gloating anticipation of the spectacle of faded beauty, and Daniel himself has toned down the element of threat and anticipated vengeance that remains even in Desportes, and has introduced at least some suggestion of that protestation

---

[1] I refer to the numbering in the convenient edition (1908) of Daniel's *Delia* and Drayton's *Idea* by Arundell Esdaile, which is that of the 1623 edition of Daniel's *Works*. With the exception of two passages to which I shall refer in footnotes, the six sonnets which I shall quote in full from Esdaile's edition remained substantially unchanged since their appearance in the first edition of *Delia* in 1592.

[2] On p. 55.

of eternal fidelity and persistent poetic service which is the main theme of
Tasso's second sonnet, *Quando avran queste luci e queste chiome*. Since
Daniel has also imitated this second sonnet, and since the first immediately
precedes it in the editions of Tasso's *Rime*, there is no reason why Daniel
should have here preferred to follow Desportes except that he found
something in Tasso's first sonnet that repelled him, something he felt
as alien to the *cor gentil*.

> Je verray par les ans, vengeurs de mon martire,
> Quel'or de vos cheveux argenté deviendra,
> Que de vos deux soleils la splendeur s'esteindra,
> Et qu'il faudra qu'Amour tout confus s'en retire.
> La beauté qui, si douce, à présent vous inspire,
> Cedant aux lois du tans, ses faveurs reprendra;
> L'hyver de vostre teint les fleurettes perdra,
> Et ne laissera rien des thresors que j'admire.
> Cet orgueil desdaigneux qui vous fait ne m'aimer,
> En regret et chagrin se verra transformer,
> Avec le changement d'une image si belle.
> Et peut estre qu'alors vous n'aurez déplaisir
> De revivre en mes vers, chauds d'amoureux desir,
> Ainsi que le phénix au feu se renouvelle.[1]

> I once may see when years shall wreak my wrong,
> When golden hairs shall change to silver wire,[2]
> And those bright rays that kindle all this fire
> Shall fail in force, their working not so strong.
> Then beauty, now the burden of my song,
> Whose glorious blaze the world doth so admire,
> Must yield up all to tyrant Time's desire;
> Then fade those flowers that deck'd her pride so long.
> When, if she grieve to gaze her in her glass,
> Which then presents her winter-withered hue,
> Go you, my verse, go, tell her what she was,
> For what she was she best shall find in you.
> Your fiery heat lets not her glory pass,
> But, Phoenix-like, shall make her live anew.

[1] *Œuvres*, ed. Michiels, 1858, p. 211.
[2] Nearer to l. 2 of Desportes's sonnet than to l. 3 of Tasso's,

> Vedrò starsi negletto e bianco il crine.

It is worth noticing how Desportes's 'Cedant aux lois du tans' (l. 6) has suggested to Daniel the characteristically Shakespearean personification of 'tyrant Time' (l. 7). The second of these two Tasso sonnets, *Quando avran queste luci e queste chiome*, contains a remarkably successful and, so far as I know, original combination of three topics: (i) 'ingrateful beauty threatened'—or rather, perhaps, in comparison with the almost Roman threatening of Tasso's preceding sonnet, 'ingrateful beauty reproached'; (ii) 'eternity in love protested'; (iii) 'immortality promised'. Daniel, perhaps because he wanted to deal more explicitly and extensively with the last of these three topics than Tasso had done in the mere three lines he had devoted to it, has expanded into two sonnets his imitation of this one of Tasso's. The first of these, 39, begins with a quatrain that contains no more than the general sense of Tasso's first four lines and whose 'sitting alone' may perhaps have been suggested by the beginning of Ronsard's *Quand vous serez bien vieille*. The next two quatrains are a close imitation of all the rest of Tasso's sonnet, except the first three lines of the sestet, where Tasso speaks of his own poetry, lines of which Daniel has incorporated a general imitation into his following sonnet; and the last four lines, which do not correspond to anything in Tasso's sonnet, may perhaps have been suggested by a line towards the end, just as the first quatrain may have been suggested by the beginning, of Ronsard's famous sonnet to Hélène:

> Regrettant mon amour, et vostre fier desdain.

In the following sonnet (40), which begins with a repetition of the last line of its predecessor, Daniel has imitated only those three lines where Tasso compares himself to a painter who emends the blemish of time, and has devoted his whole sonnet to the topic of poetry as an unfading record of beauty that must fade. Both sonnets are good examples of that decent and dignified, though almost never really splendid or memorable, plainness which Daniel sometimes achieves when he has a good model behind him.

> When men shall find thy flower, thy glory, pass,
> And thou, with careful brow sitting alone,
> Received hast this message from thy glass,
> That tells the truth, and says that all is gone:
> Fresh shalt thou see in me the wounds thou madest,
> Though spent thy flame, in me the heat remaining;

I, that have lov'd thee thus before thou fadest,
My faith shall wax when thou art in thy waning.
The world shall find this miracle in me,
That fire can burn when all the matter's spent;
Then what my faith hath been thyself shall see,
And that thou wast unkind thou mayest repent;
    Thou mayest repent that thou hast scorn'd my tears,
    When Winter snows upon thy sable hairs.

When Winter snows upon thy sable hairs,
And frost of age hath nipp'd thy beauties near,
When dark shall seem thy day that never clears,
And all lies withrèd that was held so dear:
Then take this picture which I here present thee,
Limnèd with a pencil not all unworthy;[1]
Here see the gifts that God and Nature lent thee,
Here read thyself and what I suffrèd for thee.
This may remain thy lasting monument,
Which happily posterity may cherish;
These colours with thy fading are not spent,
These may remain when thou and I shall perish.
    If they remain, then thou shalt live thereby;
    They will remain, and so thou canst not die.

In 41, together with a very un-Petrarchan and un-Shakespearean humble-ness of style, there is something of Petrarchan and Shakespearean humility and some thematic resemblance to Shakespeare's magnificent sonnet 32, concluding

    But since he died, and poets better prove,
    Theirs for their style I'll read, his for his love;

although in that sonnet Shakespeare is not specifically promising im-mortality either to his friend or to himself.

    Thou canst not die while any zeal abound
    In feeling hearts that can conceive these lines;
    Though thou, a Laura, hast no Petrarch found,

---

[1] This is far from being the only line in Daniel's sonnets that defies all attempts at scansion.

In base attire yet clearly beauty shines.
And I, though born within a colder clime,
Do feel mine inward heat as great, I know it;
He never had more faith, although more rhyme;
I love as well, though he could better show it.
But I may add one feather to thy fame,
To help her flight throughout the fairest isle;
And if my pen could more enlarge thy name,
Thou should'st then live in an immortal style.
  For though that Laura better limnèd be,
  Suffice, thou shalt be lov'd as well as she.

42, beginning

Be not displeas'd that these my papers should
Betray unto the world how fair thou art,

is a very feeble sonnet, partly imitated from Guarini, containing the hideous lines and rhymes

My Muse shall sound thy praise with mournful warble.
How many live, the glory of whose name
Shall rest in ice, when thine is grav'd in marble?

43 is a much more notable achievement, inspired not, it would seem, by any particular model, but by any or all of those great commonplaces about poetry as more enduring than buildings, pyramids, marbles and bronzes of which I have already cited so many examples from both classical and Renaissance poets:

Delia, these eyes that so admireth thine
Have seen those walls which proud ambition reared
To check the world, how they entomb'd have lien
Within themselves, and on them ploughs have eared,
Yet never found that barbarous hand attain'd
The spoil of fame deserv'd by virtuous men,
Whose glorious actions luckily had gain'd
The eternal annals of a happy pen.

> And therefore grieve not if thy beauties die;
> Though time do spoil thee of the fairest veil
> That ever yet covered mortality,
> And must instar the needle and the rail;[1]
> > That grace which doth more than enwoman thee
> > Lives in my lines and must eternal be.

Here too there is something of Shakespeare's subordination of himself and his poetic gift to the task of rescuing all that is rescuable in the beloved from oblivion and devouring Time. And the same is true of 53, where the topic of perpetuation is combined with a characteristically Petrarchan and occasionally Shakespearean profession that the poet's verses have been inspired entirely by the person to whom they are dedicated:

> Let others sing of knights and paladins
> In aged accents and untimely words,
> Paint shadows in imaginary lines
> Which well the reach of their high wits records;
> But I must sing of thee, and those fair eyes
> Authentic shall my verse in time to come,
> When yet the unborn shall say, 'Lo, where she lies,
> Whose beauty made him speak that else was dumb'.

---

1 'Rail' means 'gown', as in 'night-rail', but the whole line is what the Germans call an 'un-thing'; for, as Professor C. Schaar has shown in an article in *English Studies*, October 1959, Daniel is here misunderstandingly imitating a passage in a sonnet on his dead wife by Bernandino Rota (1509–1575), who imagines Vittoria Colonna as welcoming her into Heaven with the words:

> Tu dico, in cui bella honestà s'indonna
> > D'ogni gran lode in terra, ultimo segno
> > Solinga andrai; tu nata a scettro, a regno,
> > Tra le Stelle alzerai l'ago e la gonna,

which I take to mean: 'You in whom fair honesty reigns mistress of all great praise on earth, as last of the celestial signs you shall proceed alone; born for sceptre and sway, you shall exalt among the stars the needle and the wifely gown.' Daniel does not seem to have perceived that for Rota the needle and the gown are emblems of domestic virtue, and he has mistaken the intransitive verb *indonnarsi*, 'be, or make oneself, mistress of', for a transitive one, and has rendered it by 'enwoman'.

It is true that between 1592 and 1601 Daniel had made some considerable verbal improvements both in the last six lines of this sonnet and in lines 2 and 5; nevertheless, his misunderstanding of Rota remained as a serious blot.

> These are the arks, the trophies, I erect,
> That fortify thy name against old age,
> And these thy sacred virtues must protect
> Against the dark and Time's consuming rage.
> > Though th' error of my youth in them appear,
> > Suffice they show I liv'd and lov'd thee dear.[1]

In these seven sonnets it is only occasionally that Daniel achieves something like the Shakespearean resonance and the Shakespearean phrase. They do not communicate anything like the range and intensity of inner vibration that Shakespeare's do, and they seem almost shallow in comparison with that profound concernment, not only about the friend's transience, but about human transience in general, that we feel in Shakespeare's. Nevertheless, they constitute the fullest and finest treatment of this topic in English poetry before Shakespeare, and, although their tone is so much fainter, their accent is not perhaps greatly different from Shakespeare's own.

Without lingering over Constable's single and very feeble sonnet on this topic,[2] I will proceed to Drayton. He published his first collection of fifty-three sonnets and quasi-sonnets with the title *Ideas Mirrour: Amours in Quatorzains* in 1594, but between then and 1619 he was continually omitting from, adding to and revising his sequence, which, with the title *Idea*, he republished, each time with larger or smaller alterations, in the 1599, 1600 and 1602 editions of *Englands Heroicall Epistles* and in the 1605 and 1619 editions of his *Poems*. In the final version of 1619, which contained sixty-four sonnets, only twenty of the original fifty-three, many of them in a much-revised form, were retained. Between 1594 and 1619 Drayton published five sonnets in which poetic immortality is the main theme,[3] but of these only the first (17 in the final

---

[1] The couplet first reached this, its final form, in the 1601 edition of Daniel's *Works*; in 1592 it read:

> Though th'error of my youth they shall discouer,
> Suffice they shew I liu'd and was thy louer.

[2] 'My tears are true: though others be divine', *Diana*, 1594, Decade viii, Sonnet 4.

[3] Besides these he also published five sonnets in which the topic at least makes an appearance. In the opening sonnet of *Ideas Mirrour* (54 in 1619), after declaring that his whole life has been devoted to her service, he begs her to accept

> My soules oblation to thy sacred name:
> Which name my Muse to highest heauen shall raise
> By chast desire, true loue, and vertues praise.

In *Amour 4* in *Ideas Mirrour* (rejected from *Idea* after 1602), 'My faire, had I not erst adorned my Lute', he declares that she will be immortalised by verse she has herself inspired; in *Amour 23* (never afterwards reprinted), 'Wonder of Heauen, glasse of diuinitie', he asks

order) can be said with absolute confidence to have been written by one of
Shakespeare's predecessors. Of the two (10 and 44) which first appeared
in 1599 and of the one (47) which first appeared in 1605, we can only guess
whether Drayton, before he wrote them, may or may not have seen some
of Shakespeare's sonnets in manuscript, and we can only guess which of
his sonnets on this topic Shakespeare may or may not have written
before those dates. The only sonnet we can describe with absolute
confidence as post-Shakespearean is the one (6) first published in 1619,
ten years after the publication of Shakespeare's sonnets in 1609. Since
there are only five of them, a brief review of them all, in the order of
their publication, will not be out of place.

In thematic material, if not, perhaps, in style, the most Shakespearean
of these five sonnets is the earliest of them all, for there Drayton invites
Time to behold 'in this Celesteall glasse', that is to say, in his sonnets,
which are 'Ideas Mirrour',[1] a reflection of the beauty of the early world
and of Time's own youth. This recalls those many sonnets, without, so
far as I know, any parallels elsewhere, in which Shakespeare declares that
all beauty described by earlier poets was a prophecy of his friend's
(59, 106), that in a declining age his friend is a reminder of what beauty
once was (67, 68), and that all those whom he had supposed lost live
again in his friend (30, 31). It is true that Shakespeare does not speak of
his own poetry in these almost religiously hyperbolical sonnets and that
Drayton only metaphorically and very unemphatically does so, his whole
emphasis being, not upon the 'glasse', but upon what is reflected in it:
nevertheless, it does not seem altogether impossible that the idea of the
beloved as a reflection and reincarnation of all past beauty may have been
at least partly suggested to Shakespeare by this sonnet of Drayton's.[2]

Beauty why she has made him immortalise one who disdains to look upon him; and in
Amour 38 (never reprinted, though one of his best sonnets), 'If chaste and pure deuotion of my
youth', he mentions among his many claims on her gratitude 'A Muse that vnto heauen hath
raised her fame'. In sonnet 25 (both in 1619 and in 1599, where it first appeared), recalling
perhaps that sonnet (146, O d'ardente vertute ornata e calda) in which Petrarch had declared that,
although the vernacular he was using prevented him from filling the whole world with
Laura's praise, he would at least make sure that Italy heard it, Drayton declares that, since
English has no reputation among Southern (later 'foreign') nations, his muse must be content
with such glory as it can gain (whether for her or for himself he does not say) in Scotland and
in Ireland.

    [1] The idea of his poetry as a mirror may perhaps have been suggested to Drayton by
lines 9–12 of the second of Tasso's famous sonnets (Quando avran queste luci e queste chiome),
where Tasso declares that neither her coldness nor the loss of her beauty will diminish his
passion or impair his fidelity, and that 'like a painter who emends the blemish of time, I shall
show in lofty songs your beauties in no part harmed'.
    [2] As we shall see later (p. 110), there is another topic that seems to be peculiar to Shakes-
peare and Drayton: the contrast between the stability of the poet's love and the instability
of the political scene.

In subsequent editions Drayton very greatly improved it (can one possibly imagine Shakespeare addressing Time the enemy as 'sweet Time'?), but, because of its thematic interest, I will quote it both as it first appeared in 1594 and in the final version of 1619.

Amour 7

Stay, stay, sweet Time; behold, or ere thou passe
From world to world, thou long hast sought to see,
That wonder now wherein all wonders be,
Where heauen beholds her in a mortall glasse.
Nay, looke thee, Time, in this Celesteall glasse,
And thy youth past in this faire mirror see:
Behold worlds Beautie in her infancie,
What shee was then, and thou, or ere shee was.
Now passe on, Time: to after-worlds tell this,
Tell truelie, Time, what in thy time hath beene,
That they may tell more worlds what Time hath seene,
And Heauen may ioy to think on past worlds blisse.
Here make a Period, Time, and saie for mee,
She was the like that neuer was, nor neuer more shalbe.[1]

To Time

Stay, speedy Time, behold, before thou pass,
From age to age what thou hast sought to see,
One in whom all the excellencies be,
In whom Heaven looks itself as in a glass.
Time, look thyself in this translucent glass,
And thy youth past in this pure mirror see,
As the world's beauty in his infancy,
What it was then, and thou before it was.
Pass on, and to posterity tell this,
Yet see thou tell but truly what hath been;
Say to our nephews that thou once hast seen
In perfect human shape all heavenly bliss,

[1] *Minor Poems of Michael Drayton*, ed. Cyril Brett, 1907, p. 5.

And bid them mourn, nay more, despair with thee,
That she is gone, her like again to see.[1]

In the two sonnets first printed in 1599 (10 and 44 in the final order)
Drayton combines the promise of immortality with the un-Petrarchan
and un-Shakespearean topic of 'ingrateful beauty threatened'—a combination which, as I have already remarked, seems to have been first
introduced into European poetry by Tasso; and it is noteworthy that
while Daniel, in his combination of these two topics, has gone even
further than Desportes in toning down the element of rebuke and threat
which Desportes himself had modified in his imitation of Tasso's sonnet,
Drayton writes in a tone of plain-spoken remonstrance that is almost
outside the courtly tradition. In the first of these sonnets (10), although
there is, according to the standards of what may be called the courtly
tradition, an over-insistence upon his own 'honesty' and an absence of
proper humility and respectfulness towards his mistress, there is at least
no Ronsardian or Spenserian over-insistence on his powers as a poet.

To nothing fitter can I thee compare
Than to the son of some rich penny-father,
Who, having now brought on his end with care,
Leaves to his son all he had heap'd together.
This new rich novice, lavish of his chest,
To one man gives, doth on another spend,
Then here he riots, yet among the rest
Haps to lend some to one true honest friend.
Thy gifts thou in obscurity dost waste,
False friends thy kindness,[2] born but to deceive thee;
Thy love, that is on the unworthy plac'd;
Time hath thy beauty, which with age will leave thee:
    Only that little which to me was lent
    I give thee back, when all the rest is spent.

In the second (44) nothing could be more un-Shakespearean than the
manner in which Drayton speaks of himself and of his poetry in relation
to the mistress he is professing to immortalise, his emphasis being far
more upon the immortality he will achieve for himself than upon that

---

[1] I quote from Arundell Esdaile's convenient edition of Daniel's *Delia* and Drayton's *Idea*,
where the text of *Idea* is that of 1619. I have occasionally altered the punctuation, which, in
the original, sometimes tends to make Drayton's often obscure syntax even more obscure.

[2] 'And false friends, born only to deceive thee, waste thy kindness.'

which, in so doing, he will confer upon her. The contrast is, as it were
underlined by the fact that in line 12,

> When I, entomb'd, my better part shall save,

Drayton seems to be imitating that same passage at the conclusion of
Ovid's *Metamorphoses*,

> Parte tamen meliore mei super alta perennis
> astra ferar,

which Shakespeare, as I have suggested,[1] must surely have had in mind
when he declared in sonnet 74

> My spirit is thine, the better part of me.

I must confess that I find in this sonnet of Drayton's a mixture of
peevishness and boasting—quite different from the occasionally splendid, if shocking, arrogance of Ronsard—which seems slightly absurd
and produces an impression of something like parody (' 'Ere am I,
wearin' meself out to make you immortal').

> Whilst thus my pen strives to eternize thee
> Age rules my lines with wrinkles in my face,
> Where in the map of all my misery
> Is modell'd out the world of my disgrace.
> Whilst, in despite of tyrannizing times,
> Medea-like, I make thee young again,
> Proudly thou scorn'st my world-outwearing rhymes
> And murtherest virtue with thy coy disdain.
> And though in youth my youth untimely perish
> To keep thee from oblivion and the grave,
> Ensuing ages yet my rhymes shall cherish
> When I, entomb'd, my better part shall save;
>   And though this earthly body fade and die,
>   My name shall mount upon eternity.

Sonnet 47, first printed in 1605, one of Drayton's finest, is far more
Shakespearean both in its style and in its whole-hearted dedicatedness,

[1] See p. 33.

although it is impossible to imagine Shakespeare representing himself as sitting in the Globe playhouse and thinking, while the audience applauds *Hamlet* or *King Lear*, only of his friend. Such self-presentation and self-dramatisation is far more characteristic of Ronsard or of Sidney —the Sidney who attributed his success at the tilt-yard to the presence of Stella.[1]

> In pride of wit, when high desire of fame
> Gave life and courage to my labouring pen,
> And first the sound and virtue of my name
> Won grace and credit in the ears of men,
> With those the thronged theatres that press
> I in the circuit for the laurel strove,
> Where the full praise, I freely must confess,
> In heat of blood a modest mind might move.
> With shouts and claps at every little pause
> When the proud round on every side hath rung,
> Sadly I sit, unmov'd with the applause,
> As though to me it nothing did belong.
>   No public glory vainly I pursue;
>   All that I seek is to eternize you.

Drayton's last sonnet (6) on this theme, first printed in 1619, is also Shakespearean in its dedicatedness, its proud humility, and its occasional achievement (most notably in lines 7 to 8) of the Shakespearean phrase.

> How many paltry, foolish, painted things,
> That now in coaches trouble every street,
> Shall be forgotten, whom no Poet sings,
> Ere they be well wrapt in their winding sheet!
> Where I to thee eternity shall give,
> When nothing else remaineth of these days,
> And Queens hereafter shall be glad to live
> Upon the alms of thy superfluous praise.
> Virgins and matrons, reading these my rhymes,
> Shall be so much delighted with thy story
> That they shall grieve they liv'd not in these times,
> To have seen thee, their sex's only glory.

[1] *Astrophel and Stella*, 41.

> So shalt thou fly above the vulgar throng,
> Still to survive in my immortal song.

It may well have been from Shakespeare that Drayton learnt to speak of his own poetry in a manner appropriate to a 'servant'. Daniel had always done so, but never with such Shakespearean resonance as Drayton has achieved in these two last sonnets.

II

DEVOURING TIME AND FADING BEAUTY FROM THE GREEK ANTHOLOGY TO SHAKESPEARE

The theme of transience, which runs so continuously through Shakespeare's Sonnets, has from ancient times been one of the major themes of European lyric and elegiac poetry; and yet, the more carefully one considers Shakespeare's Sonnets, the more aware one becomes of certain significant (and perhaps characteristic) differences between his treatment of this topic and that of nearly all his predecessors.

Absence of the topics carpe diem *and* carpe florem *from Shakespeare's sonnets*

Despite occasional overlappings, it may be said that in the ancient poets (and, to a large extent, in their Renaissance imitators) there are certain immediately recognisable distinctions, which scarcely appear in Shakespeare's Sonnets, between different kinds of transience, or between different standpoints from which time and transience may be regarded, each of them appropriate to a particular kind of poetry, or poem, and to the drawing of a particular kind of moral. There is first a distinction between Devouring Time (Ovid's *tempus edax rerum*) and the brief span of time (Horace's *vitae summa brevis*) allotted to human life, and there is a further clear distinction between the brevity of human life in general and the (as it were) yet briefer brevity of youth and beauty.

In Pindar, Horace and Ovid the topic of devouring, obliterating, in-oblivion-whelming Time occurs in those passages where they proclaim the power of their poetry to obtain immortality either for themselves or for the public virtues and achievements of those they celebrate. Only very seldom, as I have remarked, do such resonantly impressive defiances of Devouring Time occur in ancient love-poetry—indeed, the only example I have been able to discover is the one already quoted[1] from Propertius (III, ii, 17 ff.).

Of poetry on the brevity of human life in general, with its subservience to Time and Fortune and the gods' inscrutable decrees, poetry with the moral *carpe diem*, seize today, enjoy the present, which alone is within our power, the great master is Horace. Sestius, in the beautiful ode on the coming of Spring (I, iv), is reminded that

Vitae summa brevis spem nos vetat inchoare longam

('Life's brief span forbids the beginning of hopes that reach beyond us');

Thaliarchus, in the Soracte ode (I, ix), is exhorted

[1] On page 42.

Quid sit futurum cras, fuge quaerere et,
quem Fors dierum cumque dabit, lucro
　　adpone, nec dulces amores
sperne puer neque tu choreas,

donec virenti canities abest
morosa

('Not taking anxious heed for tomorrow, count
　each single day dark Fortune allots to us
　　　as purest gain, nor leave unproved the
　beckoning sweetness of love and dancing

　　　　while yet from Youth's green flourish the snowy touch
　　　　of gloomy Age hangs distant')—

a passage where the topic *carpe florem*, that most characteristic topic
of ancient love-poetry, which I shall consider presently, mingles with the
clearly distinguishable topic, *carpe diem*, and where an exhortation to
enjoy the pleasures of youth while still capable of them enters into what
is not primarily an invitation to pleasure but rather the recommendation
of something like a permanent attitude to life. Leuconoë (I, xi) is not to
pry into the future, but to leave astrologers alone, to prune long hopes
from her brief span, and to put no trust in tomorrow:

　　　　Carpe diem quam minimum credula postero;

Dellius (II, iii) is reminded that he was born to die,

　　　　Seu maestus omni tempore vixeris,
　　　　seu te in remoto gramine per dies
　　　　　　festos reclinatum bearis
　　　　interiore nota Falerni

('Whether you shall have lived at all times drearily, or whether on
festal days you shall have blessed yourself, reclined on some sequestered
lawn, with an old Falernian'); Grosphus is exhorted to cultivate a *laetus
in praesens animus*, a spirit delighting in the present, which does not
torment itself about what may lie beyond (II, xvi); Hirpinus (II, xi), in a
passage which Milton imitated, is told to stop worrying about what the

Cantabrian intends and what the Scyth; Maecenas (III, viii) is invited to lay aside for once the cares of state and

> Dona praesentis cape laetus horae et
> linque severa

('Gladly accept the gifts of the present hour and leave serious things behind'); and in another invitation, in one of the finest and weightiest of all Horace's odes (III, xxix), is reminded that

> Prudens futuri temporis exitum
> caliginosa nocte premit deus
>   ridetque, si mortalis ultra
> fas trepidat

('What time will one day show, the Omnipotent
has wisely locked in deepest obscurity,
    and laughs when mortal minds are over-
anxious'),

and that, as Dryden magnificently paraphrased it,

> Happy the Man, and happy he alone,
>   He who can call to day his own:
>   He who, secure within, can say,
> To-morrow do thy worst, for I have liv'd to-day.
> Be fair, or foul, or rain, or shine,
> The joys I have possesst, in spight of fate, are mine.
>   Not Heav'n it self upon the past has pow'r;
>   But what has been, has been, and I have had my hour.

Quite distinct from this wider and more philosophic topic of *carpe diem*, which was such a favourite with Horace and which was probably suggested to him by various early Greek lyrics, of which only fragments have survived, in the form of invitations to banquets, is that favourite topic of the Greek epigrammatists and the Latin elegiac poets which, borrowing a phrase twice used by Ovid, we may call *carpe florem*. In the *Ars amatoria* (III, 59–80), in a passage beginning

> Venturae memores iam nunc estote senectae

('Be mindful now already of old age to come'), Ovid reminds women
that the years go by like water that does not return to its source; that
where now are whitening thickets were once beds of violets, and that
what is now only a thorn bush once furnished garlands; that wrinkles,
pallor and white hair will come, and that those who are now cruel
to their lovers will find themselves alone and forsaken; and he concludes

Carpite florem,
qui, nisi carptus erit, turpiter ipse cadet

('Gather the flower which, unless it be gathered, will shamefully fall of
itself.') And in the *Metamorphoses* (X, 83–5) he declares that when Orpheus
had lost Eurydice for the second time he shunned all commerce with
women, though many loved him, and taught the Thracians to love boys
instead and 'to gather the brief spring and first flowers of that time of
life which precedes youth',

citraque iuventam
aetatis breve ver et primos carpere flores.

One of the most famous and perfect examples, imitated by several
notable Renaissance Latin poets, including Marullus and Angeriano, is
an epigram of Rufinus in the *Greek Anthology* (V, 74):

Πέμπω σοί, 'Ροδόκλεια, τόδε στέφος, ἄνθεσι καλοῖς
    αὐτὸς ὑφ' ἡμετέραις πλεξάμενος παλάμαις.
ἔστι κρίνον, ῥοδέη τε κάλυξ, νοτερή τ' ἀνεμώνη,
    καὶ νάρκισσος ὑγρός, καὶ κυαναυγὲς ἴον.
ταῦτα στεψαμένη, λῆξον μεγάλαυχος ἐοῦσα·
    ἀνθεῖς καὶ λήγεις καὶ σὺ καὶ ὁ στέφανος.

('I send you, Rhodocleia, this garland, which I myself have woven of
fair flowers beneath my hands. Here is lily and chaliced rose and moist
anemone and soft narcissus and dark-glowing violet: garlanding yourself
with these, stop being boastful: you flower and you cease, both you and
the garland.')

Nec violae semper nec hiantia lilia florent,
    et riget amissa spina relicta rosa

('Neither violets nor wide-open lilies flower for ever, and stiff stands the abandoned thorn when lost the rose'),

exclaims Ovid in the *Ars amatoria* (II, 115–16);

> Vidi ego odorati victura rosaria Paesti
> sub matutino cocta iacere noto

('I have seen rose-buds of odoured Paestum, that should have lived, lying parched beneath the Southern wind at dawn'), Propertius makes the procuress Acanthis declare, in the course of her long and sophistical discourse to Cynthia (IV, v, 61–2); and the exhortation to coy or disdainful women to learn the lesson of the rose, which in ancient poetry found its most elaborate expression in the *Rosae* of Ausonius, was revived by the Latin and vernacular poets of the Renaissance, most memorably perhaps by Ronsard in *Mignonne, allons voir si la rose* and by Tasso in that song sung in Armida's garden (*Ger. Lib.*, xvi, stanzas 14–15) which Spenser imitated in his description of the Bower of Bliss; it sometimes achieved a more dialectical or 'metaphysical' expression in various poems by our own seventeenth-century poets which either were, or might be, entitled *For Fruition*; and we can perhaps hear what the Germans would call its *Ausklang* in the flower-poems of Herrick.

In Shakespeare's Sonnets the topics *carpe diem* and *carpe florem* do not occur at all. The absence of the almost specifically Horatian topic of *carpe diem* from sonnets written by Shakespeare or by any other Renaissance poet is not really surprising, for it is a topic that almost belongs to the specifically Horatian invitation, a form which Ronsard and other sixteenth- and seventeenth-century poets usually approached only in the epistle, or epistolary 'elegy', and of which the only examples I can think of in sonnet form (or in any lyrical form) are Milton's sonnets to Cyriack Skinner and to Lawrence. Shakespeare's Sonnets would indeed be even more astonishingly unparalleled than they already are did we find him occasionally inviting his friend to tear himself away from the splendours of the Court or of Wilton or of Titchfield (or wherever it was), to unbend his mind for a while from preoccupation with the purchase of new leases or of shares in the Virginia Company, or with the advantages and disadvantages of adding a new wing or building a clock-tower or installing Sir John Harington's invention in a turret, to stop worrying about the possible intentions of the Spaniard or the Turk, to abandon the idea of having his horoscope cast by Dr. Dee, and to come and eat a humble meal *sub lare pauperis* either at his lodging on the Bankside or at New Place, where Shakespeare could produce a pippin of his own graffing and a gallon or two of well-matured Worcestershire cider. (These fancies may at least serve to remind us of the astonishing range and variety of the Horatian ode in comparison with almost any lyric poetry before that of quite modern times, and of the comparative monotony, despite their splendour and intensity, even of Shakespeare's sonnets.) More surprising, perhaps, is the complete absence of any version of the topic *carpe florem*. Naturally, since Shakespeare is addressing a man, not a woman, and since his love for him is not, as Chaucer would say, *love paramours*, we should not expect to find him employing, on his own behalf, any of those pleas and arguments, those warnings and threats, which the ancient poets and their Renaissance imitators addressed to their coy mistresses and lovely boys; but Shakespeare does not even use the topic, as one might say, disinterestedly, as Horace sometimes does in odes addressed to his younger friends, allowing it to mingle from time to time with his main topic of *carpe diem*. We do not find Shakespeare reminding his friend that he will only be young once, that the time will come when those Maids of Honour will no longer be casting such melting glances upon him as they are doing today, and that he will regret that he did not 'gather the Rose of love whilst yet was time'. In fact, nowhere in Shakespeare's sonnets is there anything approaching an invitation to pleasure. In their poetry on the topics *carpe diem* and *carpe florem* the ancient poets and their imitators are, one might almost say, recommending a co-operation with Time, submission to the conditions it imposes; urging those they address to seize Time, to make the best use of Time, to be (in every sense) *in time*, to be and do what is timely, to remove, so far as they can, all possibility of later regrets for lost time, for lost opportunities. Shakespeare, though (and this is what distinguishes his sonnets from almost all other love-poetry which, unlike Petrarch's, is at all largely concerned with the theme of time and transience), will have none of this collaboration with the enemy. In comparison with the 'realistic' ancients he reveals himself (at any rate in the Sonnets) as one of the most uncompromising of idealists; for, unlike the ancients, who defy Time only in their poetry about poetry, Shakespeare always speaks of Time as an enemy to be defied, never as a power whose laws are to be accepted and submitted to. For him there is no recognisable distinction, as there seems to have been for the ancients, between the Time that destroys the mightiest monuments of stone or bronze and the Time that transfixes the flourish set on Youth;[1] for him the devouringness of Time, the swift-footedness of Time, the brevity of human life and the transience of youth and beauty are continually and inseparably associated, and what he gives us is an ever-changing series of variations upon, personifications, metaphorisations and (one might almost say) dramatisations of, the great single theme of transience. And what emerges from all these meditations on transience is not any 'moral', but a question—the question: how can what Time threatens be preserved and perpetuated? A question which receives the answer, first, in those presumably earliest sonnets, which one can scarcely avoid supposing that Shakespeare began to write as the result of some kind of external hint or suggestion: by marriage, parenthood and children; and then, more personally and profoundly: by means of enduring verse.[2]

[1] This difference between Shakespeare and the ancients is everywhere apparent, but perhaps most immediately and obviously so in the two closely related sonnets 64, beginning:

> When I have seen by Time's fell hand defaced
> The rich-proud cost of outworn buried age;

and 65, beginning:

> Since brass, nor stone, nor earth, nor boundless sea,
> But sad mortality o'er-sways their power,
> How with this rage shall beauty hold a plea,
> Whose action is no stronger than a flower?

[2] Since the exhortations to marriage, with which the sequence presumably began, are soon dropped and are not resumed, nothing like a real dialectic is developed between parenthood and poetry as means of perpetuation. On the contrary, on the few occasions when Shakespeare mentions both together in these sonnets, he feels bound to profess that poetry is a far feebler and insecurer means, and, had he ever returned to the theme of parenthood in later sonnets, it is impossible to imagine him explicitly declaring it to be, as a means of perpetuation, inferior to poetry. It seems, therefore, scarcely profitable to attempt to establish a connection between even these earliest sonnets and a passage in Plato's *Symposium* (208c–209e), much imitated by the Neo-Platonists, where Diotima tells Socrates that most human endeavours are motivated by a desire for immortality, but that, while those who are pregnant only in the body turn to women and beget children, those who are pregnant in the soul conceive and bring forth poems, works of art and, above all, wise and just laws and institutions.

Shakespeare's sonnets on Love as the Defier of Time

When Shakespeare's sonnets on the theme of poetry as perpetuation are extracted from the whole collection and considered without further reference to it, there seems to breathe from them, as I have remarked in the First Part of this study, a conviction no less strong than Horace's that it is in and through poetry alone that we can hope that anything more of us than *pulvis et umbra* will survive. There are, though, later in the collection and probably, as I am inclined to think, written later, certain sonnets in which, not poetry, but love appears as the Defier of Time, sonnets on the theme that

> Love's not Time's fool, though rosy lips and cheeks
> Within his bending sickle's compass come;

and I find it difficult to decide whether, and, if so, to what extent, we should allow these sonnets to influence our reading and interpretation of those on poetry as the Defier of Time: whether, that is to say, we ought or ought not to read into those sonnets where Shakespeare *seems* to declare that it is his friend's youth and beauty that his verse will preserve from Time an implication or undersense that this is a kind of metaphor, and that what he really loves and what his verse will really perpetuate is the meaningfulness to him of his friend's youth and beauty and charm, the spirit, the 'better part'; just as he declares that it is his own 'better part' which, if he outlives him, his friend will still possess in his verse. Is Shakespeare, that is to say, even in those sonnets where he seems closest to Horace and the ancient world, still, to some extent, rooted in the world of medieval allegory and symbol? Here I may seem to be repeating what I have said in the First Part of this study about that 'spirituality' which Shakespeare's sonnets share with Petrarch's. Perhaps, though, in such a study as this what might seem at first sight to be an excessive amount of repetition could only be avoided at the cost of distorting what is being studied; for conceptions (or whatever we prefer to call them) which in other poets are comparatively sharp and distinct are in Shakespeare's sonnets comparatively fluid and interpenetrating. In fact, it is almost a matter of comparing *kinds* of poetry written by others with *aspects* of the poetry written by Shakespeare, and those 'aspects' of his poetry which we select for comparison, flashing upon them such light as we possess, require to be continually related, or re-related, to the temporarily unilluminated portions of that whole of which they are aspects.

It is worth while to devote a little attention to those presumably later sonnets on Love as the Defier of Time, among which are some of the most 'difficult' and most 'metaphysical' in the whole collection. It is, I think, in 108,

> What's in the brain, that ink may character,
> Which hath not figur'd to thee my true spirit?

(not one of Shakespeare's best sonnets) that this conviction is first expressed.[1] He can only repeat things he has said before:

> So that eternal love in love's fresh case
> Weighs not the dust and injury of age,
> Nor gives to necessary wrinkles place,
> But makes antiquity for aye his page.

Sonnet 115, on the theme that, while Time is always changing, dimming and blunting, Love is always growing, deserves to be quoted in full:

> Those lines that I before have writ do lie,
> Even those that said I could not love you dearer:
> Yet then my judgment knew no reason why
> My most full flame should afterwards burn clearer.
> But reckoning[2] Time, whose million'd accidents

---

[1] 'First expressed': that is to say, on this page of the collection as we have it. Whether this was actually the 108th sonnet that Shakespeare wrote I can see no means of either proving or disproving.

[2] 'Reckoning', like 'fearing' at line 9, is dependent on 'I' at line 10. I am inclined to think that what chiefly makes this sonnet 'difficult' are the perhaps not ideally chosen conjunctions 'Yet', at the beginning of line 3, and 'But', at the beginning of line 5: the 'Yet' introduces an apparent justification and the 'But' proceeds to declare that this justification (now expanded and made more explicit) is no justification at all. The argument seems to be: 'It is true that at the time when I wrote those lines I could not see how I could ever come to love you more dearly. Nevertheless, even though I could have pleaded in my defence that I was taking account of Time and fearing the changes he might produce, why had I still no right to say, as I then did ("might I not then say"), "Now I love you best"?' Such argument and such syntax, with statements and qualifications expressed, not in their logical but in their psychological order, is to be found only in Shakespeare's later plays.

> Creep in 'twixt vows and change decrees of kings,
> Tan sacred beauty, blunt the sharp'st intents,
> Divert strong minds to the course of altering things,—
> Alas, why, fearing of Time's tyranny,
> Might I not then say 'Now I love you best',
> When I was certain o'er uncertainty,
> Crowning the present, doubting of the rest?
>   Love is a babe; then might I *not* say so,
>   To give full growth to that which still doth grow.

To avoid discontinuity, I have dealt in a footnote with the principal difficulties of this very difficult sonnet. The substance of what Shakespeare is saying (and this is one of the things that compels me to suppose that this and the related sonnets were written later) is that, when he was writing some of his former sonnets, he was too much afraid of the tyranny of Time and too little aware of the continually growing and counteracting power of Love. He did not then realise (or sufficiently realise) that Love, no less than Time, does not stand still. Is there perhaps some inconsistency between the argument of this sonnet and Shakespeare's habitual defiance of Time, and, if so, was Shakespeare himself aware of it? For if, as is here declared, love is continually growing, there must be at least some sense in which time is *not* its irreconcilable enemy, since growth, becoming, can take place only in time: hence it might be said that love *requires* time in order to realise its potentiality, to become, as Aristotle would express it, that which it was intended to be. There is at least some affinity, some resemblance in difference, between this sonnet and the obscurely changing and clashing arguments in two of Donne's *Songs and Sonets*: *Loves Growth*, which proceeds from the doubt-filled assertion (ll. 5–6)

> Me thinkes I lyed all winter, when I swore,
> My love was infinite, if spring make it more

to the faith-restoring conclusion

> No winter shall abate the springs encrease;

and *Lovers infinitenesse*, beginning

> If yet I have not all thy love,
> Deare, I shall never have it all,

and later declaring (ll. 23–6)

> Yet I would not have all yet,
> Hee that hath all can have no more,
> And since my love doth every day admit
> New growth, thou shouldst have new rewards in store.

Although I have called Shakespeare's sonnet 'difficult', I think it is possible, after some pondering, to reach a pretty firm assurance that one has followed and understood his argument: I doubt, though, whether I should ever be able to extract and exhibit with confidence anything like a continuous and coherent argument, or series of arguments, from *Lovers infinitenesse*, for there, as in several of Donne's poems, a certain degree of seriousness is mingled with a good deal of what I cannot but regard as mere logical, or pseudo-logical, patter.

This sonnet is followed by the immortal 'Let me not to the marriage of true minds' (116), which I have already described as both literally and metaphorically incomparable. Petrarch, it is true, often speaks of the persistence and unchangeableness of his passion for Laura, with emphasis now upon the 'sweetness' of it and now upon the 'pain', but there is almost nothing in the *Canzoniere* at all comparable with Shakespeare's defiant challenge to Time. Most comparable, perhaps, is the sonnet (145) *Pommi ove 'l sol occide i fiori e l'erba*, partly imitated from the last two stanzas of Horace's *Integer vitae* (I, xxii) and beautifully paraphrased by Surrey in 'Set me wheras the sunne doth parche the grene', where Petrarch has departed from what seems at least to be Horace's approach to the theme which I shall consider in the Third Part of this study, that of love as compensation, love as all-sufficient,[1] and has replaced it by that of 'eternity in love protested'. My impression is that in the *Canzoniere* references to time and to the flight of time are few and far between, and that Petrarch is too firmly grounded and rooted in Christian theology to be deeply concerned with the fact of human transience as such, to protest against it, or to regard it tragically. Indeed, the only allusion to it that has remained in my memory is in the famous and beautiful sonnet 248, *Chi vuol veder quantunque po natura*, in which he bids whosoever wishes to see what Nature and Heaven together can achieve among us to come and behold Laura:

---

[1] It is, I admit, not altogether possible to maintain a sharp distinction between Shakespeare's sonnets on love as the Defier of Time and those on Love as what I have called 'compensation'. Perhaps it may be said that while there Shakespeare is mainly concerned to say what his love is and what it means to him, here he is mainly concerned to defy what seems to threaten it.

E venga tosto, perché morte fura
Prima i migliori e lascia star i rei:
Questa, aspettata al regno de li dei,
Cosa bella mortal, passa e non dura.[1]

('And let him come quickly, because death steals first the better and lets
the bad remain: this fair mortal thing, awaited in the kingdom of the
gods, passes and does not last.') Although it would seem that Menander's
famous saying that those whom the gods love die young had somehow
reached Petrarch in a Latin version,[2] it has been almost completely assimi-
lated by his Christianity, and his 'thieving' Death, despite some traces of
pagan personification, is the Death whom Christ has robbed of his sting.
It is true that in Petrarch's expression, as in that of many other Christian
poets, there is not an absolute consistency (perhaps because in this world
unregenerate man is never wholly regenerated and pagan man never
wholly Christianised): if Laura 'passes' because she is awaited in Heaven,
it cannot be because she has been 'stolen' by an independently marauding
Death. Nevertheless, it is, I think, true to say that for Petrarch, as also for
Chaucer, Death has been robbed of his sting and the tragedy of transience
deprived of its edge and mitigated into, at most, sadness. Shakespeare's
faith in the values he recognised (many of them specifically Christian
values) was as great as Petrarch's or Dante's or Chaucer's, but I doubt
whether he was, in the sense in which they were, a *believer*: hence it was
that the facts of death and transience remained for him, as they had
done for the ancients, tragic facts, facts which he could not mitigate or
transform by means of a securely held theology or philosophy, but
which, nevertheless, he could confront (or could not do other than
confront) with the affirmation of something eternal within himself—
that self which, because of the intervention of Christianity, had a 'depth-
dimension' (to repeat Rudolf Kassner's phrase) which the selves of the
ancients lacked.

I doubt whether it would be possible to produce from any medieval
or Renaissance poet anything really approaching this characteristically

[1] This line was copied by Leonardo da Vinci into one of his manuscripts, and a mis-
transcription of it as *Cosa bella mortal passa e non d'arte* was ascribed to Leonardo himself, and,
although no one knew exactly how to construe it, it was treasured by many of our late
nineteenth-century poets and believers in art for art's sake as enshrining some semi-mystical
testimony to the power of art.
[2] Perhaps in Plautus's *Bacchises*, 816–17:

Quem di diligunt
adulescens moritur, dum valet sentit sapit.

Shakespearean topic of Love as the Defier of Time, and the only approach to it I can recall in ancient poetry (and even that a very distant one) is a single passage in Propertius (II, xv, 29–36):

> Errat, qui finem vesani quaerit amoris:
>   verus amor nullum novit habere modum.
> terra prius falso partu deludet arantes,
>   et citius nigros Sol agitabit equos,
> fluminaque ad caput incipient revocare liquores,
>   aridus et sicco gurgite piscis erit,
> quam possim nostros alio transferre dolores:
>   huius ero vivus, mortuus huius ero.

('He is mistaken who tries to impose a limit on frenzied love: true love knows nothing of any bound. Sooner will Earth mock ploughmen with miscarriage, the Sun-god drive the horses of Night, rivers begin recalling their waters to the source and parched fish dwell in a dried-up deep than I shall be capable of transferring to another the pains I now endure: hers will I be alive, dead hers will I be.') I call this a distant approach, because, while Propertius is merely protesting the unchangeableness of a passion, Shakespeare is affirming the existence of something unchangeable in a world of change and eternal in transient mortality. Another poet might, In language very similar to that of Propertius, have affirmed his inextinguishable thirst for a particular kind of wine. The greater universality of that whose unalterableness Shakespeare is protesting is apparent in the contrast between the metaphors in his sonnet and the list of traditional ἀδύνατα, 'impossibilities', in Propertius. Perhaps, indeed, for something even approaching an approach to Shakespeare's sonnet one would have to turn to the Old Testament—to the *Song of Solomon*, for example, (viii, 7): 'Many waters cannot quench love, neither can the floods drown it: if a man would give all the substance of his house for love, it would utterly be contemned.'

The difficult sonnet 123, 'No, Time, thou shall not boast that I do change', ought perhaps to be considered together with 106 and 59. In 106, 'When in the chronicle of wasted time', Shakespeare had declared that the praises of beauty by earlier poets had all been no more than prefigurings of his friend's, and in 59,

> If there be nothing new, but that which is
> Hath been before,

he had played with the idea of the possibility of an eternal recurrence, only to reject it because of his conviction that the subjects of earlier poets' praises had been less worthy than his friend. Here, in 123, he declares, in so many words, that the whole world of Time is a world of illusion: that Time's new 'pyramids', which seem as though they would last for ever, are merely new versions of older ones that have decayed, and that, short-lived as we are, we are deluded into supposing that the achievements of today have been created for the first time by ourselves ('born to our desire'), whereas they are merely repetitions and reproductions of things past. Nevertheless, despite all-changing and all-deluding Time, the poet protests that he will remain 'true'—true, I think he must mean, to that 'marriage of true minds', that love, which alone is eternal in this world of time and change and illusion.[1] I cannot pursue this topic further without too much anticipating what I shall have to say in the Third Part of this study about the 'religiousness' of Shakespeare's love for his friend—the fact that he habitually speaks of it in language such as other writers had (and perhaps have) only ventured to apply to Him 'with whom is no variableness, neither shadow of turning'.[2] In no other poet, perhaps in no other great secular writer except Plato, do we find such defiance of the world of Time and Appearance ('phainomena') as we do in Shakespeare—Shakespeare the creator of Juliet's Nurse and Mrs. Quickly and Falstaff, Shakespeare the creator of Prospero and author of that speech declaring that the great globe itself would fade like this insubstantial pageant and leave not a wrack behind. The greatest of realists is also the most uncompromising of idealists. The poet who has mirrored this world of ours more comprehensively than any other is also, perhaps, the most unworldly, and the most clear-sighted of poets is also the most visionary. It is perhaps only when, as I am now trying to do, one compares him where he is at all comparable that one achieves a proper awareness of his uniqueness and of what I can only regard as the inexplicability, the miracle, of his appearance.

> No, Time, thou shalt not boast that I do change:
> Thy pyramids built up with newer might
> To me are nothing novel, nothing strange;
> They are but dressings of a former sight.

---

[1] Cf. the final couplet of 125, where he tells Time's 'suborn'd informer' that

>   a true soul
> When most impeach'd stands least in thy control.

[2] James, i, 17.

Our dates are brief, and therefore we admire
What thou dost foist upon us that is old;
And rather make them born to our desire
Than think that we before have heard them told.
Thy registers and thee I both defy,
Not wondering at the present nor the past,
For thy recòrds and what we see doth lie,
Made more or less by thy continual haste.
   This I do vow, and this shall ever be,
    I will be true, despite thy scythe and thee.

The following sonnet (124) contains a probable allusion to the Jesuit
conspirators

                          ('the fools of Time,
      Which die for goodness, who have liv'd for crime')

and a possible allusion to the Gunpowder Plot ('the blow of thralled
discontent', *i.e.* of discontent breaking out of its repression into rebellion),
and its main theme is that the poet's love is not the child of Time and
Chance and Fortune and is therefore unaffected by them. It need fear
none of those conspiring 'politicians' produced by temporary circumstances and inspired by temporary aims, 'But all alone stands hugely
politic'.

If my dear love were but the child of state,[1]
It might for Fortune's bastard be unfather'd,
As subject to Time's love or to Time's hate,
Weeds among weeds, or flowers with flowers gather'd.[2]
No, it was builded far from accident;
It suffers not in smiling pomp, nor falls
Under the blow of thralled discontent,
Whereto the inviting time our fashion calls:
It fears not policy, that heretic,
Which works on leases of short number'd hours,
But all alone stands hugely politic,
That it nor grows with heat nor drowns with showers.

[1] Born of particular circumstances, the mere result of a particular state of things. Despite
this characteristic protest, there seems to lie behind much recent writing on Shakespeare a
conviction that he and all his works were 'but the child of state'.
[2] This is the reading of the Quarto, but I find it hard not to suppose that what Shakespeare
wrote was:
      Weed among weeds, or flower with flowers gather'd.

> To this I witness call the fools of time,[1]
> Which die for goodness, who have liv'd for crime.

It is interesting to compare this with the 51st sonnet of Drayton's *Idea*, first printed in the edition of 1605, where Drayton too contrasts the stability of his love with the instability of the political scene. It is the only sonnet of Drayton's and, so far as I know, of any other sonneteer where reflections similar to those in this and in some other of Shakespeare's sonnets are to be found.

> Calling to mind, since first my love begun,
> The uncertain times oft varying in their course,
> How things still unexpectedly have run
> As it please the Fates, by their resistless force:
> Lastly mine eyes amazedly have seen
> Essex' great fall, Tyrone his peace to gain,
> The quiet end of that long-living Queen,
> This King's fair entrance and our peace with Spain,
> We and the Dutch at length ourselves to sever.
> Thus the world doth and evermore shall reel;
> Yet to my Goddess am I constant ever,
> Howe'er blind Fortune turn her giddy wheel.
> > Though Heaven and Earth prove both to me untrue,
> > Yet am I still inviolate to you.

For another topic that seems to be peculiar to Shakespeare and Drayton, that of the beloved as a reflection and reincarnation of all past beauty, Shakespeare, as I have already remarked,[2] may perhaps have received a hint from a sonnet of Drayton's first printed in 1594; the present topic, though, seems more likely to have been suggested to Drayton by Shakespeare, for it first appears,[3] in combination with the topic of what I shall later describe as 'compensation', in Shakespeare's sonnet 25 ('Let those who are in favour with their stars'), where several commentators have professed, not unreasonably, to see an allusion to the disgrace of the Earl of Essex after his return from the unsuccessful Irish expedition in 1599, and which is more likely to have been written while that disgrace

---

[1] Here I cannot but agree with Beeching: 'I believe the allusion here is to the Jesuit conspirators whose object in life was to murder the King, and who when caught posed as martyrs for the faith.'

[2] See p. 86.

[3] 'First appears', I mean, on this page of the collection as we have it.

and its apparent injustice were still fresh and dominant in Shakespeare's
mind than after the rebellion, trial and execution of Essex two years later:

> Great princes' favourites their fair leaves spread
> But as the marigold at the sun's eye,
> And in themselves their pride lies buried,
> For at a frown they in their glory die.
> The painful warrior famoused for fight,
> After a thousand victories once foil'd,
> Is from the book of honour razed quite,
> And all the rest forgot for which he toil'd:
> > Then happy I, that love and am beloved
> > Where I may not remove nor be removed.

It is worth remarking that, while Drayton names names and alludes to
public events in a perfectly plain and unambiguous manner, there is not
(with the exception of one or two classical or mythological ones) a
single proper name in Shakespeare's sonnets, and that, as in the probable
allusion to Essex just quoted, all his possible or probable allusions to
public events are metaphorical and what might be called Dantesquely
periphrastic: as in sonnet 107, ll. 5–8,

> The mortal moon hath her eclipse endur'd,[1]
> And the sad augurs mock their own presage;
> Incertainties now crown themselves assur'd
> And peace proclaims olives of endless age,

where I impenitently continue to perceive an allusion to the unexpectedly
peaceful transition from Queen Elizabeth to King James, and in the
possible allusions to the Gunpowder Plot ('the blow of thralled discontent') and to the Jesuit conspirators ('the fools of time') in the sonnet
(124) with which at present we are more immediately concerned. Some
perhaps might be inclined to see in this preference for metaphorical
periphrasis to direct allusion no more than the conscious or unconscious
influence of a certain deliberately chosen hermeticism or hieroglyphical-
ness which pervades Shakespeare's sonnets, as though he were trying to

---

[1] For this use of 'endure' in the sense of 'suffer' compare *King Lear*, V, ii, 9–11:

> Men must endure
> Their going hence, even as their coming hither;
> Ripeness is all.

ensure that no reader should be able to discover from them the identity of the person addressed. This may indeed have been a contributory cause, but more important, I think, is the relation between this fact and one which I shall notice later in this study[1]—the fact, namely, that in the sonnets of the poet whom Thomas Warton rightly described as 'the universal and accurate observer of real Nature'[2] there is an abundance of metaphor and metaphorical personification, but, in comparison with the sonnets of Petrarch, Ronsard and others, very little—indeed, almost a complete absence—of detailed and direct description. Shakespeare's tendency to generalise, spiritualise and unsubstantiate was as great as his capacity to particularise and substantiate. It is therefore not surprising that, when public events enter his sonnets, they should be deprived of their local habitation and their name and become part of an unsubstantial pageant passing before and around the sole certainty and sole permanence of his love for his friend.

In the next and last of these sonnets (125) Shakespeare seems to be replying to some imaginary 'suborn'd informer' in the contest between himself and Time, and to be declaring that what he has really loved in his friend and celebrated in his verse has not been something external, visible and transient, but something inward, invisible and eternal. I say 'seems', because the first quatrain is one of many passages in the sonnets which hovers between metaphor and allegory: where, that is to say, the metaphors cannot really 'mean' anything to the reader until he has made some attempt to translate them—at any rate, to a considerable extent—into prosaic and conceptual terms, and where he can never feel sure that his translation is quite accurate. The contrast between this kind of writing (about which, even with Shakespeare, there remains something unsatisfactory) and what I may call 'pure' metaphor is immediately apparent: we do not have to puzzle about Shakespeare's 'meaning' when he speaks of the 'fell arrest without all bail', or 'the coward conquest of a wretch's knife', or when he asks

---

[1] See pp. 189 ff.
[2] Note on Milton's *Il Penseroso*, ll. 81–2:

> Far from all resort of mirth,
> Save the Cricket on the hearth:

'Shakespeare, the universal and accurate observer of real Nature, was the first who introduced the crying of the cricket, and with the finest effect, into poetry.' Warton was thinking of *Macbeth*, II, ii, 15–16:

> 'I have done the deed. Didst thou not hear a voice?'
> 'I heard the owl scream and the crickets cry.'

> How with such rage shall Beauty hold a plea,
> Whose action is no stronger than a flower?

In the first quatrain of this sonnet Shakespeare seems to 'mean' something like this: 'Could it mean anything to me if I had merely given external expression in my verse to my admiration for your external appearance, and if the eternity which I claimed both for my love and for my verse had been based upon anything so transient as this?'

> Were't aught to me I bore the canopy,
> With my extern[1] the outward honouring,
> Or laid great bases for eternity,
> Which prove more short than waste or ruining?
> Have I not seen dwellers on form and favour
> Lose all, and more, by paying too much rent,
> For compound sweet forgoing simple savour,
> Pitiful thrivers, in their gazing spent?
> No, let me be obsequious in thy heart,
> And take thou my oblation, poor but free,
> Which is not mix'd with seconds,[2] knows no art
> But mutual render,[3] only me for thee.
>   Hence, thou suborn'd informer! a true[4] soul
>   When most impeach'd stands least in thy control.

We may now return to that question which I raised at the beginning of my consideration of these presumably later sonnets on the theme of

[1] Beeching, in his edition of the Sonnets (1904, Introd., p. xxvii), has noticed that the word 'extern' only occurs elsewhere in *Othello*, I, i, 63.

[2] Flour of inferior quality.

[3] I have removed the Quarto's comma after 'art' at the end of line 11, and I take the phrase to mean 'knows no art except that of mutual render', *i.e.* 'mutual surrender'. In Shakespeare's plays there are only three other examples, all late, of the use of 'render' as a noun, or verbal noun. In *Timon of Athens*, V, i, 152, where the Senators send emissaries to Timon to 'make their sorrowed render', it seems impossible to decide whether the exact meaning is 'make their sorrowful surrender' or 'make their sorrowful confession of having been in the wrong'. In *Cymbeline*, IV, iv, 11, Belarius's fear that what has happened may 'drive us to a render Where we have lived', the meaning is clearly 'drive us into rendering an account of where we have lived'; and in V, iv, 17, where Posthumus wishes that his gaolers should 'take No stricter render of me than my all', he is speaking metaphorically, as a bankrupt, and means 'Don't trouble to work out what proportion you ought to take of what I possess—take all'. Here, if 'take of me' = 'take from me', the meaning of 'render' is as near as makes no matter to its meaning in sonnet 125, *i.e.* 'surrender'.

If 'But' in line 12 is to be taken, not as a preposition, but as a conjunction, then either (a) 'render' must be taken as an imperative dependent on 'thou', which seems impossible, or (b) it must be regarded as a corruption of 'renders' and as governed by 'oblation'.

[4] Cf. the last line of 123:

>   I will be true, despite thy scythe and thee.

Love as the Defier of Time, these sonnets in which Shakespeare declares
that what he has loved and celebrated in his friend has been that in him
which is beyond the reach of Time—we may return to the question: how
far, if at all, ought we to allow these sonnets to influence our reading of
those presumably earlier ones in which, if he does not actually declare,
Shakespeare at any rate seems to imply that it is precisely that in his friend
which *does* come within the compass of Time's bending sickle that he
most loves and that his verse will preserve? Let us remind ourselves of
some of the things he had said:

> Then the conceit of this inconstant stay
> Sets you most rich in youth before my sight,
> Where wasteful Time debateth with Decay
> To change your day of youth to sullied night;
>> And all in war with Time for love of you,
>> As he takes from you, I engraft you new
>
> (15);

> But thy eternal summer shall not fade
> Nor lose possession of that fair thou ow'st;
> Nor shall Death brag thou wander'st in his shade,
> When in eternal lines to time thou grow'st
>
> (18);

> Yet do thy worst, old Time: despite thy wrong,
> My love shall in my verse ever live young
>
> (19);

> Against my love shall be, as I am now . . .
>   when his youthful morn
> Hath travell'd on to age's steepy night,
> And all those beauties whereof now he's king
> Are vanishing or vanish'd out of sight . . .
> For such a time do I now fortify
> Against confounding Age's cruel knife,
> That he shall never cut from memory
> My sweet love's beauty, though my lover's life:[1]
>> His beauty shall in these black lines be seen,
>> And they shall live, and he in them still green
>
> (63);

[1] Rather, I think, 'the life of me the lover' than 'the life of my lover'.

O fearful meditation! where, alack,
Shall Time's best jewel from Time's chest lie hid?
Or what strong hand can hold his swift foot back?
Or who his spoil of beauty can forbid?
  O none, unless this miracle have might,
  That in black ink my love may still shine bright
                      (65);

Rise, resty[1] Muse, my love's sweet face survey,
If Time have any wrinkle graven there;
If any, be a satire to decay,
And make Time's spoils despised everywhere.
  Give my love fame faster than Time wastes life;
  So thou prevent'st his scythe and crooked knife
                      (100);

Then do thy office, Muse; I teach thee how
To make him seem long hence as he shows now.
                      (101).

On the one hand, I think it must be admitted that from these and similar utterances the 'suborn'd informer' could make out a very plausible case that Shakespeare *had* been honouring the outward and 'laying great bases for eternity' upon what Time would destroy; on the other hand, it must also be admitted that he has nowhere attempted to particularise any single one of those visible beauties and charms and graces which he declares that his verse is preserving. We do not know whether his friend was tall or short or of medium height, or what was the colour of his eyes or of his hair, or whether his voice was deep or high. We have no picture of him in the midst of any activity where his peculiar charms and graces and accomplishments were characteristically displayed: at the tilt-yard, in a court masque, at a ball, meditating under a tree like Sir Philip Sidney in Oliver's miniature, plucking a flower, playing on a lute, looking up from a book, describing something that had given him vivid pleasure, rejecting with high disdain some ignoble proposal, delivering some gracious compliment or some well-merited rebuke. Shakespeare does not attempt anything like a series of evocations of his friend's *youness*: does not say 'I shall never forget the moment when I first saw you', or 'the way you came into the room', or 'the way you suddenly looked up', or 'the way you said', or 'the way you tossed your head', or 'the way your eyes

[1] Ever-resting, torpid.

flashed', or 'the way you bit your lip', or 'the way you twisted your gloves', or 'the way you were unlike the rest'. In fact, we know nothing at all about his friend's 'ways'.

In the Third Part of this study I shall have much to say about Shakespeare's use of hyperbole, perhaps the most characteristic feature of his style both in the sonnets and in the tragedies. Here I will take the opportunity of suggesting why it is that in only one of the sonnets to his friend (21) he forswears the use of hyperboles and comparisons:

> So is it not with me as with that Muse
> Stirr'd by a painted beauty to his verse,
> Who heaven itself for ornament doth use
> And every fair with his fair doth rehearse,
> Making a couplement of proud compare
> With sun and moon, with earth and sea's rich gems,
> With April's first-born flowers, and all things rare
> That heaven's air in this huge rondure hems.
> O let me, true in love, but truly write,
> And then believe me, my love is as fair
> As any mother's child, though not so bright
> As those gold candles fix'd in heaven's air:
>   Let them say more that like of hearsay well;
>   I will not praise that purpose not to sell.

Shakespeare could only say this *once*, for, unless he was willing to describe his friend's 'ways' in detailed descriptions and evocations such as I have suggested, there was no way in which he could continue to express what his friend 'meant' to him except in and through hyperboles and comparisons, just as Milton, attempting, as someone has well said, to describe, not what Satan looked like, but what it felt like to look at him, was able to do so only in and through similes, which may be regarded as indirect or transferred descriptions. Similarly, Shakespeare has only one anti-hyperbolical sonnet (130, 'My mistress' eyes are nothing like the sun') among those addressed to the 'Dark Lady'. It is just conceivable that sonnet 21 may have been suggested to him by certain sonnets (3, 6, 15, 74) in Sidney's *Astrophel and Stella*, where Sidney declares that he does not require the inspiration of any other muse than Stella and that all he need do is to describe her as she is, without either imitating other poets or inventing elaborate similes and hyperboles: sonnets which were perhaps suggested to Sidney himself by sonnets in which both Du Bellay and

Ronsard had declared, though with very different intentions, that they were not professing, like Hesiod and others, to write as poets inspired by the Muses and by Hippocrene, the 'Pegasean Spring'. In the first four sonnets of his *Regrets* Du Bellay defends what might seem the unambitious and unadorned style of that predominantly satirical collection by declaring that he has been inspired solely by his spontaneous reaction to everyday occurrences: declares (like Persius, the Prologue to whose *Satires* he imitates at the beginning of sonnet 4) that he is writing, not as a muse-inspired poet or as a candidate for immortality, but as a satirist, and that, accordingly, he is not trying to write elaborately and learnedly like Ronsard, and like himself in his love-poetry. Ronsard, in sonnet 175 of his first *Livre des amours*, 'Je ne suis point, Muses, accoustumé,[1] imitating Persius's apology for the style of his *Satires*, Horace's compliment to Melpomene in *Odes*, IV, iii (*Quod spiro et placeo, si placeo, tuum est*), and Petrarch's declaration in 71 of the *Canzoniere* that his 'feeble style' has owed its whole achievement to the inspiration of Laura's eyes, declares that he needs no help from the Muses, since he is sufficiently inspired by the eyes of Cassandre. Sidney, in the four sonnets I have mentioned, is trying to combine things that are perhaps not really *in pari materia*, Du Bellay's defence of a style appropriate to satire and Ronsard's hyperbolical compliment to Cassandre. These sonnets of Ronsard and Sidney cannot properly be described as 'anti-Petrarchan', since they all conclude with characteristically Petrarchan compliments to the power of the beloved's beauty, and Sidney's anti-hyperbolism, such as it is, is really a new kind of hyperbole. Sidney, it is true, does not, like Shakespeare in these two sonnets, say, in so many words, that Stella, though not as beautiful as the sun, is as beautiful as any other woman, but even Shakespeare seems to have perceived that this was something he could only say once, and that to forswear the use of hyperboles and to confine himself, like his own Biron, to 'russet yeas and honest kersey noes' would be to condemn himself to silence.

Shakespeare, then, tells us nothing about his friend's 'ways'. 'Your day of youth', 'thy eternal summer', 'his youthful morn', 'those beauties whereof now he's king', 'my sweet love's beauty', 'my love's sweet face': in these phrases there is absolutely nothing that is individualising or particularising—so might any young and beautiful person of either sex seem to any older person of either sex by whom he or she was deeply or purely loved; loved with a love in which some effluence of *il primo amore* transcended, not merely Chaucer's distinction between 'love paramours'

[1] Vaganay, I, p. 190.

and 'love of friendship', but even that between these and brotherly, sisterly or parental love. If Blake, whose authority with modern writers on poetry seems to become ever more absolute, was right in believing that 'he who generalises is an idiot', then very many of Shakespeare's sonnets are idiotic, for no love could be more generalised than that which is there expressed. Indeed, I must confess to some surprise that they have not already provoked objections similar to those brought against Milton's unparticularised ploughman in *L'Allegro*. Certainly, the whole tendency of the best modern poetry and the best modern novels has been towards the individualisation and particularisation of love, and in Yeats's poems about Maud Gonne it is notable how greatness and particularity advance together. We may perhaps perceive in modern poetry a tendency, beginning, as it were gropingly, in Keats's Odes and reaching full awareness and explicitness in Rilke's *Duino Elegies*, to accept transience (with no matter what heart-rending sadness) as the necessary price of uniqueness, whereas in Shakespeare's sonnets and elsewhere we may perceive a tendency, a willingness, to sacrifice uniqueness for the sake of permanence. The following sonnet of Elizabeth Barrett Browning, which might seem sentimental to many modern readers, is nearer to Shakespeare than to Yeats and Rilke:

> If thou must love me, let it be for nought
>   Except for love's sake only. Do not say
>   'I love her for her smile—her look—her way
> Of speaking gently,—for a trick of thought
> That falls in well with mine, and certes brought
>   A sense of pleasant ease on such a day'—
>   For these things in themselves, Belovèd, may
> Be changed, or change for thee,—and love, so wrought,
> May be unwrought so. Neither love me for
>   Thine own dear pity's wiping my cheeks dry:
> A creature might forget to weep, who bore
>   Thy comfort long, and lose thy love thereby!
> But love me for love's sake, that evermore
>   Thou mayst love on, through love's eternity.

The notion of 'love for love's sake' would probably be regarded by many modern readers as on a par with being 'in love with love' and dismissed as sentimental, romantic or adolescent. Shakespeare seems to have felt differently: it is *because* his love is for love's sake that it can defy Time.

3

The instinctiveness and unphilosophicalness of Shakespeare's 'idealism' and 'spirituality': contrast with Michelangelo and other men of Geist

Nowhere, I think, has Shakespeare approached anything like a philosophical expression of the distinction I have just formulated. He was surrounded by 'Platonism' and by 'men of ideas', or, at any rate, by men who made much use of ideas in which they at least professed to believe; but I think it is not going too far to say that of 'ideas' in the Platonic sense there is scarcely any trace in his sonnets. He thought, I am inclined to say, in terms rather of feeling and conviction, memory and imagination, than in terms of doctrine and idea, and almost all his statements are metaphors, or in process of becoming metaphors. We never find him declaring that his friend's beauty is a manifestation of the eternal and unchangeable beauty, or that what he loves in his friend is the immaterial and invisible soul that will survive the material and visible accidents it is temporarily informing, or that his love of what is heavenly in his friend is weaning his own soul from the love of terrestrial things and guiding it to heaven. Indeed, I think there is only one sonnet in the whole collection where even the distinction between body and soul, terrestrial and celestial, finds clear and memorable expression, 146, which I will quote with the anonymous and generally accepted emendation of its corrupt second line:

> Poor soul, the centre of my sinful earth,
> Thrall to these rebel powers that thee array,
> Why dost thou pine within and suffer dearth,
> Painting thy outward walls so costly gay?
> Why so large cost, having so short a lease,
> Dost thou upon thy fading mansion spend?
> Shall worms, inheritors of this excess,

Eat up thy charge? Is this thy body's end?
Then, soul, live thou upon thy servant's loss,
And let that pine to aggravate thy store;
Buy terms divine in selling hours of dross;
Within be fed, without be rich no more:
     So shalt thou feed on Death, that feeds on men,
     And Death once dead, there's no more dying then.

If it were possible to use the word 'conventional' in an unpejorative sense, I think it might be said that this is Shakespeare's nearest approach to an expression both of conventional Platonism and of conventional Christianity. It is unique among his sonnets, and is the only one having some real affinity with some of those sonnets full of *suspiria de profundis* written towards the close of his life by Michelangelo, the only sonnets, I think, except perhaps for some of Donne's *Holy Sonnets*, with which it is really comparable: true though it be that the sonnets both of Michelangelo and of Donne are full of clear and explicit expressions and professions of Christian doctrine and Christian faith which we do not find in this sonnet of Shakespeare's. It is also, I think, illuminating to compare some of Shakespeare's sonnets to his friend with some of those which the old sculptor addressed to the young Tommaso de' Cavalieri and the widowed poetess Vittoria Colonna. It is not really illuminating to insist on the contrast between Shakespeare's sonnets and those of various almost professional dealers in Platonism and idealism, concerned rather to express (often with great brilliance and accomplishment) what was fashionable and what they thought their dedicatees would most like to hear than with that wherein they themselves 'must either live or bear no life'. Michelangelo, though, one of the greatest men of the Renaissance, was not a professional writer, was writing only for himself and for his friends, without thought of publication,[1] and, continually aware as he was of the imminence of death, could have said with Goethe, 'The fashion of this world passes away, and henceforth I would concern myself only with those relationships that are abiding.' With perhaps even greater sincerity than Petrarch he could have claimed that he was writing

[1] Both the autographs and the copies of Michelangelo's poems swarm with variants; they are often ungrammatical, their syntax is often tortured and uncertain, and they are formidably difficult to construe. They were first printed, in a well-intentioned but dreadfully garbled and 'improved' edition, by his grand-nephew, Michelangelo the Younger, in 1623. The edition published by Cesare Guasti in 1863 has now been superseded by that of E. N. Girardi (Bari, 1960), to whose numbering I refer. I have tried to provide absolutely literal versions of the sonnets I quote, but there are places in them about whose exact meaning I cannot feel wholly certain.

Pur di sfogare il doloroso core
In qualche modo, non d'acquistar fama

('Only to find some way of discharging my sad heart, not to acquire fame'), for his fame already, like that of Homer's Odysseus, 'ascended to heaven'. In the strength and depth and reality of the love they express, and in the absence from them of anything like pleading or courtship, there is a real affinity between many of Michelangelo's sonnets to Vittoria Colonna and Shakespeare's sonnets to his friend, but, at the same time, both Michelangelo's experience and his expression of it are indissolubly associated and integrated with specifically Christian and specifically Platonic doctrines in a manner which reveals that he was both a 'man of ideas' and a 'believer' in a sense Shakespeare never was.

105

Non vider gli occhi miei cosa mortale
    Allor che ne'bei vostri intera pace
    Trovai; ma dentro, ov'ogni mal dispiace,
    Chi d'amor l'alma a sè simil m'assale.
E se creata a Dio non fusse eguale,
    Altro che 'l bel di fuor, ch'agli occhi piace,
    Più non vorria; ma perch'è sì fallace,
    Trascende nella forma universale.
Io dico, ch'a chi vive quel che muore
    Quetar non può disir; nè par s'aspetti
    L'eterno al tempo, ove altri cangia il pelo.
Voglia sfrenata el senso è, non amore,
    Che l'alma uccide; e'l nostro fa perfetti
    Gli amici qui, ma più per morte in cielo.

('My eyes were not beholding something mortal when in your fair ones I found entire peace; but within, where all evil displeases, [they were beholding] Him who assails my soul with love like to himself. And if it [the soul] had not been created equal to God, anything more than the fair outside, that pleases the eyes, it would not wish for; but, because that is so deceiving, the soul passes beyond into the universal form. I say that for who lives that which dies cannot appease desire; nor does it seem that the eternal has anything to do with time, where one changes one's hair [but not one's habits].[1] Sense is unbridled will, not love, which kills the

---

[1] Petrarch, sonnet 122, ll. 5–6, quotes the proverb in full.

soul; and ours [*i.e.* our love] makes friends perfect here, but still more so, through death, in Heaven.')

106 (To Cavalieri)

Per ritornar là donde venne fora,
   L'immortal forma al tuo carcer terreno
   Venne com'angel di pietà sì pieno
   Che sana ogn'intelletto, e 'l mondo onora.
Questo sol m'arde, e questo m'innamora;
   Non pur di fora il tuo volto sereno:
   Ch'amor non già di cosa che vien meno
   Tien ferma speme, in cui virtù dimora.
Nè altro avvien di cose altere e nuove
   In cui si preme la natura; e'l cielo
   È ch'a lor parto largo s'apparecchia.
Nè Dio, suo grazia, mi si mostra altrove,
   Più che'n alcun leggiadro e mortal velo;
   E quel sol amo, perch' in lui si specchia.

('To return thither whence it came forth, the immortal form to your terrene prison came, angel-like, so full of pity that it heals every intellect and does honour to the world. This alone inflames me, and this makes me in love; not merely from without your serene face: for never does love in which virtue dwells hold firm hope of thing that grows less [*i.e.*, is transient]. Nor does it otherwise happen with things lofty and rare in which Nature exerts herself, and Heaven it is that for their birth liberally prepares. Nor does God, of his grace, elsewhere show himself more to me than in some charming and mortal veil; and that alone I love because in that He is mirrored.') Shakespeare, it is true, declares that he has not 'built great bases for eternity' on his admiration for his friend's external beauty, but he does not declare, like Michelangelo, that in loving his friend he has been loving God.

259 (version Ib)

Ben può talor col casto e buon desio
   Di par la speme non esser fallace;
   Ch'ogni affetto fra noi s'al ciel dispiace,
   A che fin fatto arebbe il mondo Iddio?
S'i' t'amo e reverisco, o signor mio,
   Anzi s'i'ardo, è per divina pace

Che ne'begli occhi tuoi s'alberga e giace,
Nimica e schiva d'ogni pensier rio.
Non è amor quel che qui nasce e muore
Con la beltà ch'ogni momento scema,
Ond'è suggetto al cangiar d'un bel viso:
Ma quello è ben, che'n un pudico core
Nè per cangiar di scorza o d'ora estrema
Non manca, e qui caparra il paradiso.

('Well may at times with chaste and good desire Hope be keeping step and not be deceiving; for if every affection among us were displeasing to Heaven, to what end would God have made the world? If I love and reverence you, O my Lady [*lit.* 'my Lord': perhaps with some suggestion of the co-presence and co-activity of Lord Love], if, rather, I burn for you, it is for the sake of divine peace that lodges and lies in your fair eyes, hater and avoider of all wicked thought. That is not love which is born and dies with the beauty that every moment grows less, whence it [love] is subjected to the changing of a fair face: but that is indeed [love] which in a pure heart neither through changing of outward cover nor through [coming of] last hour diminishes, and here gives earnest [= foretaste] of Paradise.')

In the sestet of this sonnet Michelangelo is indeed saying something very like what Shakespeare is saying in sonnet 116:

Love's not Time's fool, though rosy lips and cheeks
Within his bending sickle's compass come;
Love alters not with his brief hours and weeks,
But bears it out even to the edge of doom.

But even here, where Michelangelo, like Shakespeare, is content with pure negation ('Non è amor quel che . . .', 'Love is not love that . . .') and pure affirmation ('Ma quello è ben . . .', 'It is an ever-fixed mark'— notice, though, how Shakespeare instinctively falls into metaphor), even here Michelangelo concludes with that clear and sharp distinction between Here and There, Now and Then, terrestrial and Celestial which so seldom makes anything like a clear and explicit appearance in Shakespeare's sonnets. One might almost say that, while Shakespeare merely has a conviction, an ultimately inexplicable conviction, that Love is not Time's fool, Michelangelo has not merely a conviction but a proof; that while Shakespeare, as Plato might have said, merely has δόξα, opinion, belief, Michelangelo has ἐπιστήμη, knowledge, and his conviction can give a reason, λόγον διδόναι. Someone once defined philosophy as the attempt to find reasons for what we believe upon instinct: certainly, Michelangelo would seem to have felt a much greater need than Shakespeare to find reasons for his deepest convictions and intuitions, to give them a rational and intellectual basis. I have said that the word 'spiritual' best defines what Shakespeare's sonnets and Petrarch's have in common. Michelangelo's sonnets too are deeply spiritual, but in a manner different from Shakespeare's. It is significant that while Shakespeare's tend, in the main, to be a series of metaphorical variations upon or expansions of fairly simple statements, Michelangelo's are in the main close and continuous arguments, from which, except for occasional illustrations and analogies wholly subordinated to the argument, metaphor and imagery are conspicuously absent. I am reminded of Grimm's words, quoted by Pater,[1] about the great artist and sculptor: 'When one speaks of him, woods, clouds, seas, and mountains disappear, and only what is formed by the spirit of man remains behind.' Grimm (I have not verified the quotation) was presumably employing the German word *Geist*, that word often so difficult to translate, which can mean sometimes 'spirit', sometimes 'mind', and sometimes both together.[2] Our own use of the word 'spirit', when we speak of 'a great spirit' or 'a noble spirit', is difficult to define and perhaps not very clearly distinguishable from our use of the word 'soul'; and with our adjective 'spiritual' there is, so far as I know, with the possible exception of Italian *spirituale*, no exactly corresponding word in any other language. Of the German adjectives derived from *Geist*, *geistig* normally means 'mental' or 'intellectual', *geistreich* 'witty', and *geistlich* 'clerical', 'ecclesiastical' and (in the merely nominal or organisational sense) 'religious', and the adjectival noun *ein Geistlicher* means 'a clergyman'. It is true that our old official distinction of the members of the House of Lords into Lords Spiritual and Lords Temporal still remains, but in other contexts 'spiritual' has never become, like German *geistlich*, merely nominal and external, and has retained its original and powerful sense of 'concerned with the things of the spirit as distinct from the things of time, with unworldly as distinct from worldly things'. Indeed, no doubt under the influence of Protestantism and Pauline theology, the depth and inwardness of this original meaning has even increased, and the word has come to mean, or at least to imply,

---

[1] 'The Poetry of Michelangelo' in *The Renaissance* (Pocket Edition, 1925, p. 76).
[2] The article on *Geist* by Rudolf Hildebrand in Grimm's *Wörterbuch* occupies well over a hundred closely printed columns and has been published separately as a book.

a private, personal, inward and real concernment with unworldly things, as distinct from a merely public, official, external and professed concernment. We *hope* that *ein Geistlicher* may be so concerned, but we do not assume it, for that is an assumption which might easily lead to the further assumption that these things are merely the concern of *die Geistlichen, die Geistlichkeit*, and not of us all. In considering some figure of the past, whether writer, artist or musician, soldier or statesman, cleric or layman, we often say of him that he either had or had not any 'deep spiritual life'. My point is that, although both Shakespeare's and Michelangelo's sonnets are in this sense 'spiritual', there is in Michelangelo's more of *Geist*, in the German philosophical sense, than there is in Shakespeare's.

I have remarked that our use of the word 'spirit' is not easily distinguished from our use of the word 'soul': on the other hand, for many German thinkers and philosophers there is, if not exactly a clear, at any rate a very important, distinction between *Geist* and *Seele*. It is a distinction which often appears in the writings of that great though neglected modern author, Rudolf Kassner. Kassner has said, for example, of Rilke, of whom he was an intimate friend and whose poetry he greatly though critically admired, that his world was not that of the spirit (*Geist*) but that of the soul (*Seele*). By 'the world of the soul' Kassner means a kind of naïve or pre-lapsarian world; a world where, instead of a sense of sin or a sense of guilt, there is only a sense of greater or lesser participation in 'being'; a world of absolute continuity. From this world Kassner distinguishes 'the world of the spirit', a world full of discontinuities: between pleasure and work, between inclination and duty, between what we are and what we might be, or ought to be; discontinuities that can be bridged only by faith, by imagination, by (above all, and in the Platonic sense) the Idea. He has described Rilke as being essentially un-Platonic, and for him Rilke's world is a world without ideas, a world in which man has not yet reversed his direction and turned[1] to a life in and through faith and the idea. One may perhaps be reminded of the views of R. G. Collingwood and some other philosophers about the

---

[1] The word and idea of *Umkehr*, which appears so often in Kassner's writings, comes from Luther's translation of *Matthew*, xviii, 3: *Es sei denn, dass ihr euch umkehret, und werdet wie die Kinder*, 'Except ye *turn*, and become as little children, ye shall not enter into the kingdom of heaven': a passage where the Authorised Version's pedantic translation of the passive form but active meaning of the Greek ἐὰν μὴ στραφῆτε and of the Vulgate *nisi conversi fueritis* by 'Except ye be converted' has deprived Christ's command of its immediacy, as though it were to be obeyed, not here and now, on the spot, but at some future time, through some eventually to be established machinery of 'conversion'. Tyndale (1526) correctly rendered the phrase 'except ye tourne'. Turn round, turn back, from the way you are going, which leads *from* the kingdom of heaven, into the way that leads *to* it.

logical (though not necessarily the temporal) priority of the life of art to the life of history and of thought; but Kassner's distinction between the World of the Soul and the World of the Spirit cuts across these distinctions. Both Rilke and Michelangelo were great artists, but, while it is clear that Rilke belongs (in Kassner's sense) to the World of the Soul, it is also clear that Michelangelo belongs (in Kassner's sense) to the World of the Spirit—belongs to it more than Shakespeare does, although it would be absurd to place the author of *King Lear*, *Othello*, and *Macbeth* together with Rilke in the pre-lapsarian World of the Soul. These attempted distinctions can only help us so long as we are content to allow them to remain fluid and provisional.

Keats, I think, was groping towards some such distinction, or trying to express his awareness of some such distinction, in certain passages in his letters. One of these has been much quoted by modern critics, who have often seemed to attribute to it a kind of absolute validity and have used it as ammunition in the long battle to exalt Shakespeare at the expense of Milton—that passage where Keats reports that, in the course of a long discussion with Dilke, it suddenly struck him

> what quality went to form a Man of Achievement especially in Literature and which Shakespeare possessed so enormously—I mean *Negative Capability*, that is when man is capable of being in uncertainties, Mysteries, doubts, without any irritable reaching after fact and reason.[1]

Here Keats has certainly succeeded both in perceiving and in expressing something of fundamental importance about Shakespeare, something which distinguishes him from many other great poets; nevertheless, the fact remains that Dante and Michelangelo and Milton were, if that phrase has any meaning at all, 'Men of Achievement', and also that they were less capable than Shakespeare of remaining in 'uncertainties, Mysteries, doubts'; that they had more need of certainty, and that their attempts to reach it cannot properly be described as 'irritable'. Keats continues this train of thought in another famous passage, behind which, as behind so many of his remarks about poetry, one can hear, I think, some of the characteristic paradoxes and exaggerations of Hazlitt, whom Keats regarded as something of a mentor and guide and whose influence upon him was far greater than has been generally recognised. Indeed, Hazlitt's favourite word 'gusto', which I think he was the first to introduce from

---

[1] To George and Thomas Keats, 22 December 1817, *Letters*, ed. Buxton Forman, 1952, p. 71.

the criticism of painting into that of literature, here appears, togetherwith something of Hazlitt's ambivalent attitude towards Wordsworth, for whose poetry Keats has elsewhere (like Hazlitt himself) professed the greatest admiration.

> As to the poetical Character itself (I mean that sort of which, if I am anything, I am a Member; that sort distinguished from the wordsworthian or egotistical sublime; which is a thing per se and stands alone) it is not itself— it has no self—it is every thing and nothing—It has no character—it enjoys light and shade; it lives in gusto, be it foul or fair, high or low, rich or poor, mean or elevated—It has as much delight in conceiving an Iago as an Imogen. What shocks the virtuous philosopher, delights the camelion Poet. It does no harm from its relish of the dark side of things any more than from its taste for the bright one; because they both end in speculation. A Poet is the most unpoetical of any thing in existence; because he has no Identity—he is continually informing and filling some other Body.[1]

In these and other remarks about poetry Keats is pursuing, expanding and clarifying various insights, intuitions and *aperçus* that have come to him from time to time, and we should not attempt, as too many modern critics have done, to rigidify them into something like dogmas. There are other passages in his letters where he reveals an awareness of the limitations of this view of the 'poetical Character', or, at any rate, of the dangers and temptations to which it is exposed. A few months before he wrote thus he had also written:

> An extensive knowledge is needful to thinking people—it takes away the heat and fever; and helps, by widening speculation, to ease the Burden of the Mystery. . . . The difference of high sensations with and without knowledge appears to me this—in the latter case we are falling continually ten thousand fathoms deep and being blown up again without wings and with all ⟨the⟩ horror of a bare shouldered creature—in the former case, our shoulders are fledge, and we go thro' the same air and space without fear.[2]

And about a year later he wrote:

> Though a quarrel in the Streets is a thing to be hated, the energies displayed in it are fine; the commonest Man shows a grace in his quarrel—By a superior

---

[1] To Richard Woodhouse, 27 October 1818, *op. cit.*, pp. 226–7. Although he actually wrote, as the last words on a page, something like 'in for . . .', I think there can be no doubt that what Keats intended was 'informing'.

[2] To John Hamilton Reynolds, 3 May 1818, *op. cit.*, p. 139.

being our reasoning⟨s⟩ may take the same tone—though erroneous they may
be fine—This is the very thing in which consists poetry; and if so it is not so
fine a thing as philosophy—For the same reason that an eagle is not so fine a
thing as a truth.[1]

In these and in many other passages we can see Keats himself reaching
(not 'irritably' but compulsively) after 'fact and reason'. Is he at the same
time revealing some awareness of the difference between what Kassner
calls the World of the Soul and the World of the Spirit? Certainly, that
passage about the fearful falling and fearful rising of one who has 'high
Sensations' without knowledge reminds me of one in which Kassner
has conveyed his impressions of much modern literature which he
classifies as 'surrealist', and which includes at least portions of the work
of Rilke, Proust, D. H. Lawrence and Kafka:

> For the surrealist, though, there are no longer any ideas in the Platonic
> sense, but instead an emerging and submerging, the emerging and submerging
> of the phallic man, pleasure and displeasure, evaporation, dissolving, expiration
> of one's being in pure enjoyment, a relishing of things to their core, complete
> analysis to the very bottom, where even the swindle, even the lie, are obvious,
> become graspable and therewith permissible. This isolated being with nothing
> behind him believes in nothing, and consequently, the only adventure left for
> him is to believe in everything.[2]

And in the centre of this World of Surrealism, declares Kassner, there is
lodged, as in its bitter kernel, the atomic bomb. This World of
Surrealism, as described by Kassner, is not really the World of the Soul,
but rather the World of the Senses—that 'life of sensations rather than of
thoughts' for which Keats was sometimes tempted to long. Had Keats
some premonition that for modern man it would not be possible, not at
any rate without disaster, to live without *Geist* and without ideas, and are
those contrasts and antitheses that run through so many of his remarks
about poetry not merely between, let us say, Shakespeare's kind of poetry
and Milton's or Wordsworth's kind, but between the claims of sensation
and the claims of thought, between a life of sensations and a life of
ideas, between something like a conception of 'pure' poetry (which,
admittedly, Shakespeare is sometimes made to symbolise) and what
Keats called 'philosophy'—between, in fact, ways not merely of writing

[1] To George and Georgiana Keats, 14 February–3 May 1819, *op. cit.*, p. 316.
[2] *Transfiguration*, 1946, pp. 60–1.

but of living and being, neither of which in itself seemed ultimately satisfactory?

I do not know what progress (if any) I may seem to have made in my attempt to answer the question: What is it that distinguishes the 'spirituality' of Michelangelo's sonnets from the 'spirituality' of Shakespeare's? 'Ideas', in the sense in which they are operative in Michelangelo's sonnets, are scarcely present at all in Shakespeare's, and while *Geist*, in the German philosophical sense, pervades Michelangelo's, its presence in Shakespeare's is at least hard to detect. Is there, perhaps, in Shakespeare's inner world some union, analogous to that in the mystic, some perhaps never to be repeated union, between *Geist* and *Seele*, spirit and soul?

About both the word and the conception of *Geist*, as employed by Kassner and many other German thinkers and philosophers, there is something Promethean, some conviction that they are speaking of what is most representatively and specifically human. To illustrate this, I will quote the concluding words of Hegel's inaugural address to his students at Heidelberg in 1816, leaving in my translation the word *Geist*, each time it occurs, untranslated:

> The courageousness of truth, the belief in the power of *Geist*, is the first stipulation of philosophy. Man, because he is *Geist*, may and ought to consider himself worthy of the highest, of the greatness and power of his *Geist* he cannot think highly enough; and so long as he has this belief there is nothing, however harsh and hard, that will not open itself to him. The at first hidden and taciturn nature of the universe has no power that could resist the courage of knowing; it is bound to open itself before the knower and lay its riches and its depths before his eyes and surrender them for his enjoyment.

I think it is true to say that, of those great artists, whether in words or in music, in painting or in stone, whom we think of not merely as great artists but as great representative figures, all were, in their admittedly very different ways, men, in this sense, of *Geist*. Dante, Michelangelo, Milton, Dr. Johnson (whom I include with some hesitation, because he should, perhaps, be regarded rather as a moralist than as an artist), Goethe, Beethoven—they all have this in common, that we cannot dissociate them from their work, that we cannot read or hear or see their work without thinking of them; that they tower up behind (and even, perhaps, sometimes, above) their work, with a kind of monumental and representative greatness. This is a quality that transcends the differences between their different arts,[1] as it also transcends what with some other artists remains for us an unbridgeable gulf between what they achieved and what they at least seemed to be, or not to be. Despite his glaring defects of character and temper, we cannot dissociate Beethoven the man from Beethoven the composer—the greatness of his music somehow returns upon the man and transfigures him, transfigures him into an eternal representative of struggling and suffering humanity, struggling from chaos to cosmos, from darkness to light. About all these great artists there was something arrogant, something of *hybris* (the *hybris* of Prometheus): one thinks of Michelangelo walking the streets of Rome 'like an executioner', as Raphael said, and treating the Pope 'as the King of France himself would not dare to treat him'. And yet, mingled with this great arrogance, there is a great humility, a humility before an ideal of perfection; and our abiding impression is that what these men fashioned was achieved largely in and through a fashioning, or refashioning, of themselves, or in and through a perpetual struggle with themselves. It is only a few great artists who possess this representative and monumental quality; some of the very greatest are wholly without it. Who that has seen a reproduction of Waldmüller's portrait can ever forget the face of Beethoven, or fail to recall it when listening to the *Eroica* or the *Missa Solemnis*? Who retains any distinct impression of the face of Mozart, of whom Kassner has said, with equal wit and profundity, that he might have had any face? Everything about Mozart seems, as Kassner has remarked,[2] mythical and improbable: does not the story of his dismissal, his finally, after a long series of unendurable insults and humiliations, requested and obtained dismissal, by the Archbishop of Salzburg sound like something from a myth about the boyhood of some ancient hero, Achilles or Hercules?—'Then your Holy Grace is not satisfied with me?'—'What, are you trying to threaten me, you blockhead? Oh, you blockhead! There's the door, look, I'll have nothing more to do with such a miserable boy.'[3] And this cashiered blockhead (*Fex*) then goes to Vienna, to create works that are among the chief glories of humanity. Shakespeare's achievement is no

---

[1] The differences between different kinds of artist seem to me in some ways more important than the differences between the different arts: hence (for me, at any rate) the unprofitableness of most attempts to discuss and define art in general. I am inclined to regard Pater's remark (in his essay on 'The School of Giorgione' in *The Renaissance*) that 'all art constantly aspires towards the condition of music' either as a witticism, on a par with the Oxford don's remark that 'every claret would be port if it could', or as yet another of those identities, those 'terrible simplifications', which have so bedevilled the modern world: World as Will, as Will to Power, as Eternal Recurrence; the purpose of life as Productivity, Equality, Classless Society, etc.

[2] 'Das Gesicht Beethovens' in *Geistige Welten*, 1958, p. 54.

[3] Letter from Mozart to his father, 9 May 1781.

less miraculous than Mozart's, but what little we know of him lacks this mythical and improbable quality, and, although our only dim records of it are the Droeshout portrait and the Stratford bust, it could perhaps scarcely be said of Shakespeare that he might have had any face. Nevertheless, as regards the relation between the man and his work, Shakespeare seems nearer to Mozart than to those great monumental and representative figures I have mentioned.

> With this key
> Shakespeare unlocked his heart,

said Wordsworth, of the Sonnets. We do indeed come close to a heart and its treasure (*ubi thesaurus*), to a spirit, to a soul, but not to a figure or (in any normal sense of that word) to a personality. Is there anything in Shakespeare's sonnets that conjures up before us the creator of the great tragic figures in a manner comparable with that in which certain of Michelangelo's suddenly bring before us, not merely the sculptor of so many unforgettable forms, but also, one is almost tempted to say, his innermost secret? That sonnet,[1] for example, in which he declares that, just as the sculptor first makes a clay model of the form he intends to carve, so he himself was born the mere model of what he was intended to be, the model of that *cosa più perfetta* into which he hopes, under the gracious influence of Vittoria Colonna, to be reborn; or that very difficult sonnet,[2] written after her death, in which he seems to declare that he will be left imperfect and unfinished unless that divine hammer, as which Heaven employed her, is permitted to continue from Heaven the work it began upon Earth. It has been said that, while the saint is concerned with the perfecting of himself, the artist is concerned with the perfecting of his work. There is much in this distinction, and it is a useful preservative against superficial attempts to equate art with religion; nevertheless, it is not absolute, and there are some artists whose work seems to us, and has sometimes seemed to them, to have been achieved largely in and through a long struggle with themselves, so that we cannot but regard its greatness as at least in part the reflection of a kind of greatness which they had themselves achieved. I do not think that we can feel in this way about the relation between Shakespeare and his work. It is only very occasionally in the Sonnets (most notably in 'Poor soul, the centre of my sinful earth') that we find him struggling with himself. In some of the sonnets to or

---

[1] 236, II, *Da che concetto ha l'arte intera e diva.*
[2] 46, *Se'l mie rozzo martello i'duri sassi.*

about the 'Dark Lady' there is deep self-loathing, but I think the total impression produced by the Sonnets is that Shakespeare was not so much concerned to reforge and refashion his self as to escape from it, to transcend it, to leave it behind. In sonnet after sonnet we find him declaring what his friend *means* to him, but never (or almost never) declaring what his friend has *made* of him, or may make of him. The heart of one whose chief effort, whose chief need, was to lose himself in the being of another—is that the heart which in the Sonnets we find 'unlocked'? To escape from the self, to escape from time, to find some perpetual source of compensation for a thousand sickening and saddening spectacles ('Tir'd with all these, for restful death I cry'): I can see, or think I can see, a clear relation between the poet of this desire and the creator of Prospero (and of Ariel), but I must admit that I can only make dim guesses at the nature of the relationship between this poet and the author of the Comedies, Histories and Tragedies. There is, nevertheless, one link which seems to me especially worth pondering—uncomfortable as may appear the conclusions to which it might seem to lead. When, in sonnet 71, Shakespeare exclaims

> No longer mourn for me when I am dead
> Than you shall hear the surly sullen bell
> Give warning to the world that I am fled
> From this vile world, with vilest worms to dwell,

is 'vile' a merely conventional epithet and the phrase 'this vile world' the mere husk of a half-forgotten orthodoxy, like the phrase 'filthy lucre'? I do not think so, for it makes two notable appearances in the plays: first, in the Second Part of *Henry VI* (V, ii, 40), in young Clifford's passionate outburst at the sight of his dead father, one of those passages that must be regarded either as a remarkable anticipation, in this early play, of Shakespeare's maturer style, or as something which Shakespeare added during some later revision:

> O, let the vile world end,
> And the premised flames of the last day
> Knit earth and heaven together!

Then, much later, and in one of the most unforgettable of contexts, in *Antony and Cleopatra* (V, ii, 314–21):

Cleopatra As sweet as balm, as soft as air, as gentle—
O Antony!—Nay, I will take thee too:
What should I stay—
Charmian In this vile world? So, fare thee well!
Now boast thee, death, in thy possession lies
A lass unparallel'd! Downy windows, close;
And golden Phoebus never be beheld
Of eyes again so royal!

Beside these three exclamations about 'this vile world' we may place
Hamlet's about 'this harsh world':

Absent thee from felicity a while
And in this harsh world draw thy breath in pain
To tell my story,

and Kent's about 'the rack of this tough world' on which only a hater of
Lear could wish to stretch him out longer. And beside all of them,
perhaps, we might place Edgar's exclamation at the sight of his blinded
father led by an old man (*King Lear*, IV, i, 10-12):

World, world, O world!
But that thy strange mutations make us hate thee,
Life would not yield to age.

Shakespeare was indeed a worshipper, but he was far from being, in
the modern sense, a 'Life-worshipper'; and perhaps his tragedies may in
some sort be regarded as dramatisations, incarnations, of that visionary
pageant which passes before us in the sonnet beginning, 'Tir'd with all
these, for restful death I cry'. If the impulse and moral and meaning
behind their 'strange mutations' is not precisely the sad Greek reflection
that 'the best of all is never to have been born', it is perhaps very largely
an attempt to reconcile himself and us to our departure from the hateful
dominion of Time and

Of fate and chance and change in human life.[1]

---

[1] *Paradise Regained*, IV, 265.

4

Personifications of Time, Age and Youth by Ovid, Horace and Shakespeare

This may perhaps be as appropriate a place as any to introduce into these reflections on Shakespeare's treatment of the topics of Devouring Time and Fading Beauty some remarks on a subject I have already incidentally mentioned, that of the resemblances between many of his personifications and metaphorical descriptions of Time, Age and Youth and those of various ancient poets, especially Horace.

Since I have already remarked that the phrase 'Devouring Time' in the first line of sonnet 19 was almost certainly suggested by the phrase *Tempus edax rerum* in the Pythagorean passage in the last book of Ovid's *Metamorphoses* (XV, 234), I will begin by noticing a few other passages and phrases in the Sonnets which may perhaps have been suggested by this and other passages in Ovid. In the line already referred to,

Devouring Time, blunt thou the lion's paws,

Mr. J. W. Lever may well be right in suggesting[1] (so far as I know, for the first time) that the second phrase was also inspired by a passage in Ovid, one in the *Tristia* (IV, vi, 1–18), where, following a very familiar rhetorical pattern, Ovid declares that Time, who weakens everything, does not weaken his grief:

Tempore Poenorum compescitur ira leonum,
nec feritas animo, quae fuit ante, manet.

('By Time the rage of Phoenician lions is fettered, nor does that fierceness in their spirit, which was there before, remain.') Mr. Lever has also, I think, devoted more attention than any previous commentator to Shakespeare's possible (or even probable) appropriation and transformation of Ovidian 'parallels' in sonnet 60:

[1] *The Elizabethan Love Sonnet*, 1956, p. 201.

Like as the waves make towards the pebbled shore,
So do our minutes hasten to their end;
Each changing place with that which goes before,
In sequent toil all forwards do contend.
Nativity, once in the main of light,
Crawls to maturity, wherewith being crown'd,
Crooked eclipses 'gainst his glory fight,
And Time that gave doth now his gift confound.
Time doth transfix the flourish set on youth
And delves the parallels in beauty's brow,
Feeds on the rarities of nature's truth,
And nothing stands but for his scythe to mow:
    And yet to times in hope my verse shall stand,
    Praising they worth, despite his cruel hand.

The first four lines, like several similar passages in Shakespeare's sonnets
(e.g. in 64 and 65), may well have been suggested by the following lines
from Pythagoras's long discourse (*Metamorphoses*, xv, 181–5):

                    Ut unda impellitur unda
    urgueturque eadem veniens urguetque priorem,
    tempora sic fugiunt pariter pariterque sequuntur
    et nova sunt semper; nam quod fuit ante relictum est,
    fitque quod haud fuerat, momentaque cuncta novantur.

('As wave is impelled by wave and the same wave is both urged [by that
behind it] in its coming and urges that before it, so times at once flee and
follow and are always new; for what has been before is left behind and
there comes to be what has not been, and all moments are being
renewed.') I think Mr. Lever may also be right in supposing that the
next four lines of this sonnet were also suggested by something in Ovid's
Pythagorean passage (*Metamorphoses*, xv, 221–7):

    Editus in lucem iacuit sine viribus infans:
    mox quadrupes rituque tulit sua membra ferarum,
    paualatimque tremens et nondum poplite firmo
    constitit adiutis aliquo conamine nervis.
    inde valens veloxque fuit spatiumque iuventae
    transit et, emeritis medii quoque temporis annis,
    labitur occiduae per iter declive senectae.

('Outgiven into light, lies without force the infant: soon on all fours he trails his limbs in the manner of beasts and gradually, quivering and not yet with steady legs, stands upright, his muscles aided by some prop. Then he grows strong and swift of foot and passes through the stage of youth and, the years of middle life also having reached the end of their term, slides down the declining path of setting age.') If, as seems likely, Shakespeare had this passage in mind, the manner in which he has transfigured and 'Shakespeareanised' it is very characteristic. Beginning by rendering (if that word does not seem too question-begging) Ovid's *infans editus in lucem* by

Nativity, once in the main of light,

he has generalised and, at the same time, intensified the whole passage. For 'the main of light' he might perhaps, had the rhyme been more convenient, have written 'the lucid main' or 'the shiny main', just as in sonnet 64 (l. 7) he had spoken of 'the watery main'—a good example, incidentally, of that 'poetic diction', those 'elegances or flowers of speech', those 'combinations of words which distinguish poetry from prose', which Dr. Johnson rather astonishingly declared to have been 'rarely attempted' before the time of Dryden.[1] It may well be Shakespeare's own coinage, for I do not remember to have met with it in Sylvester's translation of Du Bartas, one of the great sources of this kind of diction. Shakespeare does not, like Ovid, confine his attention to the infant and his terrestrial progress and decline: he thinks of the planets that 'govern' nativities, of 'the glorious planet Sol', of eclipses, and of kings whose glory is like that of the sun and, like the sun's, may be eclipsed. Mr. Lever is not, I think, seeing more than is really there when he writes:

> Nativity, a sun rising over the horizon, crawls as an infant up the path of the sky; at its noontide zenith of maturity it is crowned king; whereupon the eclipses that stain both moon and sun, 'crooked' by transferred epithet from the shape they impose, also personified with the infanticidal malice of a Richard Crookback, fight like usurpers against a glory denoting at once the sun's light and the king's majesty.[2]

There remains a less demonstrable but still probable trace of Ovid in this great sonnet, for, although the unforgettable metaphor of Time 'delving

[1] *Lives of the Poets*, ed. Birkbeck Hill, I, p. 420.
[2] *The Elizabethan Love Sonnet*, p. 253.

the parallels in beauty's brow' may not have been directly inspired by
him, there seems every reason to suppose that what might seem the fairly
obvious and, as it were, at hand, metaphorical use of the noun *furrow* for
'wrinkle' and of the verb *furrow* for 'to make wrinkles' was first suggested
to the Elizabethans by Ovid, their favourite Latin poet, in whose works
the metaphor occurs at least five times. It was, I think, first used in surviving Latin poetry by Horace (who did not repeat it), in an obscene
Epode (viii, 3–4) addressed to an elderly and probably imaginary *matrona*,
who had professed to be unable to understand why he had for so long
rejected her advances:

> Cum sit tibi dens ater et rugis vetus
>   frontem senectus exaret.

('When your teeth are black and ancient age is ploughing up your brow
with wrinkles!') Virgil used the metaphor once (*Aen.* VII, 417), in his
description of the Fury Allecto's disguising herself as an aged priestess of
Juno before her appearance to Turnus: *Et frontem obscenam rugis arat* ('And
ploughs her loathsome brow with wrinkles'). Whether Virgil borrowed
the metaphor from Horace, and Ovid from either or both of them, or
whether it was already traditional, seems impossible to discover, although
Ovid's frequent use of it suggests that for him it was something of a
novelty. His uses of it, in chronological order, are as follows: *Medicamina
Faciei* ('Cosmetics') 45–6:

> Certus amor morum est; formam populabitur aetas,
>   et placitus rugis vultus aratus erit.

('Love of character is secure; age will ravage beauty, and the face that
pleased will be ploughed by wrinkles'); *Ars amatoria*, II, 117–18:

> Et tibi iam venient cani, formose, capilli,
>   iam venient rugae, quae tibi corpus arent.

('Soon to you too, lovely boy, will come white hairs, soon will come
wrinkles to plough your body'); *Metamorphoses* III, 276 (Juno disguising
herself as Semele's old nurse): *Sulcavitque cutem rugis* ('She furrowed [as
with a plough] her skin with wrinkles'); *Metamorphoses* XIV, 96 (Jupiter's
transformation of the Cercopes into monkeys): *Et rugis peraravit anilibus
ora* ('And ploughed their faces through with old-womanly wrinkles');
Ex Ponto I, iv, 2:

> Iamque meos vultus ruga senilis arat.

('And now the senile wrinkle ploughs my face'). It may well have been Ovid's metaphor of 'ploughing with wrinkles' that suggested to Shakespeare and others the metaphors of Time and Age ploughing furrows, digging trenches, and delving parallels. The *Oxford Dictionary*'s earliest example of *furrow* for 'wrinkle' (sense 4b) is from Greene's *Tullies Loue* (1589), and of the verb *furrow* for 'to make wrinkles in' (sense 2b) from Shakespeare's *Richard II* (I, iii, 229):

> Thou canst help Time to furrow me with age.

In sonnet 2 we have

> When forty winters shall besiege thy brow,
> And dig deep trenches in thy beauty's field,

and in sonnet 22 (l. 3)

> But when in thee Time's furrows I behold.

In the first and third of these quotations I have restored the capital to Time: its absence in nearly all modern editions tends to conceal from us the fact that for Shakespeare this was a new and living metaphor, not an old and dead one.

I have remarked that the themes *carpe florem* and *carpe diem* do not appear at all in Shakespeare's sonnets and that, while the ancient poets might be called 'realistic' in their perpetual recommendation of submission to the conditions imposed by Time, Shakespeare, in his consistent defiance of Time, seems, in comparison, uncompromisingly 'idealistic'. Nevertheless, Shakespeare and the ancients have this in common, that to them, although they recommend submission, Time and Age are as hateful as they are to him, who persists in his defiance. Let us remind ourselves of some of the characteristic personifications of Time and Age in Horace's Odes.

I, ix, 14–18 (the Soracte ode):

> Quem Fors dierum cumque dabit, lucro
>   adpone nec dulcis amores
> sperne puer neque tu choreas
>
> donec virenti canities abest
> morosa

('Each single day that Fortune shall give, count as gain, and, boy that you are, do not disdain sweet lovings and dances while from spring-green flourishing winter-white hoariness with its morosity is absent');

I, xi, 7–8 (To Leuconoë):

> Dum loquimur, fugerit invida
> aetas

('While we are talking like this, grudging Time will escape');

II, xi, 5–8 (To Hirpinus):

> Fugit retro
> levis iuventas et decor, arida
>   pellente lascivos amores
> canitie facilemque somnum

('Escaping behind our backs are smooth-faced youth and beauty, while wizened hoariness is expelling playful loves and easy sleep');

II, xiv, 1–4:

> Eheu fugaces, Postume, Postume,
> labuntur anni, nec pietas moram
>   rugis et instanti senectae
> adferet indomitaeque morti

> ('Ah, how they glide though, Postumus, Postumus,
>   the years, the fleeting! Neither shall righteousness
>   cause wrinkles, cause onsetting Age or
> unovercomable Death to falter.')

It is not necessary to collect, in order to set beside these, all Shakespeare's personifications of Time in the Sonnets—a few representative ones will do:

> For never-resting Time leads summer on
> To hideous winter and confounds him there
>   (5, l. 5);

Then the conceit of this inconstant stay
Sets you most rich in youth before my sight,
Where wasteful Time debateth with Decay
To change your day of youth to sullied night
                    (15, ll. 9–12);

But wherefore do not you a mightier way
Make war upon this bloody tyrant Time?
                    (16, ll. 1–2);

But you shall shine more bright in these contents
Than unswept stone, besmear'd with sluttish Time
                    (55, ll. 3–4);

Against my love shall be as I am now,
With Time's injurious hand crush'd and o'erworn
                    (63, ll. 1–2);

When I have seen by Time's fell hand defaced
The rich-proud cost of outworn buried Age
                    (64, ll. 1–2);

Thou by thy dial's shady stealth may'st know
Time's thievish progress to eternity
                    (77, ll. 7–8).

In every allusion to it in the sonnets Age, or even, one might almost say, non-Youth, appears, without, I think, a single exception, as something utterly hateful and repulsive.

So thou through windows of thine age shalt see
Despite of wrinkles this thy golden time
                    (3, ll. 11–12);

But when from highmost pitch, with weary car,
Like feeble Age, he reeleth from the day,
The eyes, 'fore duteous, now converted are
From his low tract and look another way
                    (7, ll. 9–12: the
young man's course compared to the sun's);

urging the young man to marriage and parenthood:

> Herein lies wisdom, beauty, and increase;
> Without this, folly, age and cold decay:
> If all were minded so, the times should cease
> And threescore year would make the world away.
> Let those whom Nature hath not made for store,
> Harsh, featureless and rude, barrenly perish
>
> (11, ll. 5–10).

Particularly significant are those passages where Shakespeare, who was only forty-five in 1609, when the Sonnets were printed, and who must have written at least some of them during his thirties, refers to what he calls his own 'antiquity'. The depth of tone, the inner vibration, in most of these passages makes it necessary to take them as 'seriously' as we can take anything in the Sonnets, and forbids us to explain them away as mere hyperbolical and flattering self-depreciation.

> But when my glass shows me myself indeed,
> Beated and chopp'd with tann'd antiquity
>
> (62, ll. 9–10);

> Against my love shall be as I am now,
> With Time's injurious hand crush'd and o'erworn;
> When hours have drain'd his blood and fill'd his brow
> With lines and wrinkles; when his youthful morn
> Hath travell'd on to Age's steepy night,
> And all those beauties whereof now he's king
> Are vanishing or vanish'd out of sight,
> Stealing away the treasure of his spring;
> For such a time do I now fortify
> Against confounding Age's cruel knife
>
> (63, ll. 1–10);

and 73, which, familiar though it is, it will be desirable to have freshly in mind. Before he wrote it, Shakespeare must have been, at most, in his early forties, although an uninstructed foreign reader, meeting with this sonnet in an anthology, might pardonably suppose that the author of it must have been at least in his late nineties. I think one can say with confidence that, even in their extreme old age, neither Sophocles nor Goethe nor Verdi ever felt anything like so old as this. Indeed, although he did not even reach forty, I think the only modern poet to whom the

passing of youth seemed so consistently desolating and irreplaceable, and
the prospect of age so unmitigatedly disastrous and horrible, was Leopardi.

> That time of year thou mayst in me behold
> When yellow leaves, or none, or few, do hang
> Upon those boughs which shake against the cold,
> Bare ruin'd choirs where late the sweet birds sang.
> In me thou see'st the twilight of such day
> As after sunset fadeth in the west;
> Which by and by black night doth take away,
> Death's second self, that seals up all in rest.
> In me thou see'st the glowing of such fire
> That on the ashes of his youth doth lie,
> As the death-bed whereon it must expire,
> Consum'd with that which it was nourish'd by.
>   This thou perceiv'st, which makes thy love more strong,
>   To love that well which thou must leave ere long.

5

Shakespeare and Chaucer: Tragedy and the Whole Truth

In Shakespeare's plays there are many attractive and sympathetic
presentations of both maturity and old age, and it is only in deliberately
comic, or semi-comic, creations, such as Juliet's nurse, Shallow, Verges,
Pandarus and (to some extent) Polonius, that the characteristic weaknesses
of age predominate. But in the Sonnets, although he says much about the
compensations of love and friendship for the evils of life, he says nothing
whatever about the compensations which maturity and age are often
supposed to bring with them for the loss of youth. There is not a word
about the 'mellowness', 'maturity', 'experience', 'balance', and so forth,
which come, or should come, with advancing years, and not a word
about the inexperience, immaturity, rashness, excessive hopes and
excessive despairs of youth. And this raises a further question: despite
Socrates's success (or apparent success, for they had gone to sleep before

he had finished) in persuading Aristophanes and Agathon, in the *Symposium*, that a great writer of tragedy must necessarily be also a great writer of comedy, is there anything at all in Shakespeare's Sonnets which evokes the creator of the great comic characters and comic scenes? Anything at all which evokes that fascinated observer of men's 'humours' and of all those 'little things' of which Dr. Johnson spoke in a memorable conversation with Boswell, all those innumerable details of life in which, as well as in love and friendship, he must have found compensation? Is there here, perhaps, some resemblance between Shakespeare and Thomas Hardy—some resemblance between this seeming contradiction between Shakespeare's sonnets and Shakespeare's comedies and the seeming contradiction between the Hardy who wondered whether Nature, when she crossed the line from invertebrates to vertebrates, did not exceed her mission, and who so often seems to agree that the best of all is never to have been born, and Hardy the inexhaustible observer and enjoyer of every detail in the world around him? Is, perhaps, such a cyclic mode of living and experiencing, such prolonged submergence in moods of desolation and dejection and near-despair, moods in which so many of the normal compensations seem to be obliterated and forgotten, a necessary condition, or limitation (for it may be regarded in either of these ways), for the production of a great tragic writer? Is this why Chaucer, although a great master of pathos, never achieves the intensity (I am almost tempted to say, the intense one-sidedness) of tragedy? For Chaucer, it would seem, the whole of his experience, his total impression of life, was more completely and habitually present with him than Shakespeare's was with him. Mr. Eliot, in a famous and often quoted passage, once remarked that the characteristic 'wit' of our seventeenth-century poets 'involves, probably, a recognition, implicit in the expression of every experience, of other kinds of experience which are possible'.[1] If we choose to regard the Sonnets as expressions of a part of Shakespeare's experience, it is certainly not possible to detect in them an implicit recognition by Shakespeare himself that what he is expressing is only part of his total experience of life—not possible to detect anything like an admission, or hint, or warning that much of what he is saying is to be regarded as hyperbolical, or as what an Irishman would call 'a manner of speaking'. With Chaucer it was quite otherwise. Chaucer (it may be regarded either as a virtue or as a defect) would have been quite incapable of taking either himself or anything else so seriously for so long as Shakespeare was able to do (or unable not to do) in his sonnets and in the intensest of his tragedies. He

[1] 'Andrew Marvell' in *Selected Essays*, 1932, p. 289.

would, for example, have been incapable of taking the loss of his own youth so 'tragically' as Shakespeare does in the sonnet beginning 'That time of year thou may'st in me behold'. It is at least conceivable that Chaucer himself, under the influence and example of 'the laureat poetë', might have begun to write a series of sonnets, but I fancy that he would not have proceeded very far, that before long he would have roundly declared that he was beginning to get 'agroted', bored, with 'allë thise sonettës', and that, perhaps after a certain amount of self-laughter and self-parody, he would have broken off. Perhaps because, although he experienced things intensely, he did not experience them with such overwhelming and submerging, such isolating and insulating, intensity as Shakespeare did, Chaucer was far more continuously aware of 'other kinds of experience which are possible', of other points of view, of other voices, of the voice of Harry Bailly, about to exclaim 'No more of this, for Goddes dignitee'. No sooner has Chaucer achieved something like the intensity and one-sidedness of the tragic point of view than cheerfulness, often very inappropriately, comes breaking in. Perhaps his nearest approach to tragedy, certainly his longest passage of sustained intensity, is that in *The Knight's Tale* describing the death of Arcite and his commendation of his friend 'Palamon, the gentil man' to her whom he himself has won only to lose. But how does that passage conclude?

> Dusked his eyen two, and failled breeth,
> But on his lady yet caste he his eyë;
> His lastë word was, 'Mercy, Emelyë!'
> His spirit chaunged hous, and wentë ther,
> As I cam nevere, I can not tellen wher.
> Therefor I stinte, I nam no divinistrë;
> Of soulës finde I nat in this registrë,
> Ne me ne list thilke opiniouns to tellë
> Of hem, though that they writen wher they dwellë.
> Arcite is coold, ther Mars his soulë gyë;
> Now wol I speken forth of Emelyë.

Mr. Aldous Huxley, in an interesting essay, suggests that tragedy and what he calls 'the whole truth' are not really compatible.[1] He begins with the description given by Homer's Odysseus, in the course of his long narrative to King Alcinoüs, of how Scylla seized and devoured six of his

[1] 'Tragedy and the Whole Truth' in *Music at Night*, 1931.

companions as their ship was passing through the straits, how they stretched out their hands to him in the terrible struggle, and how it was the most lamentable of all the sights he had seen in all his 'explorings of the passes of the sea'; how later they went ashore for the night, prepared their supper, and 'having satisfied their thirst and hunger, thought of their dear companions and wept, and in the midst of their tears sleep came gently upon them'. This, if not, as Mr. Huxley calls it, 'the whole truth', is perhaps as near to it as anything in literature, and it is also nearer to Chaucer than to Shakespeare. Mr. Huxley then notices the common English antithesis between the 'abstractness' of Racine's tragedies and the supposed all-comprehensiveness of Shakespeare's, and remarks that even the world of Shakespeare's tragedies is abstract and selective in comparison with the world of the *Odyssey*, and that tragedy and 'the whole truth', as Homer there gives it, are not compatible. The correctness of this view seems to be confirmed by some of the characteristic differences between *Hamlet* and its three great successors. Dr. Johnson declared that

> If the dramas of Shakespeare were to be characterised, each by the particular excellence which distinguishes it from the rest, we must allow to the tragedy of *Hamlet* the praise of variety.

He then proceeded to review the play, with its scenes 'interchangeably diversified with merriment and solemnity', in a passage we should do well to remember whenever we are tempted to concentrate our attention too exclusively upon the Prince and his 'problems'. The variety of *Hamlet* is indeed wonderful, and it reflects perhaps more of Shakespeare's total experience of life than any other single play; at the same time, there can be no doubt that it is the least intense, the least 'tragic' of the great tragedies, and that, although it contains more of 'the whole truth', it contains less that is distinctively tragic than *Othello*, *King Lear* and *Macbeth*. For all his too often and too superficially attributed 'universality', it was perhaps only because he was unable to see, if not more than just one thing, at any rate not more than a few things, at the same time and with equal intensity that Shakespeare was able to write great tragedies.[1] And

[1] It might, I am aware, be objected that the distinction I have been trying to make between Chaucer and Shakespeare is ill-founded, and that Shakespeare was deliberately circumscribing his versatility in obedience to his conception of what was and what was not appropriate to the forms of the sonnet and of tragedy. Although I am ready to admit that there is force in this objection, I cannot but regard most attempts to 'explain' Shakespeare's poems and plays in terms of contemporary 'conventions' as superficial and unsatisfactory; for, the more I look into the matter, the more I seem to perceive that most of Shakespeare's so-called 'conventions' were of his own making. This is particularly true of his mature comedies, which no other Elizabethan comedies remotely resemble; but even his sonnets and his tragedies differ in so

this, I think, is the true relation between what one might be tempted to call the one-sided intensity of the sonnets and that of the great tragedies. Philosophic writers on Shakespeare's tragedies have spoken much of 'reconciliation', but is such reconciliation as we can there spontaneously experience really different from the kind of reconciliation Shakespeare himself reaches in the sonnets? And is there not a very close relation between the irreconcilability of the sonnets and that of the tragedies? Just as in the sonnets there is no suggestion that Time and Age and the transience of youth and beauty are no more than necessary shade in the masterpiece of what eighteenth-century Deists called 'the Great Artificer', even so in the tragedies there is no suggestion that Shakespeare is reconciled to the existence of Iago and Edmund, Goneril and Regan, or to the fates of Othello, Desdemona and Cordelia. The only recon-ciliation which Shakespeare's tragedies can properly be said to offer us is akin to that which he offers himself in the sonnets: that, on the one hand, 'this vile world' is so vile that we should be glad that death will eventually take us out of it, and that, on the other hand, there appear in it and, as it were, in despite of it, incarnations in human form of lovablenesses which are a compensation for all its evils and to which nothing can prevent us from being 'true'.

Most of our small biographical knowledge of Elizabethan poets and dramatists has been derived from legal documents, and because Shakes-peare was seldom concerned with the law, or the law with Shakespeare, except as a comparatively inconsiderable buyer of property, we tend to think of him, often in close association with the Stratford bust, if not as, first and foremost, a man of property, a business man, who somehow contrived to write poems and plays in his spare time, at any rate as a much more equable, phlegmatic and 'normal' person than in all probability, and as the sonnets so strongly suggest, he really was. No doubt he was always as 'civil' and 'gentle' as some of his contemporaries have recorded, and no doubt he was often exceedingly good company, but there must surely have been times when he seemed to his friends to be rather under a cloud, times when perhaps 'some severals of head-piece extraordinary' inferred that he must be in one of his 'tragic periods'.

many important respects from those of his contemporaries that such 'conventions' as remain in them seem to have been accepted rather in obedience to instinctive needs than from a mere desire to conform. Did he, moreover, begin to write tragedies because of an increasing public demand for them and because more *kudos* was to be gained by them, or because, since he had to write plays anyhow, there came a time when it was more congenial to him to write tragedies than comedies? And can we feel at all sure that it was in obedience to some more developed theory of what a tragedy should be (developed, perhaps, in conversations with Ben Jonson!) that he exchanged the greater variety of *Hamlet* for the greater intensity of *Othello*, *King Lear*, and *Macbeth*?

III

'HYPERBOLE' AND 'RELIGIOUSNESS' IN SHAKESPEARE'S EXPRESSIONS OF HIS LOVE

For the matters which I propose to discuss in this Third Part of my study I have been unable to discover any obviously correct order of procedure, and I fear it will be impossible to avoid some appearance of both repetition and digression. Consider, for example, some of Shakespeare's sonnets written during absence from his friend. As I shall attempt to show, it is possible to distinguish in Classical and Renaissance poetry at least four varieties of, or variations upon, the general topic of 'The Solitary Lover recalling the Beloved'. Two of these variations do not occur in Shakespeare's sonnets, while the two that do occur do so in close association both with the peculiarly Shakespearean conception of the beloved as the archetype and pattern of all other beauty and also with a topic which, though characteristically Shakespearean and developed by Shakespeare with a fullness not to be found elsewhere, is not without certain parallels and analogues in Classical and Renaissance poetry: the topic, namely, of compensation, or, rather, a special variety of it which may be termed 'the catalogue of uncompensating delights', of delights, that is to say, which are no compensation for one that is withheld. And, again, the characteristic conception of the beloved as the archetype of all beauty is also a characteristic manifestation of that 'religiousness' (some might say 'idolatrousness') which distinguishes Shakespeare's sonnets from most other love-poetry; and so too is the catalogue of uncompensating delights, for it is, after all, but the obverse and corollary of Shakespeare's characteristic conception of love as a compensation for all the evils of life, for all his own deficiencies, and for all he has supposed lost. In a sense, therefore, it is not really possible for me to say what I think worth saying about even these sonnets written during absence except in relation to almost everything else that I propose to discuss, and without either anticipating something I have still to say or repeating something I have already said—let alone to reach any firm assurance that there is one particular stage in my discourse more appropriate than another to a consideration of these particular sonnets. And further: the 'catalogues', as I have called them, in these sonnets afford a particularly good opportunity to contrast Shakespeare's predominantly metaphorical description with the predominantly unmetaphorical description of other poets, and in taking this opportunity I may well appear to digress from my main theme. But what is my main theme? Is it not that of the resemblances and differences between Shakespeare and other poets—or, rather, of the difference, the *differentia*, the *thisness* that becomes most strikingly apparent in and through the occasional resemblances? In my pursuit of this theme during the two preceding Parts I have perhaps been able to preserve some appearance of systematic and logical procedure, but from now onwards I fear that too much concern for systematic presentation would do violence to the complexity and delicacy of the subject. I must therefore ask the reader to be patient and to allow things, as it were, to emerge.

1

Shakespeare's 'un-Platonic hyperbole'

I have put the phrase in inverted commas, and I feel that each of the two members of it ought really to be so placed. What I mean is this: there is much in Shakespeare's sonnets which may be described, sometimes perhaps with confidence and sometimes perhaps only question-beggingly, as 'hyperbole', and which is often closely associated with something that, *at first sight*, may seem to resemble what, in other Renaissance poets, we are accustomed to call 'Platonism'. When, though, we look into the matter we find that what in Shakespeare too seems to be 'Platonism' is really inverted 'Platonism', 'Platonism' standing on its head.

Before proceeding, it will be well to say a word or two about the difference between the kind of 'Platonism' we find in Renaissance love-poetry and the true doctrine of Plato. For Plato the sole justification of visible and terrestrial beauty is that it can sometimes lead the soul to 'remember' those eternal 'forms' or 'ideas' of truth, beauty and goodness which it knew in its pre-natal state. When, though, the soul has once started 'remembering', when it has become, in Plato's sense, 'philosophic', 'wisdom-loving', it proceeds, as Plato so continually and passionately insists, 'altogether without aid of the senses'. All Plato's language about the ascent, or the re-ascent, of the soul and about 'the way of dialectic' is penetrated by a passionate hostility to sense, and he never really explains why the world of what he contemptuously calls 'appearances', *phainomena*, should exist and why the soul should have been separated from the objects of its first contemplation and imprisoned in the body. There is, in fact, an absolute gulf between the pure 'forms', the pure 'ideas', the pure λόγος and the defiling and imprisoning body. This gulf was bridged by the Christian doctrine of the Incarnation, of the Word, the λόγος, become flesh, and by the Christian proclamation that the sole revelation of God was in and through the person of Christ. All poetic 'Platonism' is more or less Christianised Platonism, Platonism not only modified but transformed by the conscious or unconscious influence of the belief that the highest of all revelations of the divine had been in and through a *person*. The presence in this 'Platonic' love-poetry of more or less recognisable Platonic doctrines, notions and terms is less fundamental than that of the Christianity which has modified them. Dante was not, could not have been, a student of Plato, and Michelangelo was; nevertheless, although the direct influence of Plato is very apparent in Michelangelo's sonnets, the affinity between his way of regarding Vittoria Colonna and Dante's way of regarding Beatrice is far more profound and important than any differences between the framework of ideas which those two poets employed. The fact that some Christian poets do and some do not speak of 'ideas' and 'patterns' and of an ascent from terrestrial to celestial beauty is not in itself a matter of great significance, for the use which the Christian poets make of these Platonic notions is so different from Plato's that they can only be called 'Platonic' within the inverted commas which I am continuing to employ. Indeed, even in Petrarch there are traces of such Platonic notions, which may have reached him through Cicero. What all these philosophically or 'Platonically' Christian love-poets, from Dante onwards, or even from some of the predecessors of Dante onwards, believe, or profess to believe, is that in loving the divine beauty and goodness manifested in and through a person they are loving and being led towards that personal God of which it is a manifestation; that they are being guided *by* a person *to* a person; that a personal God, through a person, is drawing them to himself. For all these poets the body is not, as it ultimately is for Plato, 'the tomb of the soul', but 'the Temple of the Holy Ghost', and the beloved is an actual manifestation and incarnation of the divine; whereas for Plato the beauty of the beloved, like all visible beauty, is no more than a shadowy likeness or appearance, no more than, at most (to coin a really modern metaphor), a kind of propelling rocket, which falls away after it has lifted the soul of the 'philosophic' lover into the orbit of the eternal 'forms', or 'ideas'.

In all this essentially Christian love-poetry, whether mainly 'Petrarchan' or mainly 'Platonic', the beloved object, though never superseded or transcended by the lover, is itself transcended by that archetype of which it is a type, by that transcendence which is immanent within it, and from which it is represented as deriving its authority over the lover. This poetry, like Plato's philosophy, is transcendental in that the distinction between human and divine, terrestrial and celestial, remains, although this distinction is no longer, as in Plato, an absolute separation, but exists only within the great Christian paradox of Incarnation. Now what distinguishes Shakespeare's sonnets, or those among them with which I am mainly concerned, from the love-poetry I have been trying to describe, is this: that although they are *in a sense* 'transcen-dental', just as they are also, *in a sense*, 'spiritual' and 'idealistic', or even 'metaphysical', they are so only within the limits of the terrestrial. In all Shakespeare's expressions of the meaningfulness to him of his friend and of his love for his friend the distinction between human and divine, terrestrial and celestial, nowhere appears. The friend is represented as transcending all other objects of desire or ambition or contemplation, but never (never, at any rate, with anything like even an approach to explicitness) because of the immanence within him of that which tran-scends him even as he himself transcends. Indeed, he is sometimes explicitly described, not as *a type* of beauty and excellence, but as *the archetype* of all other beauty and excellence.

Before proceeding to illustrate this, I will return to my use of the word 'hyperbole' in my descriptive phrase 'un-Platonic hyperbole', a phrase of which I said that I felt each of its two members should be placed within inverted commas. I have perhaps sufficiently explained what I mean by calling Shakespeare's expressions of his love 'un-Platonic'. No doubt they are also, *in some sense*, 'hyperbolical', but in what sense? And is the relation between their 'un-Platonicness' and their 'hyperbole' essential or merely, so to speak, incidental? By which I mean, is Shakespeare's representation of his friend as the archetype of all beauty and excellence to be regarded as on a par with contemporary poetic descriptions of Queen Elizabeth as a phoenix, or rather, as *the* phoenix? Is it to be regarded simply as the *ne plus ultra* of hyperbolical compliment? Is, in other words, the un-Platonicness, the inverted Platonism, to be regarded, not as a characteristic expression of Shakespeare's way of thinking and feeling, not as an expression of something essentially un-Platonic and untranscendental in Shakespeare himself, but simply as a piece of audacious and deliberately devised hyperbole? No doubt the suggestion, when so expressed, seems inconceivable, and I will admit right away that I cannot believe that Shakespeare is being 'hyperbolical' merely in this sense, or 'merely hyperbolical' to this extent. Nevertheless, it will be desirable to consider for a little what we mean by 'hyperbole'.

The primary meaning of the noun ὑπερβολή was 'a fling beyond', and it was derived from the verb ὑπερβάλλω, whose primary meaning was 'to fling, or hurl, or cast one's spear or discus beyond that of one's competitor in the contest'. The word then came to be used, first as a conscious metaphor, and then, like so many similar words, as a mere dead metaphor whose primary meaning had been forgotten, to describe any kind of 'excess' or 'exaggeration'. Needless to say, its use in this secondary and dead-metaphorical sense as a rhetorical or literary-critical term represents an attempt by rhetoricians and 'grammarians' to describe something which had struck them in the practice of great poets, not an attempt by great poets to realise something which had been first suggested as a possibility by rhetoricians and grammarians. This may perhaps seem too obvious to require insistence, but I think it is not so at a time when so many scholars, especially in America, seem to have persuaded them-selves, not only that we can learn something really valuable from a study of medieval, or semi-medieval, textbooks on rhetoric which great Renaissance poets may or may not have read at school, but also that it was from such textbooks that great poets learnt to use rhetorical devices which, long before any textbooks existed, had been used by Homer and Aeschylus and Pindar. It is too often forgotten that the ancient treatises on rhetoric, from Aristotle onwards, were primarily intended for the training of public speakers in law-courts and assemblies, not for the training of would-be poets, although they often recommended public speakers to employ devices which had been instinctively discovered by great poets. It was, I think, only in late Latin and medieval times that the belief arose that poetry was an art that could be acquired from textbooks, whereas the great ancient poets knew that a true poet could learn only from other true poets, or from his Muse. This is not to deny that from the first century B.C. elaborate lists of tropes and figures, suitable for use in poetry, began to appear, and that Horace, Virgil and other Roman poets had received a rhetorical training that was doubtless not without influence upon their poetry. Nevertheless, while Virgil's indebtedness to Homer and Theocritus and Horace's enormous indebtedness to the early Greek lyric poets are clear and demonstrable, the precise nature and extent of their poetical indebtedness to their training in formal rhetoric must remain conjectural. And this is true of most of the great Renaissance poets from Petrarch to Milton. There are, for example, literally hundreds of places in Ronsard where he is imitating particular passages in particular poets, ancient and modern, but I doubt whether he carried in his head and habitually tried to exemplify all the innumerable and pedantic classifications of formal rhetoric. It seems to me much more likely that he said something like: 'Here I'll do the sort of thing that so-and-so does at so-and-so', or 'There was a good "turn" in one of those sonnets of Serafino's I was reading the other day—let me see if I can find it'. In fact, what these poets carried in their memories were not lists and classifications, but passages of what seemed to them good poetry. About these medieval, or semi-medieval, 'Arts of Poetry', such as Puttenham's, there is something

fundamentally illiterate and misconceived, something of that same belief
in the possibility and value of short-cuts which inspires treatises on 'How
to win friends and influence people'. They are interpenetrated with and
tend to disseminate fundamental misunderstandings about the nature of
great poetry. They assume that a great poet, like any advocate or public
orator or, as Milton would say, 'rhyming parasite', has in mind some
perfectly plain and simple 'thing', idea or conception, which he proceeds
to decorate, dress up and 'beautify' in whatever manner best suits his
immediate purpose and the clearly conceived object he wishes to attain
or effect he wishes to produce. Consider, for example, Puttenham on
hyperbole:

> . . . when we speake in the superlatiue and beyond the limites of credit,
> that is by the figure which the Greeks call *Hiperbole*, the Latines *Dementiens*
> or the lying figure. I for his immoderate excesse cal him the ouer reacher right
> with his originall, or *lowd lyar*, and me thinks not amisse: now when I speake
> that which neither I my selfe thinke to be true, nor would haue any other
> body beleeue, it must needs be a great dissimulation, because I meane nothing
> lesse then that I speake,[1] and this manner of speech is vsed, when either we
> would greatly aduance or greatly abase the reputation of any thing or person,
> and must be vsed very discreetly, or els it will seeme odious, for although a
> praise or other report may be allowed beyond credit, it may not be beyond
> all measure, specially in the proseman, as he that was speaker in a Parliament
> of king *Henry* the eights raigne, in his Oration which ye know is of ordinary
> to be made before the Prince at the first assembly of both houses, should seem
> to praise his Maiestie thus. What should I go about to recite your Maiesties
> innumerable vertues, euen as much as if I tooke vpon me to number the
> starres of the skie, or to tell the sands of the sea. This *Hyperbole* was both *vltra
> fidem* and also *vltra modum*, and therefore of a graue and wise Counsellour
> made the speaker to be accompted a grosse flattering foole: peraduenture
> if he had vsed it thus, it had bene better and neuerthelesse a lye too, but a
> more moderate lye and no lesse to the purpose of the kings commendation,
> thus. I am not able with any wordes sufficiently to expresse your Maiesties
> regall vertues, your kingly merites also towardes vs your people and realme
> are so exceedingly many, as your prayses therefore are infinite, your honour
> and renowne euerlasting: And yet all this if we shall measure it by the rule
> of exact veritie, is but an vntruth, yet a more cleanely commendation then
> was maister Speakers.[2]

Underlying this dreary trash (as I am tempted to call it) is the unshakable
conviction that the 'real' or 'true' meaning, significance, importance,

---

[1] *i.e.* 'because there is nothing I mean less than what I am actually saying'.
[2] *The Arte of English Poesie*, 1589, Bk. III, ch. xvi (Arber's *English Reprints*, 1906, p. 202).

appearance of any thing at any time, what it 'really' is, is precisely the same for, let us say, Shakespeare as for Puttenham; that the only difference between Shakespeare and Puttenham is that Shakespeare can decorate, dress up, bedizen and 'beautify' this thing with greater effectiveness and in a greater variety of ways; that, despite all this 'beautification', Shakespeare knows as well as Puttenham that nothing could be more remote from his real 'meaning' than what he is actually saying, or from how the thing 'really' appears to him; that, for example, Shakespeare knows quite well that the friend to whom he is addressing his sonnets does not 'really' mean to him any more than he might mean to Puttenham; that there is, in fact, a kind of normal or average meaningfulness which, 'by the rule of exact veritie', any thing in the world has, or ought to have, for all persons at all times. No poet worthy of the name could learn to be a better poet from books such as Puttenham's; at the best, a 'Speaker' such as he has described might learn to make his compliments and commendations a degree less inappropriate and absurd.

Let us turn from this dreary Alexandrianism, or Byzantinism, to the beginnings of European poetry, to that speech in the ninth *Iliad* (378–91) where the aggrieved and retired Achilles, nursing his wrath, contemptuously rejects what Agamemnon, through Odysseus, has offered him if he will resume his place in the battle-line:

> I loathe his gifts. I care nothing for them. Not if he gave me ten, twenty times over all that he now has, not if there were added to that all that goes into Orchomenos or Egyptian Thebes, where most treasure is stored in the houses,— Thebes of the seven gates, through each of which emerge two hundred men with horses and chariots; not if he gave me as many gifts as there are grains of sand and dust, not even then shall Agamemnon appease my spirit until he has paid in full for all the outrage that stings it. And I will not marry the daughter of Agamemnon son of Atreus, not though she vied with golden Aphrodite in beauty and equalled grey-eyed Athene in handiwork—not even then would I marry her.

The allusions to Orchomenos and hundred-gated Thebes, to Aphrodite and Athene, are not just decoration: Achilles, as Homer imagines him, thinks and feels in and through such images, such hyperboles, just as so many modern men seem to think and feel in and through -isms and -ologies, and 'the wrath of Achilles', the main subject of the *Iliad*, *is* the emotion that expresses itself in and through such hyperboles. Aristotle, in the *Rhetoric* (III, xi, 16), remarks that

There is something youthful about hyperboles, for they show vehemence: that is why those in a rage most frequently utter them.

And Aristotle quotes, as an example, part of the speech which I have quoted at greater length. 'Something youthful about them': one thinks of Marlowe, whose *Tamburlaine* is full of such hyperboles: no doubt it was of them that Drayton was thinking when (so far as we know, coining a word) he declared that Marlowe

> Had in him those brave translunary things
> That the first Poets had.[1]

'Those in a rage most frequently utter them':

> Come then, let the two-edged tress of fire be hurled upon me, let Aether be shaken by thunder and the spasm of savage winds: let the blast swing Earth by the roots from her foundations, the wave of Ocean with rude clamour confound the thoroughfares of the celestial stars: let him hurl utterly into black Tartarus this form of mine with cruel whirlings of Necessity: utterly unable shall he be to bring death upon me.[2]

Thus does Aeschylus's Prometheus hurl his defiance at Zeus, and it is in such language, in such hyperboles, that Lear curses his daughters and 'out-scorns' the elements. 'Hurls his defiance': hyperbole, as the great poets use it, recovers its original, pre-textbook meaning; the characters of Homer, of Aeschylus, of Shakespeare 'hurl' their expressions of defiance, aspiration, joy and grief like spears, hurl them beyond, far beyond, what to the Puttenhams of this world seems 'the exact veritie'; for Shakespeare-Othello, Shakespeare-Lear, Shakespeare-Macbeth knows that, however hard and high and far he hurls, he can never even reach, let alone exceed, the communicable equivalent in the external world for that which is agitating his little world within: he will still have 'that within which passeth show', that which 'into words no virtue can digest'. Hyperbole in Shakespeare's tragedies, and even in some of his more poetic comedies, is not just a rhetorical device, a *means* of expression; it is the only possible expression of what Shakespeare, in and through his characters, has to express. Othello *is* the man who says things like

[1] To Henry Reynolds Esquire, of *Poets & Poesie*, ll. 106–7.
[2] *Prometheus Vinctus*, 1043–53.

PONTYPRIDD PUBLIC LIBRARY

O my soul's joy!
If after every tempest come such calms,
May the winds blow till they have waken'd death!
And let the labouring bark climb hills of seas
Olympus-high, and duck again as low
As hell's from heaven! If it were now to die,
'Twere now to be most happy, for, I fear,
My soul hath her content so absolute
That not another comfort like to this
Succeeds in unknown fate[1]

(II, i, 186 ff.);

and like

If thou dost slander her and torture me,
Never pray more; abandon all remorse;
On horror's head horrors accumulate;
Do deeds to make heaven weep, all earth amaz'd;
For nothing canst thou to damnation add
Greater than that

(III, iii, 368 ff.).

Shakespeare's Othello *is* the man who expresses himself like this; it is only in and through expressions such as this that he exists and has a meaning for us. We have heard Puttenham declaring that when *he* makes use of hyperbole there is nothing he means less than what he is actually

[1] This speech is not only full of characteristic Shakespearean hyperbole: it also seems to contain two reminiscences and characteristic transformations of passages in Latin poets Behind the lines about the labouring bark there seem to be recollections of Ovid's description, in the story of Ceyx and Alcyone, of the storm which wrecked Ceyx's ship (*Metamorphoses*, xi, 503–6):

Et nunc sublimis, veluti de vertice montis,
despicere in valles imumque Acheronta videtur,
nunc, ubi demissam curvum circumstetit aequor,
suspicere inferno summum de gurgite caelum.

('And now, lifted aloft, it seems to look down as from a mountain crest into valleys and deepest Acheron; now, when it has been plunged down and curving walls of water have surrounded it, it seems to look up to heaven from the infernal gulf.') And there is a remarkable parallel between the last lines and a passage in Terence's *Eunuchus* (550–2), spoken by a young man emerging from a house where, disguised as a eunuch, he has contrived to gain admittance and to seduce a girl who has attracted him (it is true he subsequently marries her):

Iamne erumpere hoc licet mi gaudium? pro Iuppiter,
nunc est profecto, interfici quom perpeti me possum,
ne hoc gaudium contaminet vita aegritudine aliqua.

('May I not now give vent to this joy? By Jupiter, now is the moment I could bear to be cut off, lest life pollute this joy with some distress.') If this passage was really in Shakespeare's mind, what he has made of it is a remarkable example of the consecration of profanity.

saying; when, though, Shakespeare-Othello uses hyperbole there is nothing he means *more* than what he is saying, or trying to say. Not only what things mean to Othello, but what Othello means to Shakespeare and should also mean to us, can find expression only in and through such hyperboles. Othello, as Shakespeare conceives him, *is* the man who has that within which can only be expressed, externalised, in and through such hyperboles. Take away the hyperboles, and Shakespeare's Othello disappears. His meaning is in what things mean to him, in the inner vibration they set up in him, and it is only in and through hyperboles that this inner vibration can be communicated.

This, of course, raises the whole question of the attitude, not only of his contemporaries, but of Shakespeare himself to what are today contemptuously described as 'heroics'. I have already spoken of what seems to me Shakespeare's almost uniquely mediatorial position between the ancient and the modern, the Pagan and the Christian, worlds. Despite his parodies of the 'mighty line' through the mouth of Ancient Pistol, despite the contrast between Hotspur and Prince Hal, despite some things in *Troilus and Cressida*, Shakespeare was capable of a whole-hearted, wholly unironical, sympathy with 'heroism' as Homer and the ancients understood it—with, for example, that reply of Achilles to Agamemnon, which I have followed Aristotle in quoting as an example of Homeric hyperbole, and which a modern Social Realist might feel irresistibly impelled to reduce to something like: 'Tell that bastard I'm just not interested in his bloody money—*or* his bloody daughter.' Bernard Shaw, in his dramatic criticisms and then in the Prefaces to his own plays, never ceased to express his contempt and detestation for these Shakespearean heroics, for this 'beglamouring', as he often called it, of what seemed to him mere selfish, anarchic, idea-less, romantic individualism ('You can find Antonys and Cleopatras in every pub'); but he at least recognised the profound difference between Shakespeare's values and his own, and never tried to persuade either himself or his readers that Shakespeare's real intentions were not really very different from his: never suggested that in the history plays Shakespeare was mainly concerned to teach lessons about hierarchy, order and the miseries of civil war, or that in the tragedies he was really giving us profoundly ironical studies in self-deception—as Mr. T. S. Eliot did in some remarks about *Othello*.[1] I am convinced that in Othello's last speech Shakespeare was no more being ironical or

[1] 'Shakespeare and the Stoicism of Seneca' in *Selected Essays*, 1932, pp. 130–1. Mr Eliot, it is true, begins by describing the effect which Othello's speech produces on *him*, but at the end of the paragraph he seems to congratulate Shakespeare on having produced that effect.

satirical, no more intending us, as Mr. Eliot suggested, to recognise an utterly self-deceived and self-destroyed man 'cheering himself up', than Sophocles was being ironical or satirical in the last words he gave to Ajax, lord of Salamis:

> O light, O sacred ground of Salamis, my native land, O hearth's ancestral basis, and glorious Athens, and those brought up with me; these springs, too, and rivers here, and the Trojan plains,—I bid you, my nurses, all farewell. This is the last word Ajax calls to you, the rest I will speak in Hades to those below.[1]

There is, said Aristotle, 'something youthful' about hyperboles (εἰσὶ δὲ ὑπερβολαὶ μειρακιώδεις), and perhaps there is also something youthful about those heroes of Homer, of the Greek tragedians and of Shakespeare who make such frequent use of them. Perhaps, indeed, there was 'something youthful', something which many modern critics and educationists would call 'immature', about Shakespeare himself, about the Shakespeare of the sonnets, who took, or who professed to take, the passing of his own youth so 'tragically' and wrote of himself, while at most in his early forties, in a manner which, as I have said, might pardonably lead an uninstructed foreign reader to suppose that he must have been at least in his late nineties. Is not this what Dr. Leavis, who, following Mr. Eliot, has written a whole essay[2] revealing that he is only able to make any kind of sense of *Othello* by regarding it as a deliberate study in self-deception—is not this what Dr. Leavis, and some of his disciples, call 'immature', and what Mr. Bateson and some of his disciples call 'disturbing' or 'disquieting'? It may be that the hyperboles and 'heroics' of Homer, of the Greek tragedians and of Shakespeare have no place in the modern world, in 'The Century of the Common Man', and should be put away, with other childish things, as 'immature', 'disquieting' and 'revisionary' (in the hideous jargon of totalitarianism, 'revisionist'), as likely to cast doubt upon, to encourage revision, 'agonising reappraisal', of certain fundamental convictions of 'The Century of the Common Man'—the conviction, for example, that equality is an absolute value, and what Yeats, writing of certain books on Shakespeare which he had been reading in the library at Stratford-on-Avon, called 'the conviction that the commonplace shall inherit the earth'.[3] It may be that wise totalitarians will eventually remove the works of these poets from

---

[1] *Ajax*, 859–65.
[2] 'Diabolic Intellect and the noble Hero' in *The Common Pursuit*, 1952, pp. 136 ff.
[3] 'At Stratford-on-Avon' in *Essays*, 1924, p. 128.

circulation, as tending, in Bernard Shaw's phrase, to 'beglamour' values and ideals and tendencies which the Common Man (or, at any rate, those who rule in his name) has rejected. Meanwhile, let us at least try to see them 'as in themselves they really are', instead of trying to distort them into some kind of agreement with ideals and tendencies which are utterly alien to them.

The point of this digression, as it may have appeared to some readers, has been to suggest that we should beware of calling Shakespeare's sonnets 'hyperbolical' in the sense of being merely extravagant or exaggerated and as not really 'meaning' what they seem to 'say'—to suggest, in fact, that Shakespeare himself, like his tragic heroes, could only express what things most deeply 'meant' to him in and through hyperbole; to suggest that he was probably much more a man of moods, much more 'visionary' and 'idealistic' and 'enthusiastic', much nearer, in some ways, to the popular notion of a great poet, than too much study of the legal records of his purchases and too much contemplation of the Stratford bust have led many to suppose. He had enough strength of character, strength of mind, common-sense (call it what you will) to prevent his imagination from destroying him, to prevent his frequent submergence in indignation, dejection, or even despair, from reducing him to the opium and the absinthe, the garrets, tavern brawls and pickled herrings, the squalor and the outcastness of many a *poète maudit*, but his imagination, I am sure, was continually active, and filled, not so much with 'ideas', as with incarnated meanings, incarnations of good and evil: goodness rising and irradiating the world like sunrise, evil, 'more fell than anguish, hunger, or the sea', darkening the sun with black Apollyon wings. His vision heightened and intensified everything it beheld: the apples in his orchard at New Place must have seemed to him more golden than those of the Hesperides. Hyperbole was his most natural form of expression, and it is in and through this continuous use of hyperbole that the sonnets and the tragedies are most intimately related.

Nevertheless, although there is an absolute distinction between hyperbole as used by the great poets of the ancient world and hyperbole as used by Puttenham's 'Speaker', I will not pretend that both in later Latin and in Renaissance poetry there is not a great deal of hyperbole that is betwixt and between these two extremes. In an age of courts and patrons not only the poetaster, Milton's 'rhyming parasite', whom we may disregard, but even poets of genius were often tempted or compelled by a variety of motives to say about their patrons, or hoped-for patrons, a great deal more than they 'meant', and, by an extension analogous to that of the originally deferential form of the second person plural, more or less meaningless hyperbolical compliment tended to become an established and indispensable form of politeness and to play a distressingly large part in all forms of personal address, including love-poetry. But it does not follow that a poet who began with a fairly clear awareness that he did not really mean what he was proposing to say might not come to mean it, or half mean it, in the course of saying it, and that the original object of his compliment or adoration might not gradually be transformed into a symbol or ideal. It may even be that Shakespeare himself began somewhat in this way, began by 'meaning', in any profound sense, very little of what he was actually saying; began with statements and generalisations which, as he first expressed them, meant little more to him than the current coin of hyperbolical compliment, but which, as he proceeded, came to mean more and more to him, until at last he meant nothing more than what he was actually saying. Consider sonnet 14, beginning

> Not from the stars do I my judgement pluck,
> And yet methinks I have astronomy,

one of those sonnets urging the young man to marry, those sonnets with which the whole thing seems to have begun and which it is difficult not to suppose that Shakespeare began to write as the result of some kind of external hint or suggestion. It is a mechanical, carpentered kind of sonnet, such as almost any Elizabethan sonneteer might have written, full of clumsy inversions, without distinction of phrase, and communicating, as it were, no inner vibration. He does not, he declares, like other astronomers, study the heavens and predict therefrom the kind of things that they predict:

> But from thine eyes my knowledge I derive,
> And, constant stars, in them I read such art,
> As truth and beauty shall together thrive,
> If from thyself to store thou wouldst convert;
>   Or else of thee this I prognosticate:
>   Thy end is truth's and beauty's doom and date.

Shakespeare may well have stumbled upon the 'idea', 'conceit', or whatever we choose to call it, expressed in the concluding couplet simply

in the course of trying, perhaps not very seriously, to devise some
ingenious hyperbolical compliment; but this particular piece of hyperbole,
together with several variations upon it, seems to have become more and
more meaningful for him, more and more the only possible way of
expressing what his friend had come to 'mean' to him. It reappears at the
end of 104, one of the most beautiful of the sonnets, despite the careless
(I cannot think deliberate) 'eye I ey'd' in the second line:

> To me, fair friend, you never can be old,
> For as you were when first your eye I ey'd,
> Such seems your beauty still. Three winters cold
> Have from the forests shook three summers' pride,
> Three beauteous springs to yellow autumn turn'd
> In process of the seasons have I seen,
> Three April perfumes in three hot Junes burn'd,
> Since first I saw you fresh, which yet are green.[1]
> Ah, yet doth beauty, like a dial-hand,
> Steal from his figure, and no pace perceiv'd;
> So your sweet hue, which methinks still doth stand,
> Hath motion, and mine eye may be deceiv'd:
>   For fear of which, hear this, thou age unbred:
>   Ere you were born was beauty's summer dead.

Some would perhaps regard the final couplet as merely tagged on, and
the idea it expresses as a piece of more or less meaningless hyperbolical
compliment; I myself am convinced that Shakespeare was here expressing
something which he really felt and really 'meant'. As variations upon
this theme that all truth and beauty are incarnated in his friend and will
perish with him, or, at least, that perfect beauty ('beauty's summer') has
been once and for all reached and realised in him, and that all succeeding
beauties will be no more than shadows of this and a progressive declination
from it—as variations upon this theme we may consider those sonnets
where Shakespeare declares that all descriptions of beauty by earlier poets
were but prophecies and prefigurings of his friend's and that in a declining
age his friend is a reminder of what beauty once was:[2] 59,

---

[1] Cp. (noticed by L. P. Wilkinson) Horace, *Epodes*, xi, 5-6:
    Hic tertius December, ex quo destiti
    Inachia furere, silvis honorem decutit.
   ('The third December since I ceased to rave for Inachia is now shaking their glory from
the woods.') The only other examples of this figure I have noticed between Horace and
Shakespeare are Boccaccio, *Teseida*, II, st. 1, and Chaucer, *Troilus and Criseyde*, V, st. 2.

[2] On page 86 I have considered the possibility that this 'idea' may have been at least
partly suggested to Shakespeare by a sonnet of Drayton's.

> If there be nothing new, but that which is
> Hath been before,

where he rejects the idea of an eternal recurrence for the reason that no one can show him his friend's image 'in some antique book'; 106,

> When in the chronicle of wasted time
> I see descriptions of the fairest wights,

declaring that, while the finest descriptions of beauty by the greater poets of past ages fall short of his friend's beauty because those poets were trying to describe what they could only divine, the lesser poets of today lack the skill to celebrate worthily what they have been permitted to behold—a sonnet which, although both from the Christian and the Platonic point of view far more 'idolatrous' than anything Petrarch ever wrote, has some affinity with those two sonnets in which Petrarch declares that Laura ought to have lived in the days of Homer and Virgil; 67,

> Ah! wherefore with infection should he live,
> And with his presence grace impiety,

asking why his friend should live in this declining age, where other beauties are no more than shadows of his own and where Nature is bankrupt, and replying

> O, him she stores, to show what wealth she had
> In days long since, before these last so bad;

and its companion, 68,

> Thus is his cheek the map of days outworn,
> When beauty liv'd and died as flowers do now,

declaring that beauty today is false and borrowed, like wigs made from dead women's hair, but that

> In him those holy antique hours are seen,
> Without all ornament, itself and true,

and that

> him as for a map doth Nature store,
> To show false Art what beauty was of yore.

In all these sonnets there is some suggestion, some appearance, of the Platonic idea, pattern, or paradeigma, and of Platonic 'recollection' (anamnêsis), but it is all characteristically (and I think uniquely) Shakespearean and, as I have said, inverted. The nearest approach (and even that a rather distant one) to true Platonism, or, at any rate, to something like the Platonic doctrine of 'recollection', is in 67 and 68, where Shakespeare declares, in so many words, that in this Leaden Age his friend is a reminder of the 'Golden World': this is the nearest Shakespeare ever comes to saying that his friend is the 'reminder' of a pattern or paradeigma, although even here he is scarcely being transcendental, for the Golden Age was, after all, imagined as having once existed on earth. Nowhere does Shakespeare say that his friend is the 'reminder' of an idea, pattern or paradeigma laid up, as Plato said, 'in heaven'; and, with the exception of the two sonnets I have mentioned, he represents his friend, not as the 'reminder' or manifestation of an archetype, pattern or idea, but as himself an, or rather *the*, archetype, pattern, idea or ideal. Perhaps the most striking single expression of Shakespeare's inverted Platonism is in the opening lines of 53, a sonnet which otherwise contains much with which it is possible to produce parallels from other poets. It is in fact a sonnet where Shakespeare is both farthest from and nearest to his poetic predecessors, and where his own characteristic hyperbole in the first two lines might well, but for the fact that there is so much resembling it in his other sonnets, seem less remarkable than it really is—might seem no more than an audacious but isolated attempt to go one better, to go just a step beyond, the traditional hyperboles and *encomia* of preceding poets.

> What is your substance, whereof are you made,
> That millions of strange shadows on you tend?
> Since every one hath, every one, one shade,
> And you, but one, can every shadow lend.
> Describe Adonis, and the counterfeit
> Is poorly imitated after you;
> On Helen's cheek all art of beauty set,
> And you in Grecian tires are painted new.
> Speak of the spring and foison of the year,
> The one doth shadow of your beauty show,
> The other as your bounty doth appear;
> And you in every blessed shape we know.
> > In all external grace you have some part,
> > But you like none, none you, for constant heart.

Let us briefly consider the relation between the various kinds of hyperbole and comparison in this sonnet and those in various poetical *encomia* from ancient times until the Renaissance. What—to begin at the beginning— are the nearest approaches we can find in preceding poetry to the first two lines, the most essentially and characteristically Shakespearean; lines expressing something at once more 'ideal' and 'metaphysical' than anything in ancient love-poetry, and more religiously idolatrous, or idolatrously religious, than anything in Petrarch? The nearest approach to such 'ideality' which I can recall in ancient poetry is in an epigram of Catullus (86), where, after admitting that Quintia has some of the elements of beauty, but denying that she is beautiful because she lacks *venustas*, he declares that Lesbia is beautiful because she has stolen all graces from all other women for herself alone:

> Lesbia formosast, quae cum pulcherrima totast,
>   tum omnibus una omnis surripuit Veneres.

Here, though, it is only the extreme terseness of the encomium that lends it some appearance of ideality. It is essentially the same kind of encomium as that of which it would be possible to produce numerous examples from the *Greek Anthology* onwards, that which declares either that the beauty of the person celebrated surpasses that of various women who were famous in their day, or that she unites in herself the particular beauties for which women of the past, or even goddesses, were famous. A good example, often imitated by Renaissance poets, is the following epigram by Rufinus in the *Greek Anthology* (V, 94):

> Ὄμματ' ἔχεις Ἥρης, Μελίτη, τὰς χεῖρας Ἀθήνης,
>   τοὺς μάζους Παφίης, τὰ σφυρὰ τῆς Θέτιδος·
> εὐδαίμων ὁ βλέπων σε, τρισόλβιος ὅστις ἀκούει,
>   ἡμίθεος δ' ὁ φιλῶν, ἀθάνατος δ' ὁ γαμῶν

('You have the eyes of Hera, Melite, the hands of Athena, the breasts of the Paphian, the ankles of Thetis. Happy the beholder of you, thrice happy who listens to you, a demi-god the kisser of you, an immortal the marrier[1] of you.') Propertius (II, iii, 32 ff.) declares that Helen's beauty has reappeared with his Cynthia, and that he now understands why the Greeks demanded her return and the Trojans refused:

---

[1] γαμῶν is the reading of the Palatine manuscript, which was discovered by Salmasius in 1607 but not printed until the end of the eighteenth century. The only printed *Greek Anthology* during the Renaissance was that of Planudes, where the last word of the present epigram is συνών, 'the lier with you'.

If any desire to surpass the fame of all ancient pictures, let him take my mistress as model for his art; if he show her to the peoples of the West or to the peoples of the East, he will set the East and set the West on fire.

And Chaucer, following an old French example which may itself be regarded as a descendant of these ancient *encomia*, introduced into the prologue to his *Legend of Good Women* a 'Balade' beginning:

> Hyd, Absolon, thy giltë tresses clerë;
> Ester, ley thou thy meknesse al a-doun;
> Hyd, Jonathas, al thy frendly manerë;
> Penalopee, and Marcia Catoun,
> Mak of your wyfhod no comparisoun;
> Hyde ye your beautes, Isoude and Eleynë,
> My lady cometh, that al this may disteynë.

In the two following stanzas Chaucer declares that, in addition to the persons already mentioned, his 'Alceste' surpasses no less than thirteen other heroines of antiquity. As with many other well-established topics—a surpassing beauty or pleasure or impossibility, a surpassingly enduring love or grief—the list of persons or things surpassed might be made as long or short as the poet pleased, and such *formulae* were all too often used by minor poets to say something when they had really nothing to say. In his allusions to Adonis and Helen in this sonnet Shakespeare is writing in a thoroughly traditional, or conventional, manner, and, as so often when he is so doing, not a whit better than scores of lesser poets. Indeed, wherever he is most like his contemporaries, he is nearly always a good deal below his best. The next four lines are more characteristically his own:

> Speak of the spring and foison of the year,
> The one doth shadow of your beauty show,
> The other as your bounty doth appear;
> And you in every blessed shape we know.

(But, oh, these 'doths' and these lazy inversions!) This (although Shakespeare probably did not attain to it as such) may perhaps be regarded as a variation upon what, since its most notable ancient examples are in pastorals by Theocritus and Virgil, I have been accustomed to call the 'pastoral hyperbole'.[1] In Theocritus's eighth Idyll (ll. 45 ff. in most modern editions) one of the topics alternately elaborated by Menalcas and Daphnis in the course of their song-contest is that all things flourish at the approach and wither on the departure of the boy Milon and the girl Naïs, and Virgil, in his seventh Eclogue (ll. 53–60), makes his Corydon and Thyrsis develop the same topic. It is a topic which has a close affinity with one that often appears in ancient panegyrics upon rulers and which perhaps began with a passage in the *Odyssey* (xix, 109 ff.), where Odysseus declares that Penelope's fame ascends to heaven like that of a 'blameless king', under whose beneficent 'leadership' crops, fruit-trees, cattle and even the very fish in the sea flourish to astonishment. This related topic makes a notable appearance in Horace's great ode to Augustus, on the blessings of his reign (IV, v, 5–8), in a passage which may well have influenced some of the elaborations of what I have called the 'pastoral hyperbole' by some of our own seventeenth-century poets:

> Lucem redde tuae, dux bone, patriae:
> instar veris enim voltus ubi tuus
> adfulsit populo, gratior it dies
> et soles melius nitent.

> ('Lend, kind Leader, again light to the land you love!
> Where, like burgeoning Spring, glances your countenance,
> days pass gladlier by there for your countrymen,
> more delightfully shines the sun.')

For the 'pastoral hyperbole' was wittily elaborated by Cleveland, Marvell, Cowley and many lesser poets, and it was probably with the third stanza of *The Spring*, one of the poems in Cowley's *The Mistress*, in mind, a stanza beginning

> Where'er you walk'd, Trees were as reverent made
> As when of old *Gods* dwelt in every shade,

that Pope, in his *Pastorals*, having already imitated the Virgilian passage

---

[1] The earliest example of all, so far as I know (if indeed it can be regarded as conscious hyperbole and not rather as a piece of folklore), is not in pastoral but in Hesiod's *Theogony* (194–5), describing the birth of Aphrodite and declaring that 'grass sprang up around beneath her shapely feet'. This was magnificently elaborated by Lucretius in the great invocation to Venus at the beginning of the *De Rerum Natura*.

in his 'Spring' (ll. 69 ff.), wrote in his 'Summer' the famous lines (73 ff.):

> Where'er you walk, cool gales shall fan the glade;
> Trees, where you sit, shall crowd into a shade;
> Where'er you tread, the blushing flowers shall rise,
> And all things flourish where you turn your eyes.

Pope, though, is far less wittily extravagant on this topic than his seventeenth-century predecessors had been, and Petrarch, in his 165th sonnet, *Come 'l candido piè per l'erba fresca*, had contented himself with saying that there seemed to issue from the white feet of Laura a virtue which opened and renewed the flowers. Shakespeare's four lines might, I said, be regarded as a variation upon this topic which I have called the 'pastoral hyperbole', although I doubt whether it was as a consciously original variation on this topic that he wrote them. For what is most fundamental in Shakespeare's lines, and most distinguishes them from all the various examples to which I have alluded, is his characteristic and, so far as I know, unprecedented, conception of his friend's beauty and excellence as archetypes, to which all other beauties and excellences are no more than dim approximations. He does not say that his friend is *like* Spring and Autumn, that his presence has the *effect* of them, but that they are shadows, types, images of him. (It is a significant fact that nowhere in the Sonnets does Shakespeare praise his friend for what he *does*, but always for what he *is*). This is the poet who made Cleopatra exclaim of Antony:

> For his bounty,
> There was no winter in't; an autumn 'twas
> That grew the more by reaping—

lines in which there is something of the same suggestion of uniqueness and archetype.

And this brings me back to the opening lines of this sonnet, with whose 'ideality' and 'metaphysicality' there is nothing really comparable either in ancient love-poetry or in its Medieval and Renaissance imitations and developments. Nearer to these lines, though still essentially different, are certain passages in Petrarch, Chaucer, Ariosto and Ronsard, where those poets declare that in the person celebrated God and Nature have shown, in a never-to-be-repeated fashion, what they can achieve. Petrarch's 159th sonnet begins:

> In qual parte del ciel, in quale idea
> Era l'essempio onde natura tolse
> Quel bel viso leggiadro, in ch'ella volse
> Mostrar qua giú quanto là su potea?

('In what quarter of the heavens, in what idea, was the pattern whence Nature took that fair, delightful face, in which she wished to show here below what she could achieve there above?') His 248th, one of the most beautiful of all his sonnets, from which I have already quoted a passage in the preceding Part of this study, I will here quote in full:

> Chi vuol veder quantunque po natura
> E'l ciel tra noi, venga a mirar costei,
> Ch'è sola un sol, non pur a li occhi mei
> Ma al mondo cieco che vertú non cura;
> E venga tosto, perché morte fura
> Prima i migliori e lascia star i rei:
> Questa, aspettata al regno de li dei,
> Cosa bella mortal, passa e non dura.
> Vedrà, s'arriva a tempo, ogni vertute,
> Ogni bellezza, ogni real costume
> Giunti in un corpo con mirabil tempre;
> Allor dirà che mie rime son mute,
> L'ingegno offeso dal soverchio lume:
> Ma, se piú tarda, avrà da pianger sempre.

('Whoso wishes to see how much Nature and Heaven can among us, let him come to behold this she, who is alone a sun, not only to my eyes, but to the blind world which is careless of virtue; and let him come soon, because Death steals first the better and leaves standing the wicked: this she, awaited in the kingdom of the gods, fair mortal thing, passes and does not endure. He shall see, if he arrives in time, all virtue, all beauty, all royal manners joined in one body with marvellous tempering; then he shall say that my rhymes are dumb, my genius injured [= blinded] by that sovereign light: but if he delays longer, he shall have cause to weep for ever.')

Ariosto, perhaps with these sonnets in mind, went a step further, and spoke of Nature's having broken the mould she had used. In the tenth book of the *Orlando Furioso* Ruggiero is transported by the hippogriff to Britain, where he sees the English and Scottish nobility gathering armies to assist Charlemagne. The Scots are under the command of their king's son, the Duke of Ross:

> Non è un sì bello in tante altre persone:
> Natura il fece, e poi ruppe la stampa.
> Non è in cui tal virtù, tal grazia luca,
> O tal possanza: ed è di Roscia duca.

('Among so many other persons there is not one so fair. Nature made him and then broke the mould. There is not one in whom such worth, such grace shines, or such power; and he is the Duke of Ross'—st. 84.) Ronsard, together with a general imitation of Petrarch, has imitated this apparently original 'conceit' of Ariosto's in two of the sonnets in the Second Book of his *Sonets pour Helene*, 18 and 36, both of which I shall quote in full: the first, because in its twelfth line there is an interesting resemblance to the concluding couplet of Shakespeare's sonnet, and the second because it is one of the finest of Ronsard's more 'Petrarchan' sonnets.

> Une seule vertu, tant soit parfaicte et belle,
> Ne pourroit jamais rendre un homme vertueux:
> Il faut le nombre entier, en rien defectueux:
> Le Printemps ne se fait d'une seule arondelle.
>
> Toute vertu divine acquise et naturelle
> Se loge en ton esprit. La Nature et les Cieux
> Ont versé dessus toy leurs dons à qui mieux mieux:
> Puis pour n'en faire plus ont rompu le modelle.
>
> Icy à ta beauté se joint la Chasteté,
> Icy l'honneur de Dieu, icy la Pieté,
> La crainte de mal-faire, et la peur d'infamie:
>
> Icy un cœur constant, qu'on ne peut esbranler.
> Pource en lieu de mon cœur, d'Helene, et de ma vie,
> Je te veux desormais ma Pandore appeller.

Despite the 'conventional' allusions to Adonis and Helen in Shakespeare's sonnet, I must confess that I have always been rather surprised by the conventional triteness of the concluding couplet:

> In all external grace you have some part,
> But you like none, none you, for constant heart.

Why just here should Shakespeare 'drag in' (as one might be inclined to say) the all too familiar 'constant heart'? Perhaps because he had this sonnet of Ronsard's in mind:

> Icy un cœur constant, qu'on ne peut esbranler.

The resemblance may be no more than accidental, but, on the other hand, we have already noticed other rather surprising resemblances to passages in Ronsard, and it begins to seem unlikely that they are *all* accidental. The second of these two sonnets is as follows:

> Lorsque le Ciel te fist, il rompit la modelle
> Des Vertuz, comme un peintre efface son tableau,
> Et quand il veut refaire une image du Beau,
> Il te va retracer pour en faire une telle.
> Tu apportas d'en haut la forme la plus belle,
> Pour paroistre en ce monde un miracle nouveau,
> Que couleur, ny outil, ny plume, ny cerveau
> Ne sçauroient egaler, tant tu es immortelle.
> Un bon-heur te defaut: c'est qu'en venant ça bas
> Couverte de ton voile, ombragé du trespas,
> Ton excellence fut à ce monde incognue,
> Qui n'osa regarder les rayons de tes yeaux.
> Seul je les adoray comme un thresor des cieux,
> Te voyant en essence, et les autres en nue.

The last of these 'idealistic' passages I shall quote is one from Chaucer's *Phisiciens Tale* (ll. 7–29), where, although he is partly imitating a passage of Jean de Meun in the *Roman de la Rose* (ll. 16379 ff.) about the inability of artists to vie with Nature, Chaucer's accent is nearer to the passages I have quoted from Petrarch, Ariosto and Ronsard:

> Fair was this mayde in excellent beautee
> Aboven every wight that man may see;
> For Nature hath with sovereyn diligencë
> Y-formed hir in so greet excellencë,
> As though she woldë seyn, 'lo! I, Naturë,
> Thus can I forme and peynte a creaturë,
> Whan that me list; who can me countrefetë?
> Pigmalion noght, though he ay forge and betë,
> Or grave, or peyntë; for I dar wel seyn,

> Apelles, Zanzis, sholdë werche in veyn,
> Outher to grave or peynte or forge or betë,
> If they presumed me to countrefetë.
> For he that is the former principal
> Hath maked me his vicaire general,
> To forme and peynten erthely creaturis
> Right as me list, and ech thing in my cure is
> Under the monë, that may wane and waxë,
> And for my werk right no-thing wol I axë;
> My lord and I ben ful of oon accord;
> I made hir to the worship of my lord.
> So do I alle myne otherë creaturës,
> What colour that they han, or what figurës'.—
> Thus semeth me that Nature woldë seyë.

It was, I think, almost certainly with this passage in his memory that Wordsworth, in a manner so unparalleled elsewhere in his poetry and so uncharacteristic, personified Nature as a kind of goddess in that poem which Coleridge called 'Nature's Lady':

> Three years she grew in sun and shower,
> Then Nature said, 'A lovelier flower
> On earth was never sown;
> This Child I to myself will take;
> She shall be mine, and I will make
> A lady of my own.'[1]

But although these poets declare that the beauty of the person celebrated is a unique and never-to-be-repeated manifestation of what God and Nature can achieve, none of them, and, so far as I know, none of their imitators, ever went so far as to declare, like Shakespeare, that the beauty of the person celebrated was the substance of which all other beauties were but shadows. The only other poet who approaches Shakespeare in this respect (as well as in other respects, about which I shall have more to say later) is Donne, when he writes in *The good-morrow*:

> But this, all pleasures fancies bee.
> If ever any beauty I did see,
> Which I desir'd, and got, t'was but a dreame of thee.

---

[1] This most interesting 'parallel' was pointed out to me in 1954 by Mr. Paul Piehler, to whom I am happy to have this opportunity of expressing my indebtedness.

Even here, in one of the more 'serious' of the *Songs and Sonets*, I am not sure whether Donne is not to some extent, as he often and obviously is elsewhere, being deliberately and provocatively blasphemous—here only of 'Platonism', although elsewhere he is blasphemous not only of 'Platonism' but, if not exactly of Christianity, at any rate of scholastic theology. Of Donne's anti-Platonic blasphemy there are several examples in his *Elegies*: in, for example, the nineteenth, *Going to Bed*, where, parodying and satirising those 'Platonic' poets who profess to admire the external beauty of their mistresses only as the partial manifestation of an internal and invisible beauty which is divine and with which alone they are really in love, Donne declares (ll. 33–43) that, while a mere 'earthly' lover is arrested by gems and clothes, a true lover can be satisfied by nothing less than nakedness:

> Full nakedness! All joyes are due to thee,
> As souls unbodied, bodies uncloth'd must be,
> To taste whole joyes. Gems which you women use
> Are like Atlanta's balls,[1] cast in mens views,
> That when a fools eye lighteth on a Gem,
> His earthly soul may covet theirs, not them.
> Like pictures, or like books gay coverings made
> For lay-men, are all women thus array'd;
> Themselves are mystick books, which only wee
> (Whom their imputed grace will dignifie)
> Must see reveal'd.

Whereas the 'Platonic' poets had talked very 'spiritually' about a very 'spiritual' distinction between outward and inward beauty, Donne is talking here in a parodyingly 'spiritual' way about a very gross and carnal distinction between outward and inward beauty; and even here, although his main target is 'Platonism', Donne is also being profanely witty, not merely about the elaborately formulated doctrine of 'imputed grace', but also about the simple belief, common to all Christians, that the souls of the redeemed shall see God. He seems for long to have felt an irresistible temptation, to which he often yielded, to apply to matters of fact and to the world of the flesh the elaborate terminology, the subtle distinctions and the transcendental conceptions which those philosophers

---

[1] Donne's memory of the legend of Atalanta is inaccurate. She challenged her suitors to race with her and, as she overtook them, speared them in the back, until Hippomenes won her by a trick. Aphrodite gave him three golden apples, which he dropped as he ran, and Atalanta, through stooping to pick them up, lost the race.

and theologians with whom he was so familiar had applied to matters of faith, to matters of speculation, and to the world of the spirit. Just as writers of mock-heroic (Pope, for example, in *The Rape of the Lock*) parodied Homer and Virgil, whom they admired, and described Belinda's bodkin in the manner of Homer's description of Agamemnon's sceptre, Donne was always ready (at any rate, until up to the time of his ordination) to parody, not merely the 'Platonic' speculations of Ficino and Castiglione, which he seems rather to have despised, but also the doctrinal formulations of the Fathers and the Schoolmen, whom he admired (or came to admire) as much as any authors he ever read. Had he ever chosen to write a comparatively long poem (as long, let us say, as *The Rape of the Lock*), he might well have introduced a new *genre*, that of the mock-scholastic, or mock-theological, corresponding to the mock-heroic. Even as it is, some of his elaborate complimentary verse-letters to the Countess of Bedford (a divinity, to be apprehended partly by reason and partly by faith) and to the Countess of Huntingdon, written during the comparatively sober years preceding his ordination, give the impression of having been written chiefly in order to display his capacity for this kind of witty profanity, which he was capable of introducing at almost any time into almost any poem. Indeed, I rather suspect that the chief inspiration of *The Dreame*, by no means one of the more outrageous of the *Songs and Sonets*, may have been the sudden occurrence to him of the brilliant piece of theological wit in its second stanza, where he attributes to his mistress a power which Aquinas had denied even to angels and attributed only to God, the power to read thoughts directly:

> As lightning, or a Tapers light,
> Thine eyes, and not thy noise wak'd mee;
>   Yet I thought thee
> (For thou lovest truth) an Angell, at first sight,
> But when I saw thou sawest my heart,
> And knew'st my thoughts, beyond an Angels art,
> When thou knew'st what I dreamt, when thou knew'st when
> Excesse of joy would wake me, and cam'st then,
> I must confesse, it could not chuse but bee
> Prophane, to thinke thee any thing but thee.

Such a poem, if not actually written for an audience, was certainly written with an audience in mind—that audience of young Inns of Court men among whom Donne's poems circulated in manuscript and to whom he had revealed possibilities of poetic wit hitherto undreamt of—in England, at any rate, though not in contemporary Italy, where it seems likely that Donne first discovered them. About Donne's *Elegies* and the circulation of them in manuscript among his 'private friends' there is something of the atmosphere of a very select and sophisticated college smoking concert. One can see that the frequent profanity and the occasional obscenity were indispensable and expected ingredients, for surprise was of the very essence of the entertainment, and nothing can have been more surprising than the way in which these things were, so to speak, volatilised by Donne's wit. Many of his readers felt no doubt like Lady Plyant in Congreve's *Double-Dealer*: 'But the sin!—well, but the necessity'—the necessity of participating in Donne's sin in order to enjoy Donne's wit. (Those who tried to imitate him seldom succeeded in achieving much more than the profanity and obscenity.) Because he really enjoyed it, because he knew he could do it so well, and because, no doubt, it was still expected of him, Donne continued to indulge in this kind of witty profanity for as long as he continued to write secular poetry, and even in the apparently latest and most personal of the *Songs and Sonets* he still seems to be aware of his original audience and to be writing, at least partly, for them.

Since it is necessary to perceive the *notness* of Shakespeare's sonnets (if I may coin an addition to Hopkins's Scotian coinage) in order to perceive their *thisness*, and since it is illuminating to perceive some of the characteristic differences between their author and certain poets between whom and himself there is occasionally a deep affinity, it has seemed to me worth insisting that Donne's parodies of Platonism are utterly different from what I have called Shakespeare's inverted Platonism, and that Donne's hyperboles (those, at any rate, which I have quoted or alluded to) are utterly different from Shakespeare's. Hyperbole, both in the sonnets and in the tragedies, is Shakespeare's most natural mode of expression, his most characteristic way of expressing what things most deeply 'mean' to him, whereas many of Donne's hyperboles are, as it were, satires on hyperbole, hyperboles to end hyperbole; and in passages such as those I have alluded to Donne is not trying to say what a particular person most deeply 'means' to him, but amusing himself and proving to himself and to his never-forgotten audience how far he can go. There are indeed many poems among the *Songs and Sonets* where Donne really is (or seems to be) trying to express what his love 'means' to him and where he is more concerned with the person addressed than with an imagined audience, and, as I shall try to show later, there seems to me a real and deep affinity between these poems and some of Shakespeare's sonnets; nevertheless, many of the *Elegies* and of the *Songs and Sonets* can only be described as love-poetry in the sense that love happens to be the topic on which Donne is there exercising his wit. There is no trace of this irreverent, satirical, parodying wit in Shakespeare's sonnets, and although Shakespeare probably conceived himself, sometimes, at any rate, as writing *for* posterity as well as *to* his friend, he never conveys the impression that his eye is at least as much upon some contemporary audience as upon his friend, let alone, as Donne so often does, that his eye is mainly upon such an audience. Shakespeare's sonnets might well provoke from a Social Realist an accusation of 'personalism' and 'beglamouring', but they could never provoke, as might so much of Donne's poetry, the baffled and resentful equivalent of 'Think ye'r being funny, do yer?'.

It seems possible, as I have already suggested, that Shakespeare may first have stumbled, as it were, into the path which led him to his characteristic conception of his friend as the archetype of all beauty and excellence in the course of writing those presumably earliest sonnets urging him to marry and have children, especially 14, with its conclusion that, if his friend dies childless,

> Thy end is truth's and beauty's doom and date.

He may not have meant this very seriously; it may well have occurred to him in the course of trying, in much the same manner as so many of his contemporaries were so often trying, to devise some ingenious hyperbolical compliment. Nevertheless, even here he was trying to say something appropriate to the subject and to the occasion, whereas my impression is that Donne, in *The Dreame*, invented a situation in order to introduce a brilliant piece of profanity which had just occurred to him— the idea that his mistress possessed the more than angelic power of reading thoughts directly. Shakespeare, unlike Donne (or unlike what seems so often to have been the case with Donne[1]), required other motives for writing than the mere desire to exercise and exhibit his wit: his sonnets were occasioned by the young man who became his friend, just as his plays were occasioned by the Theatre and the Globe. Then (to continue this not implausible hypothesis), as he came to know the young

---

[1] 'I did best when I had least truth for my subjects,' he admitted to Sir Robert Carr in 1625: see *Poems*, ed. Grierson, I, 288.

man better and to love him, he came to find in the 'conceit', or in various developments of the 'conceit', which he had first hit upon in an attempt to say something appropriate to the occasion of his first addresses, the more and more adequate and ultimate expression of what his friend had come to 'mean' to him. What, one might perhaps say, began as 'wit' ended as 'meaning', and what began as hyperbole in something like the Puttenham sense ended as hyperbole in the most characteristically and indispensably Shakespearean sense.

The fact that he was being content to write endless variations on a few deeply meaningful themes seems to have struck Shakespeare himself as something which distinguished his poetry from that of others:

Why is my verse so barren of new pride,
So far from variation or quick change?
Why with the time do I not glance aside
To new-found methods and to compounds strange?
Why write I still all one, ever the same,
And keep invention in a noted weed,
That every word doth almost tell my name,
Showing their birth and where they did proceed?
O know, sweet love, I always write of you,
And you and love are still my argument;
So all my best is dressing old words new,
Spending again what is already spent:
   For as the sun is daily new and old,
   So is my love still telling what is told.

(76)

'And keep invention in a noted weed': how Donne would have disdained such a 'poeticism'! Had Shakespeare, perhaps, seen some of those precious manuscripts, or copies of them, and is it to the 'new-found methods' of Donne and some of his imitators that he is here alluding? For he must surely be alluding to some poetry very different from his own, to a poetry different not merely in degree, as Daniel's, for example, might almost be regarded, but, like Donne's, different in kind. There is indeed far more of a certain kind of 'invention' in Donne's *Elegies* and *Songs and Sonnets* than in the whole of Shakespeare's works, and it was often, I cannot but think, merely in order to exercise and exhibit such powers of 'invention' that Donne wrote his poetry. Would Donne and his friends have regarded Shakespeare's sonnets as rather old-fashioned and conventional? Were there, perhaps, moments when Shakespeare felt a little abashed by the 'art and scope' of Donne, felt a bit plain and 'traditional' and simple-minded and silly-sooth in comparison with that brilliant and audacious wit? If so, I fancy they were only moments and that his admiration for Donne's 'new-found methods' had many reserves. They were methods appropriate to a poet who 'did best when he had least truth for his subjects', and Shakespeare knew that he himself was not a poet of that kind. Moreover, like Chaucer before him and like Milton after him, Shakespeare contrived to be original within, and not, like Donne, outside of, the main tradition of European poetry. When he is being most original, one seldom has the impression that he is striving for originality as such. Apart altogether from their originality of phrasing, his sonnets, as we have seen, and shall continue to see, are full of what may be regarded as unprecedented developments of, or variations upon, traditional topics. Even this most unprecedented of all his conceptions, that of the friend's beauty and excellence as archetypal, may be related to various kinds of traditional *encomia*, and was almost certainly not arrived at as the result of a deliberate attempt to say something which, as Dr. Johnson said of those whom he called the 'metaphysical poets', he hoped had been never said before. Indeed, I am by no means certain that Shakespeare himself was consciously aware that what I have called his inverted Platonism was fundamentally different from the 'Platonism' or 'idealism' he had met with in other poets; for my impression is that he was singularly indifferent to doctrines and ideas as such, and as distinct from the values they were intended to express. His impression of such 'Platonic' or 'idealistic' poetry as he had read may well have been merely that it was a good 'method' of saying that the person celebrated 'meant' a great deal to the poet; and perhaps if someone had pointed out to him that he himself, unlike these poets, had said nothing about God or the divine pattern or the distinction between celestial and terrestrial beauty, he might have replied: 'Well, fancy that now! To tell you the truth, I just hadn't noticed it.'

2

Excursus: sonnets written during absence

> Nor did I wonder at the lily's white,
> Nor praise the deep vermilion in the rose;
> They were but, sweet, but figures of delight,
> Drawn after you, you pattern of all those.
>
> (98, ll. 9–12)

Since that characteristically Shakespearean hyperbole (or whatever we may decide to call it) of the beloved as the archetype of all beauty, which I have discussed in the preceding section, often occurs in them, this will perhaps be as convenient a place as any to consider some of Shakespeare's sonnets written during absence.

From the Roman elegiac poets to Shakespeare the situation of the Solitary Lover had been treated in at least four more or less clearly distinguishable ways by European poets, or, what amounts to the same thing, had provided four more or less clearly distinguishable topics. All four of these topics are to be found in Petrarch, Ronsard and other Renaissance poets, but only two of them are to be found in Roman elegiac poetry and only two of them (the two, characteristically enough, which are *not* in the Roman poets) are to be found in Shakespeare. We may consider first the two topics, or situations, which are to be found in the Roman poets but not in Shakespeare, and try to decide why it was that Shakespeare left them alone.

(*a*) *The unrequited lover retires to solitary places in order to conceal his distress from others*

In Roman poetry it is only in a single elegy (I, xviii) of Propertius, the most 'romantic' of the Roman poets, that I have found anything like a thorough exploitation of this characteristically romantic, this almost Wertherian, topic and situation.

> Haec certe deserta loca et taciturna querenti,
> et vacuum Zephyri possidet aura nemus.

178

> hic licet occultos proferre impune dolores,
>   si modo sola queant saxa tenere fidem
>   (1–4)

('Here indeed is a deserted and silent spot for a lamenter, only the breath of Zephyrus possesses this empty grove. Here hidden griefs may be freely uttered, if only these lonely rocks are able to keep faith.') Thus Propertius begins, and thus, after reproaching Cynthia for her fickleness, he invokes the trees:

> Vos eritis testes, si quos habet arbor amores,
>   fagus et Arcadio pinus amica deo.
> a quotiens teneras resonant mea verba sub umbras,
>   scribitur et vestris 'Cynthia' corticibus!
>   (19–22)

('You shall be my witnesses, if trees too have loves, you, beech, and you, pine, dear to Arcadia's god. Ah, how often my words resound beneath your gentle shades, and "Cynthia" is written on your barks!') After declaring that in return for his fidelity he has received only chill rocks to lie upon and broken sleep on a rugged path, and that only birds hear his laments, he concludes:

> Sed qualiscumque es resonent mihi 'Cynthia' silvae,
>   nec deserta tuo nomine saxa vacent!

('Be, though, what you will, let the woods still re-echo "Cynthia" and these lonely rocks have no rest from the sound of your name!') It may well have been partly under the influence of this elegy that Petrarch wrote what was to become one of the most famous and most imitated of his sonnets, 35:

> Solo e pensoso i piú deserti campi
>   Vo mesurando a passi tardi e lenti;
>   E gli occhi porto, per fuggire, intenti,
>   Ove vestigio uman l'arena stampi.
> Altro schermo non trovo che mi scampi
>   Dal manifesto accorger de le genti;
>   Perché ne gli atti d'allegrezza spenti
>   Di fuor si legge com'io dentro avampi:

Sí ch'io mi credo omai che monti e piagge
E fiumi e selve sappian di che tempre
Sia la mia vita, ch'è celata altrui.
Ma pur sí aspre vie né sí selvagge
Cercar non so, ch'Amor non venga sempre
Ragionando con meco, et io con lui.

('Alone and pensive, I walk [as if] measuring the most deserted plains
with paces tardy and slow, and keep my eyes, ready for flight, attentive
for where human trace may print the sand. No other means I find of
escaping from the manifest awareness of the people; for in my actions
devoid of all cheerfulness is read from without how I blaze within: so
that I finally believe that mountains and hills and rivers and forests know
of what temper is that life of mine which is concealed from others. Yet
even so I cannot search out paths so rough and savage that Love will not
ever come discoursing with me and I with him.') This topic, which
Petrarch has here treated with an exquisite economy and restraint, was
one which lent itself only too easily to a kind of rhetorical exaggeration
that could become hollow or absurd; just as did that topic which, from
Theocritus's First Idyll onwards, became one of the established topics of
pastoral elegy and which, when they came to describe how all Nature
was lamenting the dead Shepherd, tempted many poets to introduce
weeping tigers, groaning wolves, and sometimes even lists of rivers that
roared or bellowed with grief. Ronsard, in the twenty-ninth sonnet of
his second *Livre des amours*, which was almost certainly inspired by this
famous sonnet of Petrarch's, has not wholly avoided such absurdity.
Perhaps indeed it was a topic on which Petrarch, although he might be
more or less successfully imitated, could be surpassed only in absurdity.

Les Villes et les Bourgs me sont si odieux,
Que je meurs si je voy quelque tracette humaine:
Seulet dedans le bois pensif je me promeine,
Et rien ne m'est plaisant que les sauvages lieux.
Il n'y a dans ces bois sangliers si furieux,
Ny roc si endurcy, ny ruisseau, ny fontaine,
Ny arbre tant soit sourd, qui ne sache ma peine,
Et qui ne soit marry de mon mal envieux.
Un penser qui renaist d'un autre m'accompaigne
Avec un pleur amer qui tout le sein me baigne,
Travaillé de souspirs, qui compaignons me sont:

> Si bien que si quelcun me trouvoit au bocage,
> Voyant mon poil rebours, et l'horreur de mon front,
> Ne me diroit un homme, ains un monstre sauvage.[1]

Various reasons may be suggested for the absence of this topic from Shakespeare's sonnets. It presupposes the situation of the suing but unrequited lover, as which Shakespeare never represents himself, and its main subject is not, as with Shakespeare, the meaningfulness of the beloved to the poet, but the 'torment' which the poet suffers because of the beloved's coldness or infidelity, and which he escapes into solitude to hide from public gaze and to soothe among 'natural objects' and wild animals, animals which, not indeed Petrarch himself, but many of his successors, represent as less 'cruel' than the beloved and more sympathetic than indifferent and superficial men. There is bitter rebuke and bitter self-reproach in Shakespeare's sonnets to or about the 'Dark Lady', and there is deep sadness in some of his sonnets to the friend who has temporarily become estranged from him

> (Farewell! thou art too dear for my possessing,
> And like enough thou know'st thy estimate—87),

but there is no self-pity, no hopeless languishing, no 'pageant of his bleeding heart'. There is much of what might perhaps be called 'romantic idealism', but there is almost nothing of romantic egotism.

(b) The lover invokes the scenes where his beloved has played or lingered

If not the ultimate inspiration of all later verse on this topic, at any rate the earliest example I have been able to discover is in the pseudo-Virgilian *Lydia*, which in the manuscripts follows, in sequence and without separate title, the *Dirae* ('Curses'), a poem which seems to have been inspired by the distribution of lands to veterans in 41 B.C. and which was traditionally ascribed to Virgil. In the *Lydia* the poet declares that he envies the fields and meadows which retain the *puella* from whom he is separated, and the following lines (8–19) are very close to many things in Petrarch and later poets, except that Lydia (*mea cura*) is represented as sighing for her lover just as he is sighing for her:

> Invideo vobis, agri, discetis amare.
> O fortunati nimium multumque beati,

---

[1] Vaganay, II, 57.

in quibus illa pedis nivei vestigia ponet
aut roseis viridem digitis decerpserit uvam . . .
aut inter varios, Veneris stipendia, flores
membra reclinarit teneramque illiserit herbam,
et secreta meos furtim narrabit amores.
gaudebunt silvae, gaudebunt mollia prata
et gelidi fontes, aviumque silentia fient.
tardabunt rivi labentes (sistite lymphae),
dum mea iucundas exponat cura querelas.

('I envy you, fields, you will learn to love. O too fortunate and greatly blest, in which she will set the prints of her snowy foot and with rosy fingers gather the green grape . . . or among varied flowers, Venus's tributes, she will recline her limbs and crush the tender grass, and apart and stealthily relate my love. The woods will rejoice, rejoice will the soft meadows and cool springs, and there will be silences of birds. The gliding brooks will pause (stay, waters!) while my care sets forth her sweet laments.')[1] It seems very likely that Petrarch's 162nd sonnet, which, like so many of his sonnets, provided not only a theme but a pattern for later poets, was inspired by these pseudo-Virgilian lines:

Lieti fiori e felici e ben nate erbe
    Che Madonna pensando premer sòle;
    Piaggia ch'ascolti sue dolce parole,
    E del bel piede alcun vestigio serbe;
Schietti arboscelli e verdi frondi acerbe;
    Amorosette e pallide vïole;
    Ombrose selve, ove percote il sole
    Che vi fa co'suoi raggi alte e superbe;
O soave contrada, o puro fiume
    Che bagni il suo bel viso e gli occhi chiari

[1] Later (41-2) the poet asks why it is that, although, when Phoebus has departed, Luna's love Endymion is with her, his own love is not with him:

Luna, tuus tecum est: cur non est et mea mecum?
Luna, dolor nosti quid sit: miserere dolentis.

The second of these two lines must surely have been in Sidney's memory when he apostrophised the moon in the 31st sonnet of *Astrophel and Stella*:

Sure, if that long-with-acquainted eyes
Can judge of love, thou feel'st a lover's case;
I read it in thy looks; thy languisht grace,
To me, that feel the like, thy state descries.

E prendi qualità dal vivo lume;
Quanto v'invidio gli atti onesti e cari!
Non fia in voi scoglio omai che per costume
D'arder co la mia fiamma non impari.

('Joyful and happy flowers and well-born grasses, that my lady, lost in
thought, is wont to press; slope that listen to her sweet words and of
that fair foot preserve some trace; plain saplings and green leaves [yet]
unripe; lovable and pale violets; shady woods where strikes that sun that
makes you with its rays lofty and proud; O gentle landscape, O pure
river that bathe her fair face and her clear eyes and assume its quality
from that living light; how much I envy you her actions decent and dear!
There will not be among you a single rock that through habit will not
learn to burn with my flame.') We do not find this sort of apostrophe in
Shakespeare's sonnets: partly, perhaps, because it is appropriate to the
expression of a more languishing, a more self-pleasing, and even, with
many poets, a more fictitious and factitious kind of love than his, and
partly because it goes better with simple descriptive lists and catalogues
than with his own characteristic metaphors. If not by Petrarch himself,
at any rate by his imitators it is often combined with another topic, which
does not, I think, occur in ancient love-poetry, for which, perhaps, it is
already somewhat too 'ideal', or 'spiritual' or 'metaphysical', since it may
be regarded as already beginning to foreshadow the notion of the
beloved as a kind of pattern or archetype.

(c) *The lover in a place where all things remind him of the beloved*

This topic was, I think, first elaborated by Petrarch, and one of the most
classical and exemplary treatments of it is in his 112th sonnet:

Sennuccio, i'vo'che sappi in qual manera
    Trattato sono e qual vita è la mia.
    Ardomi e struggo ancor com'io solia.
    Laura mi volve, e son pur quel ch'i'm'era.
Qui tutta umile, e qui la vidi altera,
    Or aspra or piana, or dispietata or pia;
    Or vestirsi onestate or leggiadria,
    Or mansueta or disdegnosa e fera.
Qui cantò dolcemente, e qui s'assise;
    Qui si rivolse, e qui rattenne il passo;

Qui co'begli occhi mi trafisse il core;
Qui disse una parola, e qui sorrise;
Qui cangiò 'l viso. In questi pensier, lasso,
Notte e dí tiemmi il signor nostro, Amore.

('Sennuccio, I want you to know in what manner I am treated and what life is mine. I burn and melt still as I was wont. Laura whirls me [like a breeze], and I am purely what I was. Here all humble and here I saw her proud; now rough, now smooth; now dispiteous, now pitiful; now clothing herself with reserve, now with charmingness; now meek, now disdainful and fierce. Here she sang sweetly, and here she sat; here she turned and here she stayed her footing; here with her beautiful eyes she pierced my heart; here she spoke a word and here she smiled; here she changed colour. In these thoughts our Lord Love holds me outwearied night and day.') Here the half-playful languishment (as one might almost call it) of sonnet 162 and its pseudo-Virgilian prototype has passed (as had also, under the influence, conscious or unconscious, of Christian worship, so much of the poetry of the Troubadours and Minnesingers) into an almost religious adoration (or idolatry) that is foreign to ancient love-poetry. The later imitators of Petrarch often combined themes and topics and situations which he himself usually kept distinct, and Ronsard, in one of the most charming of his Cassandre sonnets, 163 in his first *Livre des amours*, has imitated both of the Petrarchan sonnets I have just quoted:

Voicy le bois, que ma sainte Angelette
Sur le printemps enchante de son chant:
Voicy les fleurs que son pied va marchant,
Quand à soymesme elle pense seulette:
Voicy la prée et la rive mollette,
Qui prend vigueur de sa main la touchant,[1]
Quand pas à pas pillarde va cherchant
Le bel émail de l'herbe nouvelette.

[1] Here Ronsard has also imitated ll. 1–4 of Petrarch's sonnet 165:

Come 'l candido piè per l'erba fresca
I dolci passi onestamente move,
Vertú che 'ntorno i fiori apra e rinove
De le tenere piante sue par ch'esca.

('As soon as her white foot becomingly moves her sweet paces through the fresh grass, virtue that opens and renews the flowers around seems to issue from her tender soles.')

Icy chanter, là pleurer je la vy,
Icy sourrire, et là je fu ravy
De ses discours, par lesquels je des-vie:
Icy s'asseoir, là je la vy danser:
Sus le mestier d'un si vague penser
Amour ourdit les trames de ma vie.[1]

Here there is far more outwardness in Ronsard than in Petrarch, far more description of a kind that may be appropriately called picturesque; and Drummond of Hawthornden, in a sonnet, one of his best, that was probably inspired both by Petrarch and by Ronsard, has gone still further in the direction of mere picturesqueness:

Alexis, here *shee* stay'd, among these Pines
(*Sweet Hermitresse*) *shee* did alone repaire,
Here did she spread the Treasure of her Haire,
More rich than that brought from the *Colchian* Mines.
Shee set Her by these musket Eglantines,
The happie Place the Print seemes yet to beare,
Her Voyce did sweeten here thy sugred Lines,
To which Winds, Trees, Beasts, Birds did lend their Eare.
Mee here *shee* first perceiu'd, and here a Morne
Of bright *Carnations* did o'respreade her Face,
Here did *shee* sigh, here first my Hopes were borne,
And I first got a Pledge of promis'd Grace:
    But (*ah*) what seru'd it to bee happie so?
    Sith passed Pleasures double but new Woe.[2]

(d) *The lover surrounded by delights which are no compensation for the absence or loss of the beloved*

In two beautiful sonnets written after the death of Laura Petrarch combines the topic (or situation) we have just been considering with what may be called the 'catalogue of uncompensating delights', and it is here that he and his imitators come closest to the pattern of some of Shakespeare's sonnets written during absence from his friend. It is true that in other sonnets, which I shall discuss in the next section of this Part, Shakespeare makes frequent use of the theme, or topic, of 'compensation',

[1] Vaganay, I, 178.
[2] *Poetical Works*, ed. Kastner, I, 41.

but in a much wider sense, and one for which it is hard to find any real precedent except in specifically religious poetry. Here, however, in some of his sonnets written during absence, he is writing, though still with characteristic differences, in a tradition which Petrarch may be said to have classicised. For what I have called 'the catalogue of uncompensating delights' Petrarch was by no means without precedent: it appears in those popular canzoni and ballate about Spring and May and in those *reverdies*, or Spring songs, by the Provençal and early Italian poets (including Guido Cavalcanti and Fazio degli Uberti) in which the lover declares that, while all things around him are rejoicing in the return of Spring, he alone is full of sadness because of the absence or loss of his lady. Here, then, are Petrarch's two sonnets:

310

Zefiro torna, e 'l bel tempo rimena,
  E i fiori e l'erbe, sua dolce famiglia,
  E garrir Progne e pianger Filomena,
  E primavera candida e vermiglia.
Ridono i prati e 'l ciel si rasserena;
  Giove s'allegra di mirar sua figlia;
  L'aria e l'acqua e la terra è d'amor piena:
  Ogni animal d'amar si riconsiglia.
Ma per me, lasso!, tornano i piú gravi
  Sospiri, che del cor profondo tragge
  Quella ch'al ciel se ne portò le chiavi;
E cantar augelletti e fiorir piagge
  E 'n belle donne oneste atti soavi
  Sono un deserto e fere aspre e selvagge.

('Zephyrus returns and brings back the fair season and the flowers and the grasses, his sweet family, and [brings back] Progne to her twittering and Philomena to her weeping, and [brings back] Spring-time white and red. The meadows laugh and the sky grows clear; Jove delights to behold his daughter; the air and the water and the earth are full of love: every creature takes new advice to love. But to wretched me return the heaviest sighs, which from the depths of my heart she draws who bore away its keys to heaven [*i.e.* who left it closed to all delight]; and birds singing and slopes flowering are for me a desert and the gentle acts of fair virtuous ladies are rough and savage beasts.')

312

Né per sereno ciel ir vaghe stelle,
  Né per tranquillo mar legni spalmati,
  Né per campagne cavalieri armati,
  Né per bei boschi allegre fere e snelle;
Né d'aspettato ben fresche novelle,
  Né dir d'amore in stili alti et ornati,
  Né tra chiare fontane e verdi prati
  Dolce cantare oneste donne e belle;
Né altro sarà mai ch'al cor m'aggiunga;
  Sí seco il seppe quella sepellire
  Che sola a gli occhi miei fu lume e speglio.
Noia m'è 'l viver si gravosa e lunga,
  Ch'i'chiamo il fine per lo gran desire
  Di reveder cui non veder fu 'l meglio.

('Neither passing through clear sky of wandering stars, nor through tranquil sea of tarred ships, nor through landscapes of armed horsemen, nor through fair groves of beasts cheerful and swift; nor fresh news of awaited good, nor discourse of love in styles lofty and ornate, nor among clear fountains and green meadows sweet singing of ladies virtuous and fair; nor aught else shall ever be that may reach my heart; so able was she to bury it with herself who alone to these eyes of mine was light and mirror. Weariness to me so burdensome and long is living that I beg its end through my great desire of seeing again whom it had been better for me not to see.')

Ronsard has imitated these two sonnets written after the death of Laura in sonnets about living mistresses, and in each of his imitations we again find, together with a far clearer and simpler syntax, less reflection and more pure description than in Petrarch. They are among Ronsard's best sonnets, although (if one may use that word unpejoratively) they are more superficial, more of the surface, than either Petrarch's or Shakespeare's. In each of them Ronsard seems to have been inspired mainly by the rhetorical pattern he has chosen, and it would be hard to find better examples of the way in which a superb craftsman can combine so much naturalness with so much artifice. In the earlier of the two, a Cassandre sonnet (60 in the first *Livres des amours*), where he has imitated fairly closely Petrarch's 312, he has applied Petrarch's *Né* formula in a manner which, had he been less successful and had he failed to pack so much vivid detail into each line, one would have called

mechanical; for, while Petrarch begins to alter the pattern at line 7 and
discards it after line 9, Ronsard begins every one of his first twelve lines
with Ny. The only approach to such a catalogue and continuously
repeated pattern in Shakespeare's sonnets (ten lines beginning with
'And') is the magnificent 'Tir'd with all these, for restful death I cry',
which, unlike the sonnets of Petrarch and Ronsard, contains, not a list of
sights and sounds, but a pageant of personifications.

> Ny voir flamber au point du jour les roses,
> Ny liz plantez sus le bord d'un ruisseau,
> Ny son de luth, ny ramage d'oyseau,
> Ny dedans l'or les gemmes bien encloses,
> Ny des Zephirs les gorgettes décloses,
> Ny sur la mer le ronfler d'un vaisseau,
> Ny bal de Nymphe au gazouillis de l'eau,
> Ny voir fleurir au printemps toutes choses,
> Ny camp armé de lances herissé,
> Ny antre verd de mousse tapissé,
> Ny des forests les cymes qui se pressent,
> Ny des rochers le silence sacré,
> Tant de plaisirs ne me donnent qu'un Pré[1]
> Où sans espoir mes esperances paissent.[2]

The later of Ronsard's two sonnets (72 in the second *Livre des amours*)
is one of those associated with Marie of Bourgueil, and should perhaps
be regarded rather as a variation upon than as an imitation of Petrarch's
310th. The repetition, at the beginnings of the second quatrain and of each
tercet, of the opening phrase 'Je mourrois de plaisir' seems to be a rhetorical
pattern of Ronsard's own invention, and it may perhaps have suggested
to Sidney his equally successful use of a similar pattern—'It is most
true' (twice) and 'True that' (twice)—in one of his finest sonnets, the
fifth in *Astrophel and Stella*. Indeed, these two sonnets of Ronsard and of
Sidney may serve to remind us how effective such formal and simple
patterns can be when the poet has been able to generate enough verbal
energy to, as it were, animate them. It is a pity that Elizabethan sonneteers
in general did not make more use of such formal patterns, instead of
continually attempting to translate their conceptions into metaphors

---

[1] '*un Pré*': an allusion to the married name of Cassandre Salviati, who in 1546 had married
Jehan Peigné, seigneur de Pré.
[2] Vaganay, I, 74.

which were not for them, as they were for Shakespeare, a natural and necessary form of expression. It was partly, perhaps, their love of such formal patterns and the inspiration they so often derived from them that gives to the best sonnets of Ronsard and his contemporaries their incomparable clarity and grace. They were great rhetoricians, and a study of French poetry in general should teach us that poetry and rhetoric can be great allies and are by no means always, as we too much tend to suppose, great enemies.

> Je mourrois de plaisir voyant par ces bocages
> Les arbres enlassez de lhyerres espars,
> Et la verde lambrunche errante en mille pars
> Sur l'aubespin fleury pres des roses suavages.
> Je mourrois de plaisir, oyant les doux ramages
> Des Hupes, des Coqs, et des Ramiers rouhars
> De sur un arbre verd bec en bec fretillars,
> Et des Tourtres aussi voyant les mariages:
> Je mourrois de plaisir, voyant en ces beaux mois
> Debusquer au matin le Chevreuil hors du bois,
> Et de voir fretiller dans le ciel l'Alouëtte:
> Je mourrois de plaisir, où je languis transy,
> Absent de la beauté qu'en ce bois je souhaite.
> 'Un demy jour d'absence est un an de soucy.'[1]

Relation of Shakespeare's sonnets to types (c) and (d)

Some of Shakespeare's sonnets written during absence have affinities with either or both of the last two types we have been considering, but none of them are so easily, obviously and unambiguously classifiable and describable as are the sonnets of Petrarch and Ronsard which I have quoted. This is partly because of the occasional presence in them of the 'metaphysical' idea that all other beauties are but shadows of the friend's, but still more because Shakespeare's sonnets are far less directly and simply descriptive and far more continuously metaphorical than those of Petrarch and Ronsard on these themes. In Petrarch and Ronsard there is a clearly recognisable distinction between means and ends, between the clear and simple (though beautiful) description and the

---

[1] Vaganay, II, 130. The last line is imitated from Theocritus, *Id.* xii, 2:

οἱ δὲ ποθεῦντες ἐν ἤματι γηράσκουσιν

('the longing grow old in a day').

clear and simple concluding statement to which it leads. In Shakespeare's sonnets there is, as it were, a much more continuous intellectual activity, and one often apprehends his very difficult metaphors as, in some sort, ideas themselves rather than as illustrations of a simple idea or theme. The variations, in fact, tend to become so striking and so elaborate that we can only faintly and tentatively recognise the theme on which they are being played.

In the course of his enumeration of what, in his great *Preface*, he took to be Shakespeare's characteristic 'faults', Dr. Johnson declared:

> It is incident to him to be now and then entangled with an unwieldy sentiment, which he cannot well express, and will not reject; he struggles with it a while, and if it continues stubborn, comprises it in words such as occur, and leaves it to be disentangled and evolved by those who have more leisure to bestow upon it.

This is a not unjust description of the kind of 'difficulty' we often find in Shakespeare, although elsewhere Johnson often seems to suppose that Shakespeare was attempting to do very much the same sort of thing that poets like Petrarch and Ronsard had done and was failing in the attempt. The fact is, though, that Shakespeare's mind often, if not always, worked in a quite different way from theirs. Often he is not describing or illustrating something that he has completely and clearly and definitely thought or felt, but attempting to convey by means of what might be called impressionistic metaphors something he cannot really apprehend, and cannot therefore express, in any other way. With these impressionistic, inexact, approximate metaphors and similes, which are so characteristic of Shakespeare, there is, so far as I know, nothing comparable either in any other Renaissance poet or in classical Latin poetry, and to find anything at all like them we must go back to Pindar's odes and to the choruses of Greek tragedy, especially those of Aeschylus.

Let us begin with sonnet 97: there is clearly a strong thematic resemblance between it and those sonnets and canzoni (together with their various prototypes and later imitations) where Petrarch declares that, since Laura's death, his heart has been closed to all delight, but how utterly different both from Petrarch and from Petrarch's predecessors and imitators is Shakespeare's style! Winter and spring, summer and autumn are indeed evoked, but, except for the concluding statement about the muteness of the birds and the paleness of the leaves, everything is metaphorical and there is not a single phrase of simple description.

How like a winter hath my absence been
From thee, the pleasure of the fleeting year!
What freezings have I felt, what dark days seen!
What old December's bareness everywhere!
And yet this time remov'd was summer's time,
The teeming autumn big with rich increase,
Bearing the wanton burthen of the prime,
Like widow'd wombs after their lords' decease:
Yet this abundant issue seem'd to me
But hope of orphans and unfather'd fruit;
For summer and his pleasures wait on thee,
And, thou away, the very birds are mute:
   Or, if they sing, 'tis with so dull a cheer
   That leaves look pale, dreading the winter's near.

This, if not one of Shakespeare's very finest sonnets, is certainly one of his most memorable, and is to be found in most anthologies. And yet, of all those who have remembered it, how many can feel sure that they have 'understood' it, or even construed it, correctly? In lines 5 to 11 the simile and each of the metaphors are beautiful in themselves and even unforgettable, but they contradict and conflict with one another at almost every point, and the more closely one examines the whole passage the more hopelessly incoherent it appears. The non-metaphorical sense, the underlying perceptual and psychological experience, seems to be something like this: 'That time during which I was removed from you was late summer, and the evidence of my senses told me that there was every prospect of a fine harvest of crops and fruit; nevertheless, I could not believe the evidence of my senses, for it did not seem like summer with you away.' Not that I feel at all certain that Shakespeare began with a clear recognition of this fairly simple mood, or experience, and then proceeded to metaphorise it. He may well have begun with the simile: 'Earth was already swelling with an abundant harvest, but somehow I felt she was like a widow, and that all she could be hoped to give birth to would be orphans.' The difficulty arises through Shakespeare's personification of Spring ('the prime'), of Summer and of Autumn: 'It was summer, *and* widowed Autumn was swelling with the progeny which had been begotten by her dead husband Spring; *but* it seemed to me that all she could be hoped to give birth to would be orphans, *because* her husband Summer had departed with you.' It is true that to the mere natural observer there is a continuity between the seasons and that it is not possible to say precisely when Summer has ended and Autumn begun; nevertheless, if the seasons are to be personified they must not be represented as being simultaneously present, unless, as in Horace's verses, the successor only enters in order to destroy its predecessor:

> ver proterit aestas
> interitura simul
> pomifer Autumnus fruges effuderit, et mox
> bruma recurrit iners.

Have we been hypnotised into admiring beautiful nonsense, or is this sonnet, like some other sonnets and some other passages by Shakespeare, in the same category as those paintings which are intended to be viewed from a certain distance? Certainly, it will not bear close and minute inspection, and in this respect it seems to me (despite its great beauties) inferior to the sonnets of Petrarch and Ronsard which I have quoted. Petrarch's sonnets are often difficult, but their difficulties are nearly always grammatical or syntactical or the result of a kind of oracular periphrasis (as when in 310 he says that Laura has carried away the keys of his heart to heaven, meaning thereby that she has left it closed to all delight), and there is almost never any want of consistency either between the parts themselves or between the parts and the whole. There is, for example, a syntactical ambiguity at the beginning of 310:

> Zefiro torna, e 'l bel tempo rimena,
> E i fiori e l'erbe, sua dolce famiglia,
> E garrir Progne e pianger Filomena,
> E primavera candida e vermiglia.

Here it is impossible to feel sure whether the nouns in lines 2 to 4 are, like Zefiro, subjects of torna or objects of rimena; whether we are to construe 'Zephyrus returns and brings back the fair season, and the flowers and the grasses return, and Progne returns to her twittering and Philomena to her weeping, and spring returns'; or 'Zephyrus returns and brings back the fair season, and brings back the flowers and the grasses, and brings back Progne to her twittering', etc. Nevertheless, whichever way we construe, the sense remains the same and the relationship of the parts to each other and to the whole is clear and consistent. This is quite different from the kind of 'difficulty' we find in lines 5 to 8 of Shakespeare's sonnet:

> And yet this time remov'd was summer's time,
> The teeming autumn big with rich increase,
> Bearing the wanton burthen of the prime,
> Like widow'd wombs after their lords' decease.

At first, perhaps, one supposes that 'the teeming autumn' is a kind of further definition of 'summer's time': 'It was summer—that is to say, it was autumn'. Then, feeling that this is really too much, one decides to regard lines 6 to 8 as a kind of ablative absolute: 'It was summer, with teeming Autumn bearing the wanton burthen of the prime'. And yet, even when we have been persuaded to admit that 'teeming' (pregnant) Autumn is not yet fully Autumn, and that Autumn only 'begins' when she has poured out, given birth to, her fruits, the attempt to hold simultaneously in the imagination a fully personified Autumn, who is somehow not yet fully Autumn, with a half-personified (soon to be fully personified) Summer, proves ultimately impossible, and we have to be content with the beautiful metaphor-cum-simile for its own sake, without trying to relate it at all closely either to what has preceded or to what follows. 'Autumn's children will be fatherless because Summer has departed with you.' But Summer always *has* departed before Autumn's children are born; and, moreover, Master Shakespeare, you have just told us that the begetter of these as yet unborn children was Spring ('the prime'). *Sufflaminandus erat*, he needed braking, as Ben Jonson said.[1]

The following sonnet (98), one of Shakespeare's very finest, is as consistently beautiful and as crystal-clear as the best of those sonnets of Petrarch and Ronsard which I have quoted:

> From you have I been absent in the spring,
> When proud-pied April, dress'd in all his trim,
> Hath put a spirit of youth in every thing,
> That heavy Saturn laugh'd and leap'd with him.
> Yet nor the lays of birds nor the sweet smell
> Of different flowers in odour and in hue
> Could make me any summer's story tell,
> Or from their proud lap pluck them where they grew:
> Nor did I wonder at the lily's white,

---

[1] Jonson (*Works*, ed. Herford and Simpson, Vol. viii, p. 584, and Vol. xi, p. 231) was quoting a phrase used by Augustus about the Roman senator and rhetorician Quintus Haterius, recorded by the elder Seneca.

> Nor praise the deep vermilion in the rose;
> They were but, sweet, but figures of delight,
> Drawn after you, you pattern of all those.
> Yet seem'd it winter still, and, you away,
> As with your shadow I with these did play.

The metaphors, or metaphorical personifications, in the first quatrain are characteristically Shakespearean, and quite unlike anything to be found in Petrarch or Ronsard or, for that matter, in any other Renaissance poet. In what follows the absence of descriptive detail, of what may properly be called picturesqueness, of any attempt to provide a crowded catalogue of particular sights and sounds, is also, I am inclined to say, characteristically Shakespearean and strikingly different not only from Ronsard's sonnets on this theme but even from Petrarch's. The Shakespeare of the sonnets is usually vivid, not through detailed description, but through metaphor and personification, and sometimes through a wonderful use of what may be called concentrated generalisation, as in the unforgettable lines

> Nor did I wonder at the lily's white,
> Nor praise the deep vermilion in the rose,

lines which linger in the memory long after all the picturesque detail and particularisation in the sonnets I have quoted from Ronsard and Drummond have been forgotten; lines in which, without a single inversion or departure from prose order, the operative words are as much isolated and emphasised as in the most elaborately successful stanza of Horace, and evoke all the whiteness and redness of all the flowers in all the summers we have known, and all the wonder and all the praise which they excited; lines which may be compared with Wordsworth's evocation of

> the bare trees and mountains bare
> And grass in the green field.

We may say of such lines, as Beethoven said of his Pastoral Symphony, that they are *mehr Ausdruck der Empfindung als Malerei*, 'more an expression of sensibility than a depiction'. In the concluding lines appears that pseudo-Platonic hyperbole, or whatever we are to call it, which I have

discussed at length in the preceding section of this Part, and with which
I can find no real parallel in any preceding poet. Shakespeare, unlike
Petrarch and Ronsard, says *more* than that these things remind him of his
friend and *more* than that they are no compensation for his absence:
he declares that they are but shadows of his friend's substance. They
remind him in the sense in which terrestrial beauty reminds the Platonic
lover of celestial. Indeed, perhaps no single one of Shakespeare's best
sonnets can be so profitably and so illuminatingly compared with those
of his predecessors; for nowhere more than in some of these sonnets
written during absence does he come so close to writing within an
established convention, to accepting a traditional theme and situation;
and yet in this, the finest of them, the differences from the sonnets of
Petrarch, Ronsard and others on this theme are more striking than the
resemblances.

Whether the remark seem recondite or obvious, a paradox or a
commonplace, I am inclined to say that where Shakespeare is most like
other poets he is least like himself. Sonnet 99 has (astonishingly enough)
the appearance of being a continuation of its magnificent predecessor—
so much so that Beeching and most other editors have replaced 1609's
full stop at the end of 98 by a colon. There could not be a greater contrast,
for 99 is simply a mechanical and tiresome piece of ingenuity, such as
almost any Elizabethan sonneteer might have written, with a metaphorical list of flowers which have 'stolen' their beauties from his friend.
It has, admittedly, the appearance of being a rough draft, which Shakespeare for some reason never revised, for it contains fifteen lines, the
fifth line, which repeats a rhyme already used twice in the preceding
quatrain, being extra-metrical. Perhaps he could think of no theft to
attribute to the violet that would substantially differ from the thefts he
had too carelessly proceeded to attribute to the other flowers; for, after
the lily had stolen the whiteness of the friend's hand, the marjoram his
hair, and the roses both the red and white of his complexion and the
sweetness of his breath, what was there left for the poor violet to steal,
unless perhaps Shakespeare had been willing to say that the violet had
stolen its 'purple pride' from the friend's eyes? There was nothing to be
done except to rewrite the whole sonnet, which Shakespeare probably
(and rightly) decided was not worth rewriting.

> The forward violet thus did I chide:
> Sweet thief, whence didst thou steal thy sweet that smells,
> If not from my love's breath? The purple pride

Which on thy soft cheek for complexion dwells
In my love's veins thou hast too grossly dyed.
The lily I condemned for thy hand,
And buds of marjoram had stol'n thy hair;
The roses fearfully on thorns did stand,
One blushing shame, another white despair;
A third, nor red nor white, had stol'n of both
And to his robbery had annex'd thy breath;
But, for his theft, in pride of all his growth
A vengeful canker eat him up to death.
    More flowers I noted, yet I none could see
    But sweet or colour it had stol'n from thee.

The man who wrote these two sonnets (the second of them perhaps immediately after the first) was indeed, as Dryden said of him, 'the very Janus of poets'. Does it not seem almost incredible that the author of those tired, those merely line-filling and rhyme-supplying, phrases, 'thy sweet that smells', 'for complexion dwells', 'had annex'd thy breath', the author of the poetasterish, the not-very-bright-school-boyish

The roses fearfully on thorns did stand,
One blushing shame, another white despair,

was the author (perhaps only a day or two before) of the unforgettable

Nor did I wonder at the lily's white,
Nor praise the deep vermilion in the rose?[1]

---

[1] This is but one example among the sonnets of the fact that inferiority or apparent immaturity of style cannot in itself be regarded as a proof of earlier composition. When he wrote in languid or uninspired mood Shakespeare was at any time liable to slip back into a style similar to that of the less distinguished rhymed portions of his early comedies and of the average level of the average Elizabethan sonneteer. If, therefore, one attempts to use 'parallels' with passages in particular plays as evidence for the dates of particular sonnets, it is only where Shakespeare is at his best and most characteristic that such parallels are worthy of serious consideration. It is the parallels with passages in the maturer plays that are really significant: such parallels as that between 'that fell arrest Without all bail' in sonnet 74 and Hamlet's

            as that fell serjeant Death
    Is strict in his arrest
                    (V, ii, 347).

It is, incidentally, worth remarking that in the two passages just mentioned Shakespeare, for once, is almost certainly doing what we so often find Milton doing in his earlier poems: appropriating and unforgettably transforming phrases he had found in far lesser English poets. In Sylvester's translation of Du Bartas, First Week, Second Day (ed. 1621, p. 70),

In sonnet 113 Shakespeare seems to be translating, as it were, into the language of semi-scientific psychology and in 114 into what might be called psychological allegory the 'thoughts' (or whatever we are to call them) of 98, that the beauties of the season seem to him but shadows of his friend's substance, and of 97, that his actual experience, as distinct from his mere perception, of the seasons is infinitely modified by the presence or absence of his friend. This translation, or allegorisation, is very different from the spontaneous apprehension in and through metaphor which we find in 97 (despite the inconsistencies and contradictions in that sonnet) and in 98, and, like the mechanical metaphors of 99, it is far closer to the general practice of other Elizabethan sonneteers. Neither sonnet can give much pleasure or satisfaction, although 113 can perhaps yield rather more than its successor.

> Since I left you mine eye is in my mind,
> And that which governs me to go about[1]
> Doth part his function and is partly blind,
> Seems seeing, but effectually is out;
> For it no form delivers to the heart

in a passage, largely inspired by Virgil, praising the country life, it is said of the countryman:

> And Death, drad Seriant of th'eternall Iudge,
> Comes very late to his sole-seated Lodge.

In the original (*Works*, ed. Holmes, Lyons, Linker, vol. II, 1938, p. 302, ll. 949–50),

> et la mort redoutee
> N'approche que bien tard de sa loge escartee,

there is almost no suggestion of this personification, and it may well be that the exuberant Sylvester hit upon the phrase 'drad Seriant of th'eternall Iudge' in the course of an attempt to find a rhyme (or near-rhyme) for 'Lodge'. A little later in the poem, *First Week, Fourth Day* (ed. 1621, p. 89), Sylvester again introduced this personification where there was no suggestion of it in his original. Du Bartas (*op. cit.*, p. 334, ll. 757–9) had reminded the sun that God prolonged the life of Hezekiah by making it go backwards (*Isaiah*, xxxviii, 5–8):

> pour tesmoigner du midi jusqu'au nord
> Que ton Dieu revoquoit le triste arrest de mort
> Donné contre Ezechie.

Here *arrest de mort* means simply 'decree' (sentence) of death', and there is no suggestion of personification; but Sylvester, probably because the phrase reminded him both of the English word 'arrest' and of his earlier 'drad Seriant', rendered the passage:

> to make apparant
> That God revoak't his Serieant Death's sad Warrant
> Gainst *Ezechias*.

Shakespeare's indispensable and unforgettable additions are the words 'fell' and 'arrest'.

[1] That eye which directs my movements.

Of bird, of flower, or shape, which it doth latch:[1]
Of his[2] quick objects hath the mind no part,
Nor his[2] own vision holds what it doth catch;
For if it[3] see the rud'st or gentlest sight,
The most sweet favour or deformed'st creature,
The mountain or the sea, the day or night,
The crow or dove, it shapes them to your feature:
    Incapable of more, replete with you,
    My most true mind thus maketh mine untrue.

Capell and Malone emended the last line to

My most true mind thus makes mine eye untrue,

and Onions (*A Shakespeare Glossary*) and several modern editors have supposed that 'untrue' is a noun, with the meaning 'untruth'. No other example of this usage has been produced, but Shakespeare was capable of transforming any adjective, or any verb, into a noun.

In sonnet 114 Shakespeare continues these reflections, translating them, as I have expressed it, partly into metaphor and partly into allegory. Is his eye merely flattering when it reports to his mind that all things reflect his friend's beauty, or has love enabled it to effect a real, alchemical transmutation? The eye is indeed flattering and proffering illusion, but (this, though not explicitly stated, seems to be implied) to no evil or ulterior end, since the eye itself loves the illusion it is proffering. Shakespeare allegorises this in terms of a taster proffering to a monarch a poisoned cup which he has himself prepared, tasted and enjoyed.

Or whether doth my mind, being crown'd with you,
Drink up the monarch's plague, this flattery?
Or whether shall I say, mine eye saith true,
And that your love taught it this alchemy,
To make of monsters and things indigest
Such cherubins as your sweet self resemble,
Creating every bad a perfect best,
As fast as objects to his beams assemble?
O 'tis the first; 'tis flattery in my seeing,

[1] Take hold of.
[2] The eye's.
[3] The eye.

And my great mind most kingly drinks it up:
Mine eye well knows what with his gust is 'greeing,
And to his palate doth prepare the cup:
  If it be poison'd, 'tis the lesser sin
  That mine eye loves it and doth first begin.

Not even Shakespeare can develop long allegorical metaphors of this sort without falling into inconsistencies and absurdities, and the suggestion in the last lines, that a poisoner's guilt is lessened if he himself genuinely loves poison, is one which 'no virtue can digest'. But before commenting further on the style of these two sonnets, I will remark that they make explicit what in other sonnets written during absence is so merely implicit, so fleetingly present, that we may well fail to notice it, namely the element of recognised but loved illusion. In many of the sonnets to or about the 'Dark Lady' the fact of recognised and often *hated* illusion is clearly and explicitly present (for example, at the beginning of 148,

O me, what eyes hath love put in my head,
Which have no correspondence with true sight!),

but perhaps there is some element of recognised though *loved* illusion, some recognition that the poet's happiness is what Swift called 'a perpetual possession of being well deceived', in many of those apparently whole-hearted sonnets where the friend appears as the archetype of all other beauties. Certainly, in the sonnets I have quoted from Petrarch and Ronsard there is no similar suggestion of illusion, or of possible illusion: they declare that all the beauties they have been describing are no compensation for the loss or absence of the beloved, or that they can no longer enjoy these things without her, but they never either declare or suggest that love has made them no longer capable of seeing things as they really are. Is it, in fact, possible to perceive in Shakespeare, who seems to have had little interest in doctrines and ideas for their own sakes and to have been little troubled by apparent inconsistencies and contradictions between the various patterns he perceived in the carpet of life or between the images which appeared at different times in the mirror he held up to Nature—is it possible to perceive in him, together with so much else, some anticipation of that elaborate philosophy of illusion as the only good and the only source of happiness that was to be developed by Leopardi? Such a defence of illusion, of inwardness against outwardness, would be by no means experientially or emotionally inconsistent with the strong element of defiance which I have noticed in my examination of Shakespeare's sonnets about Time. Be that as it may, sonnets 113 and 114, though far below Shakespeare's best, would seem to be valuable as commentaries upon many where his actual poetic achievement is far greater.

In these two sonnets, as in several others, Shakespeare is not spontaneously apprehending in and through metaphor, but, as it were, translating into metaphor or metaphorical allegory 'thoughts' which could be fully expressed in prose. This is what most other Elizabethan sonneteers were almost continually doing: consider, for example, the following lines (5–8) from the eighth[1] of Daniel's *Delia* sonnets, the one beginning 'Thou, poor heart, sacrific'd unto the fairest':

> And you, mine eyes, the agents of my heart,
> Told the dumb message of my hidden grief,
> And oft with careful tears, with silent art,
> Did 'treat the cruel fair to yield relief.

Contrast this with lines 9–10 of Shakespeare's sonnet 23 ('As an imperfect actor on the stage'):

> O, let my looks be then the eloquence
> And dumb presagers of my speaking breast.

Shakespeare is here speaking a language that comes naturally to him, whereas Daniel is simply translating prose statement into metaphors that get neither him nor us any further. Daniel's *Delia* is full of such translation, and he often tediously extends this translated metaphor into allegory, as in sonnet 45, a sufficiently typical example:

> Read in my face a volume of despairs,
> The wailing Iliads of my tragic woe,
> Drawn with my blood and painted with my cares,
> Wrought by her hand that I have honour'd so;
> Who, whilst I burn, she sings at my soul's wrack,
> Looking aloft from turret of her pride;
> There my soul's tyrant joys her in the sack

---

[1] I again quote from Arundell Esdaile's edition, where the numbering is that of the 1623 edition of Daniel's *Works*.

Of her own seat, whereof I made her guide.
There do these smokes that from affliction rise
Serve as an incense to a cruel dame,
A sacrifice thrice-grateful to her eyes
Because their power serves to exact the same.[1]
    Thus ruins she, to satisfy her will,
    The temple where her name was honour'd still.

It is when Shakespeare writes like this, or in a manner approaching this, that he is most Elizabethan and least Shakespearean.[2] Here there is an interesting and characteristic difference between him and the two great poets with whom I have been comparing and contrasting him. Petrarch and Ronsard, especially Ronsard, are often at their very best, and also, in a profound sense, most original, when they are most traditional, when they are employing, with variations, some well-established pattern or formula, or elaborating upon some well-established and immediately recognisable topic—when, in fact, they are writing in a manner which some foreign poet might, in a happy moment, successfully imitate, or even equal, as Surrey did in 'Set me wheras the sun doth parch the green', a beautiful imitation of Petrarch's sonnet 145, *Pommi ove 'l sole occide i fiori e l'erba*, where Petrarch himself was partly imitating the last two stanzas of Horace's *Integer vitae* (I, xxii),

> Pone me pigris ubi nulla campis
> arbor aestiva recreatur aura, *etc*.[3]

Shakespeare, on the other hand, is nearly always at his worst when he is most like other Elizabethan sonneteers, or when he is (or seems to be) most imitable. This may partly be because, with the exception of Sidney at his very best, there was no other Elizabethan sonneteer of anything like the stature of Petrarch or Ronsard, but I think it is chiefly explained by the fact that what distinguishes Shakespeare's best sonnets is his use of metaphor, that he so habitually thought and felt in metaphors that he

---

[1] The unhappy phrase 'the same' too often supplies Daniel with a rhyme.

[2] Some of the worst examples of this kind of writing in Shakespeare's sonnets are numbers 24, 45, 46 and 47. It is worth remarking that 44 is immensely superior to its three successors, and that this generally undistinguished group (43–52) of sonnets written during absence concludes with the magnificent 'So am I as the rich, whose blessed key'. If, as seems not unreasonable to suppose, all the sonnets in this group were written during the same period of absence, here is further proof that Shakespeare was always capable of slipping back into a manner which he might be supposed to have outgrown.

[3] For a detailed examination of the relations between these three poems see my *Translating Horace*, 1956, pp. 94 ff.

could not do without them, and that, when he had been unable to accumulate a sufficient imaginative pressure, he collapsed into mechanical similes, mere 'translation' into metaphor, and cumbrous allegories such as are so frequent in Daniel and others, for whom metaphor was not really a natural and necessary mode of expression. Partly, no doubt, because of the preoccupation of so much modern criticism with what is called 'imagery', and of a tendency to describe almost anything but the plainest statement of fact as an 'image', the distinction between predominantly metaphorical and predominantly unmetaphorical writing, together with the distinction between those poets for whom metaphor is and those for whom it is not a natural and necessary mode of expression, has been too often overlooked. Many, perhaps most, of the best sonnets of Petrarch and Ronsard contain little of what can properly be described as metaphor, which also plays only a small part in the best Latin poetry,[1] but for Shakespeare, as for Pindar and Aeschylus, metaphor was a natural and necessary mode of expression.

3

The theme of 'compensation'

A natural transition from the preceding excursus to the subject of what I can only call the 'religiousness' of so many of Shakespeare's sonnets may be provided by a further consideration of the frequently recurring topic of 'compensation'. Hitherto I have referred to it only in connection with what I have called the 'catalogue of uncompensating delights', which we find in sonnets and poems written during the absence or after the loss of the beloved by Shakespeare, by Ronsard and Petrarch, and by Petrarch's medieval predecessors, both courtly and popular. This, though, is only the negative expression (and, with Shakespeare, only one of the negative expressions), only the obverse or corollary, of those great positive affirmations which are so characteristically Shakespearean and

---

[1] It is true that in reading much Latin poetry one sometimes gets the impression that the Latin language itself is mainly composed of dead metaphors, but with dead metaphors and such traditional and commonplace ones as 'smiling meadows', etc., I am not here concerned: I am concerned with new and striking metaphors which have spontaneously occurred to the poet as the only possible expression of what he has to say.

for which it is hard to find any real precedent in earlier poetry. Familiar as
they are, or should be, it will be well to have them before us, so that we
may become sufficiently penetrated with a sense of their uniqueness.

In at least three sonnets, two of which are among his very finest,
Shakespeare declares that his friend is a compensation for all his own
deficiencies of talent and fortune and for all his failures and disappointments.

25

Let those who are in favour with their stars
Of public honour and proud titles boast,
Whilst I, whom fortune of such triumph bars,
Unlook'd for[1] joy in that I honour most.
Great princes' favourites their fair leaves spread
But as the marigold at the sun's eye,
And in themselves their pride lies buried,
For at a frown they in their glory die.
The painful warrior famoused for fight,
After a thousand victories once foil'd,
Is from the book of honour razed quite,
And all the rest forgot for which he toil'd:
 Then happy I, that love and am beloved
 Where I may not remove nor be removed.

29

When, in disgrace with fortune and men's eyes,
I all alone beweep my outcast state,
And trouble deaf heaven with my bootless cries,
And look upon myself, and curse my fate,
Wishing me like to one more rich in hope,
Featur'd like him, like him with friends possess'd,
Desiring this man's art and that man's scope,
With what I most enjoy contented least;
Yet in these thoughts myself almost despising,
Haply I think on thee, and then my state,
Like to the lark at break of day arising
From sullen earth, sings hymns at heaven's gate:
 For thy sweet love rememb'red such wealth brings
 That then I scorn to change my state with kings.

[1] Probably = 'unheeded'.

In sonnet 37 there is a less memorable but perhaps more explicit treatment of the theme of 29: the contemplation, and as it were, appropriation of his friend's abundance is a compensation for all his own deficiencies:

> As a decrepit father takes delight
> To see his active child do deeds of youth,
> So I, made lame by fortune's dearest[1] spite,
> Take all my comfort of thy worth and truth.
> For whether beauty, birth, or wealth, or wit,
> Or any of these all, or all, or more,
> Entitled in thy parts do crowned sit,[2]
> I make my love engrafted to this store:
> So then I am not lame, poor, nor despis'd,
> Whilst that this shadow doth such substance give[3]
> That I in thy abundance am suffic'd
> And by a part of all thy glory live.
>   Look, what is best, that best I wish in thee:
>   This wish I have; then ten times happy me!

In sonnet 30 he declares that his friend is a compensation, not merely for many disappointments and unrealised hopes, but also for the loss of earlier friends:

> When to the sessions of sweet silent thought
> I summon up remembrance of things past,[4]

---

[1] Direst, hardest, most grievous. The adjective is of a different origin from *dear* = precious etc., although Spenser (who may have revived it), Shakespeare and other poets seem to have regarded it only as a peculiar poetic sense of the more familiar adjective.

[2] I have accepted, with some hesitation, this generally accepted emendation of the Quarto's

> Or any of these all, or all, or more
> Intitled in their parts, do crowned sit.

This would presumably mean: 'or others with a still better title to the parts allotted them.' If this reading were accepted, the place where these gifts and graces were 'sitting crowned' would remain unstated and would have to be inferred.

[3] The mere shadow, or image, of his friend's substance in the poet's imagination enormously substantiates and transubstantiates the poet.

[4] With Shakespeare's legal metaphor of a summoning to the sessions of thought I have long associated Rilke's theatrical metaphor, in the fourth of the *Duino Elegies*, of one sitting before the stage of his heart:

> Wer sass nicht bang vor seines Herzens Vorhang?
> Der schlug sich auf: die Szenerie war Abschied.

> ('Who's not sat tense before his own heart's curtain?
> Up it would go: the scenery was Parting.')

While, though, what comes to Shakespeare's sessions of thought inspires only pure lament

I sigh the lack of many a thing I sought,
And with old woes new wail my dear time's waste:
Then can I drown an eye, unus'd to flow,
For precious friends hid in death's dateless night,
And weep afresh love's long since cancell'd woe,
And moan the expense of many a vanish'd sight:
Then can I grieve at grievances foregone,
And heavily from woe to woe tell o'er
The sad account of fore-bemoaned moan,
Which I new pay as if not paid before.
    But if the while I think on thee, dear friend,
    All losses are restor'd and sorrows end.

The subject of lost friends and lost loves, which in this sonnet emerges only from a more general evocation of things loved and lost, becomes the main subject of sonnet 31, which may well have been written almost immediately afterwards and in which Shakespeare declares that all those he has lost and lamented are, as it were, reincarnated in his friend:

Thy bosom is endeared with all hearts,
Which I by lacking have supposed dead;
And there reigns Love, and all Love's loving parts,
And all those friends which I thought buried.
How many a holy and obsequious tear
Hath dear religious love stol'n from mine eye,
As interest of the dead, which now appear
But things remov'd that hidden in thee lie!
Thou art the grave where buried love doth live,
Hung with the trophies of my lovers gone,
Who all their parts of me to thee did give,
That due of many now is thine alone.
    Their images I lov'd I view in thee,
    And thou, all they, hast all the all of me.

Finally, in the magnificent sonnet 66 Shakespeare proclaims that his friend is a compensation, not merely for his own deficiencies and disappointments and losses, but for all that 'sea of troubles', those 'whips

over human transience, what appears on the stage of Rilke's heart inspires self-reproach and satire on the inadequacy and triviality of most human 'heart-work'. In the contrast between these two passages there is something of the contrast, not merely between Shakespeare and Rilke, but between Shakespeare's age and Rilke's age, an age in which the very significance of man and of his place in the world had been called in question.

and scorns of Time', which Hamlet declared that only fear of what might come after death could restrain a wise man from escaping once and for all by committing suicide:

> Tir'd with all these, for restful death I cry,
> As, to behold desert a beggar born,
> And needy nothing trimm'd in jollity,
> And purest faith unhappily forsworn,
> And gilded honour shamefully misplac'd,
> And maiden virtue rudely strumpeted,
> And right perfection wrongfully disgrac'd,
> And strength by limping sway disabled,
> And art made tongue-tied by authority,
> And folly, doctor-like, controlling skill,
> And simple truth miscall'd simplicity,
> And captive good attending captain ill:
>> Tir'd with all these, from these would I be gone,
>> Save that, to die, I leave my love alone.

Where, in previous European poetry, from the Greeks until Shakespeare's own day, can we find any form whatever of this topic of 'compensation', let alone anything approaching Shakespeare's treatment of it? The only form of the topic in ancient poetry which I myself have been able to discover occurs in two passages where the poet declares (not perhaps very seriously) that, in order to be completely happy, he requires nothing whatever except the company of his beloved. The first of these passages, in which alone perhaps the topic clearly emerges as a topic and finds really memorable expression, occurs in the last two stanzas of Horace's *Integer vitae* (*Odes*, I, xxii), where the poet declares that he would continue to adore his Lalage even if he were condemned to live in the Frozen or in the Torrid Zone:

> Pone me pigris ubi nulla campis
> arbor aestiva recreatur aura,
> quod latus mundi nebulae malusque
> Iuppiter urget;

> pone sub curru nimium propinqui
> solis in terra domibus negata:
> dulce ridentem Lalagen amabo,
> dulce loquentem.

('Place me where on frozen expanses not one
tree's revived again with the breath of Summer,
region where all times a malign and cloud-filled
heaven is brooding;

place me where beneath a too closely earthwards
charioteering sun not a dwelling rises,
I'll adore my Lalage's pleasant laughter,
pleasant discoursing.')

The second passage occurs in one of the elegies traditionally, though
probably falsely, ascribed to Tibullus (III, xix, 9–12; IV, xiii in the
Renaissance editions):

Sic ego secretis possum bene vivere silvis,
    qua nulla humano sit via trita pede.
tu mihi curarum requies, tu nocte vel atra
    lumen, et in solis tu mihi turba locis.

('Thus I am able to live well in the secrecy of forests where no path is
worn by a human foot. You for me are rest from cares, you even in
dark night are light, and in solitary places you for me are crowd.') The
phrases in the last two lines of this passage (*tu mihi curarum requies*, etc.)
are not characteristic of ancient love-poetry and are much nearer to what
we often find in hymns and invocations to the gods. There is, however,
a curious passage in the *Agamemnon* (896 ff.), where Clytemnestra (perhaps
with what Aeschylus intended to appear as hypocritical and impious
hyberbole) addresses her returned husband as 'the stabling's watch-dog,
ship's saving cable, high roof's long-robed column, father's only son,
land shown past hope to sailors, fairest day beheld after storm, well-
spring to thirsty traveller'. It is significant that, of the one or two passages
I have been able to discover in ancient love-poetry where there is some
approach to the Shakespearean topic of 'compensation', one should
contain that religious, or semi-religious, phraseology which, though
highly uncharacteristic of ancient love-poetry, is most characteristic of the
medieval poets of Courtly Love and their successors. Nevertheless, despite
their religious phraseology, it is difficult to feel certain about the exact
meaning and emphasis of these lines ascribed to Tibullus, for the poet
has previously expressed the wish that his beloved may seem lovely

to him alone, so that he may be free from jealousy, and has exclaimed:

> Nil opus invidia est; procul absit gloria vulgi,

a line which seems to mean: 'There is nothing here to excite envy, and as for me, I can dispense with that vulgar fame which depends on the mere possession of something envied by others.' Hence his declaration that his beloved's society will be sufficient even in solitude may well be mingled with the reflection, wholly inadmissible for a medieval courtly lover, that he can well dispense with the pleasure which envious admiration of her might excite in him in return for being free from the jealousy which such pleasure would certainly exact as its price. In other words, it is difficult to decide whether the main topic here is that of the all-sufficingness of love or that of the advantages of loving one who excites neither admiration nor envy in others—a paradoxical topic which may be said to culminate in Tasso's famous stanzas *Against Beauty* and Donne's Second Elegy, *The Anagram*, on the advantages of marrying an old and ugly woman rather than a young and handsome one.[1] It is, then, only in the Horatian stanzas that some approach to the characteristically Shakespearean topic of love as compensation clearly and unambiguously emerges and finds memorable, if not very serious, expression. These stanzas, as I have already remarked, were imitated and expanded by Petrarch in his 145th sonnet, *Pommi ove 'l sole occide i fiori e l'erba*; although, while Horace seems to imagine himself as sitting side by side with Lalage in these uncomfortable situations, Petrarch (how could he do otherwise?) merely declares that throughout these and all possible situations he will be what he has been and live as he has lived, continuing that sighing which has now lasted for three lustres:

> Sarò qual fui, vivrò com'io son visso,
> Continuando il mio sospir trilustre.

In Petrarch's sonnet, therefore, and in Surrey's charming paraphrase of it, which I will quote, the topic is rather that of 'eternity in love protested', the topic of Shakespeare's

---

[1] Because I have found it so difficult to follow the line of thought in this not very good or serious poem, and to decide on which topic the emphasis chiefly falls, I have consulted a far better classical scholar, who is inclined to think that the chief topic is, after all, what I have here called 'compensation', and who has offered the following summary: 'You are everything to me. I wish I were everything to you. I need only you. I swear no other woman would interest me—Fool that I am! I've made you realise your power. But even if you *are* notorious, I shall stay your slave.'

> Let me not to the marriage of true minds
> Admit impediments,

than that which I have called 'compensation'. For Petrarch's (and Surrey's) emphasis is not, like Shakespeare's in the sonnets we have been considering, upon the transfiguring and transubstantiating, redeeming and reincarnating, power of his love, but upon its mere persistence.

> Set me wheras the sunne doth parche the grene,
> Or where his beames do not dissolue the yse,
> In temperate heate where he is felt and sene,
> In presence prest of people madde or wise;
> Set me in hye or yet in lowe degree,
> In longest night or in the darkest daye,
> In clearest skye or where clowdes thickest be,
> In lusty youth or when my heeres are graye;
> Set me in heauen, in earth or els in hell,
> In hyll or dale or in the fomyng flood:
> Thrall or at large, aliue where so I dwell,
> Sicke or in health, in euyll fame or good,
> Hers will I be, and only with this thought
> Content my selfe, although my chaunce be nought.

There is, then, no real precedent in previous love-poetry either for Shakespeare's topic or for Shakespeare's treatment of it. There is perhaps something rather more like precedent for his development of a kind of corollary to this topic, for his declarations, in certain sonnets, that all he has, or might have, is not, or could not be, a compensation for the absence or loss of his friend. A special and limited form of this obverse or negative treatment of the topic of compensation is what I have called the 'catalogue of uncompensating delights', which we have found in sonnets written by Petrarch, Ronsard and Shakespeare during the absence or after the loss of the beloved. I have remarked that for this special and limited topic and situation I have found no precedent in ancient love-poetry; there is, though, an old Greek formula, often imitated by the Roman poets and by no means confined to love-poetry, of the type: 'A is good, B is better, but C is best of all', or 'Some prefer A to everything else, others prefer B, but I prefer C'. There is a fragment of Sappho in which she declares, 'Some say a troop of horsemen, some of footmen, some of ships is the finest thing upon black earth, but I say that it is whatsoever one loves.'[1] Horace, in the first ode of his First Book, *Maecenas atavis edite regibus*, after reviewing various ways of life that differ from his own, declares that, as for himself, the ivy crown of poetry links him with the gods above; and in the seventh ode of the same Book, *Laudabunt alii claram Rhodon aut Mitylenen*, declares that, while others may praise Rhodes or Mitylene, Ephesus or Corinth, Thebes or Delphi or Tempe, Argos or Mycenae, not even Lacedaemon or the plain of Larisa have so taken his own fancy as has Tibur, with its grotto and its stream, its grove and its orchards. But perhaps the most memorable use of this formula in all ancient poetry is in that passage beginning *Suave mari magno* with which Lucretius opens the second book of his *De Rerum Natura*, a passage thus rendered by Bacon towards the end of the First Book of his *Advancement of Learning*:

> It is a view of delight (saith he) to stand or walk upon the sea shore side and to see a ship tossed with tempest upon the sea; or to be in a fortified tower, and to see two battles join upon a plain. But it is a pleasure incomparable, for the mind of man to be settled, landed, and fortified in the certainty of truth; and from thence to descry and behold the errors, perturbations, labours, and wanderings up and down of other men.

Shakespeare comes very close to this formula in sonnet 91, by no means one of his least distinguished sonnets, but one where, as so often when he is most comparable with other poets, he is a good deal below his best:

> Some glory in their birth, some in their skill,
> Some in their wealth, some in their body's force;
> Some in their garments, though new-fangled ill;
> Some in their hawks and hounds, some in their horse;
> And every humour hath his adjunct pleasure,
> Wherein it finds a joy above the rest:
> But these particulars are not my measure;
> All these I better in one general best.
> Thy love is better than high birth to me,
> Richer than wealth, prouder than garments' cost,
> Of more delight than hawks or horses be;
> And having thee, of all men's pride I boast:
>   Wretched in this alone, that thou may'st take
>   All this away and me most wretched make.

---

[1] *Poetarum Lesbiorum Fragmenta*, ed. Lobel and Page, 1955, 16.

Far more characteristically Shakespearean is this sonnet's predecessor (90):

> Then hate me when thou wilt; if ever, now;
> Now, while the world is bent my deeds to cross,
> Join with the spite of fortune, make me bow,
> And do not drop in for an after-loss:
> Ah, do not, when my heart hath 'scap'd this sorrow,
> Come in the rearward of a conquer'd woe;
> Give not a windy night a rainy morrow,
> To linger out a purpos'd overthrow.
> If thou wilt leave me, do not leave me last,
> When other petty griefs have done their spite,
> But in the onset come: so shall I taste
> At first the very worst of fortune's might,
> And other strains of woe, which now seem woe,
> Compar'd with loss of thee will not seem so.

One can almost imagine the substance of this transposed into blank verse and delivered in some passionate adjuration by a Hamlet who, as the very crown of his misfortunes, had found reason to suspect the fidelity of Horatio. Indeed, the latter part of it recalls one of the soliloquies of Edgar in *King Lear* (IV, i, 3–6):

> The lowest and most dejected thing of fortune
> Stands still in esperance, lives not in fear.
> The lamentable change is from the best;[1]
> The worst returns to laughter.

In sonnet 92 Shakespeare goes even further in superlative, hyperbole, absoluteness, vehemence, sweepingness and generality (for any and all of these terms are equally appropriate), and declares that, since his life depends on the continuance of his friend's love, he need not fear the loss of it, for with that loss his life too will end:

[1] The change to be lamented is that from the best to anything less than the best; a change from the worst can only be a change for the better. Behind this speech lie, perhaps, recollections, conscious or unconscious, of Ovid's *Ex Ponto*, II, ii, 31–2, which Shakespeare may well have found in some book of extracts:

> Fortuna miserrima tuta est,
> nam timor eventus deterioris abest.

('Fortune at its most wretched is safe, for fear of a worse outcome is absent'); and perhaps also of *Metamorphoses*, xiv, 488–90.

> But do thy worst to steal thyself away,
> For term of life thou art assured mine;
> And life no longer than thy love will stay,
> For it depends upon that love of thine.
> Then need I not to fear the worst of wrongs,
> When in the least of them my life hath end.
> I see a better state to me belongs
> Than that which on thy humour doth depend:
> Thou canst not vex me with inconstant mind,
> Since that my life on thy revolt doth lie.
> O, what a happy title do I find,
> Happy to have thy love, happy to die!
>   But what's so blessed-fair that fears no blot?
>   Thou may'st be false, and yet I know it not.

In ll. 7–8,

> I see a better state to me belongs
> Than that which on thy humour doth depend,

the way in which a kind of pagan Stoicism, a deliberate and willed exaltation of the self and of that with which it has become identified above the reach of change and fortune, mingles with that almost religious adoration of a person which would have been impossible before the advent of Christianity is characteristically and perhaps uniquely Shakespearean, and is magnificently repeated in one of Cleopatra's speeches (V, ii, 1–8):

> My desolation does begin to make
> A better life. 'Tis paltry to be Caesar;
> Not being Fortune, he's but Fortune's knave,
> A minister of her will; and it is great
> To do that thing that ends all other deeds,
> Which shackles accidents and bolts up change,
> Which sleeps, and never palates more the dung,
> The beggar's nurse and Caesar's.

Indeed, the 'hyperbolical', the universalising, the all-else-annihilating expressions of their love by Antony and Cleopatra, together with the occasional recognition by Antony (far more clearly and shatteringly, it is true, than by Shakespeare in the sonnets to his friend) that his happiness has been 'a perpetual possession of being well deceived', are often closer than anything else in the plays to some of the most characteristic expressions in the sonnets; and the concluding couplet of this sonnet may recall the reflections already suggested by sonnets 113 and 114,[1] that perhaps even in many of Shakespeare's most whole-hearted sonnets, where his friend appears as the archetype of all other beauties, there may be some element of recognised, though loved, illusion, some willingness to be what Swift called 'well deceived'. Be that as it may, it is perhaps significant that it is only in sonnets written, apparently, during some temporary misunderstanding or estrangement that we find this obverse or negative treatment of the topic of compensation, find Shakespeare declaring, not that his friend *is* a compensation for all that he himself lacks or has lost, but that the loss of his friend's love *would not be* compensated for by all that he has or might have. I have suggested that for this obverse or negative treatment of the topic there is perhaps something more like precedent in earlier poetry; nevertheless, it is only in sonnet 91, the least characteristically Shakespearean of these sonnets, that it is possible to perceive any real resemblance to the passages from Sappho, Horace and Lucretius which I have quoted. In comparison with Shakespeare's other sonnets, either on love as compensation or on love as a pre-eminent and irreplaceable good, the passage from Horace's *Integer vitae*, and even that from Sappho, are light and almost trivial. In weight and seriousness only, among the passages I have quoted, that from Lucretius on the supremacy of knowledge is at all comparable, and the only approaches in ancient poetry to anything like Shakespeare's passionately hyperbolical vehemence, intransigence, sweepingness, etc., are to be found, not in love-poetry, but in passages in epic or tragedy expressing hatred or defiance, passages like those where Achilles expresses his hatred for Agamemnon and Prometheus hurls his defiance at Zeus. It is almost impossible not to feel that in these and in most of the other sonnets I have been discussing Shakespeare is expressing what meant most to him, the faith he chiefly lived by, the values in which he most passionately believed, and that these were all centred upon the eternal miracle of human personality. Whether, both over and beyond this and in association with it, he had any other deep religious faith I find it impossible to decide: the one thing about which I am certain is that, for any real parallel with what he has written about the meaningfulness for him of his friend, we must turn to what certain religious poets have written about the all-compensatingness and all-sufficingness of their Master.

[1] See p. 199.

4

The 'religiousness' of Shakespeare's Love.
Shakespeare and Donne

> How many a holy and obsequious[1] tear
> Hath dear religious love stol'n from mine eye,
> As interest of the dead, which now appear
> But things remov'd that hidden in thee lie!
>
> (31, ll. 5–8)

It is interesting to observe how, from *A Lover's Complaint* to *Antony and Cleopatra*, Shakespeare, no doubt with varying degrees of seriousness and sometimes, perhaps, almost instinctively, no less than five times associates love with religion. In *A Lover's Complaint*, which was definitely ascribed to Shakespeare when it was printed with the Sonnets in 1609 and which, bad though it often is, I think we must regard as his, even if his very earliest poem, the woman making the 'complaint' relates how the young Don Juan who ruined and deserted her declared that she was the only woman he had ever loved, and that he had only pretended to love all the other women who had pursued him, among whom was a nun, with whom

> Religious love put out Religion's eye.
>
> (l. 250)

When Benvolio offers to show him beauties in comparison with whom his Rosaline will seem a crow, Romeo replies:

> When the devout religion of mine eye
> Maintains such falsehood, then turn tears to fires!
>
> (I, ii, 93–4)

In reply to his mother's question, 'What have I done?', Hamlet exclaims:

---

[1] A combination of the senses 'dutiful' and 'proper to obsequies'.

O such a deed
As from the body of contraction plucks
The very soul, and sweet religion makes
A rhapsody of words.

(III, iv, 45–8)

Dolabella says to Cleopatra:

Madam, as thereto sworn by your command,
Which my love makes religion to obey,
I tell you this.

(V, ii, 198–200)

Mention of *Antony and Cleopatra* prompts me to ask whether any ancient poet could possibly have written anything approaching Antony's exclamation:

Let Rome in Tiber melt, and the wide arch
Of the rang'd empire fall! Here is my space.
Kingdoms are clay; our dungy earth alike
Feeds beast as man; the nobleness of life
Is to do thus, when such a mutual pair
And such a twain can do't.[1]

(I, i, 33–8)

When the young Yeats declared that 'Shakespeare cared little for the State, the source of all our judgements, apart from its shows and splendours, its turmoils and battles, its flamings out of the uncivilised heart',[2] he was no doubt indulging in unscholarly exaggeration, but I think he was much nearer the truth than those many modern scholars who have tried to represent Shakespeare as a kind of continuer of *The Mirror for Magistrates*. This, though, is a digression: what I am here concerned with is what I can only call the 'religiousness' of so many of Shakespeare's expressions of his love.

---

[1] A passage that may perhaps be illuminatingly compared with one of the characteristic utterances of a later individualist: 'I hate the idea of causes, and if I had to choose between betraying my country and betraying my friend, I hope I should have the guts to betray my country.' (E. M. Forster, 'What I believe' in *Two Cheers for Democracy*, 1951, p. 78.)

[2] 'At Stratford-on-Avon' in *Essays*, 1924, p. 130.

There is indeed a certain kind of religiousness in the love-poetry of other sonneteers and other love-poets, from the Troubadours and Minnesingers and early Italian poets onwards, but partly, though by no means mainly, because it is addressed to women, it does not seem to me really comparable with Shakespeare's. A detailed comparison and contrast between Shakespeare's sonnets and those of Petrarch, the chief model and inspiration of so many later sonneteers, would be both interesting and profitable, but I cannot here attempt it, and must confine myself to the briefest possible enumeration of some things in Petrarch that we do not find in Shakespeare: courtship, languishing adoration, protests against Laura's 'cruelty'; many expressions of a kind of Christianised 'Platonism', declaring that Laura's beauty of form and spirit has raised his thoughts and his soul from earth to heaven, together with occasional expressions of a desire to escape from this bondage of passion, which, as he made St. Augustine, in his dialogue the *Secretum*, lead him to confess, was not really raising his soul to heaven, but confining it to earth. Of all this, so frequent in later sonneteers, there is nothing in the sonnets which Shakespeare addressed to his friend. On the other hand, even apart from Shakespeare's characteristic manner of expression, I can find nothing in other love-poetry really comparable with his many variations on the theme of what I have called 'compensation', and I think the only things in other poetry of which they really 'remind' me are some of those poems where George Herbert expresses or, as it were, revivifies his conviction that his 'pearl of great price' is a more than sufficient compensation for all that either he himself or the world may have supposed him to have resigned or forgone; perhaps, too, certain things in Henry Vaughan, such as the beautiful conclusion of the poem 'Silence and stealth of dayes!', one of those commemorating the death of his younger brother:

> Yet I have one *Pearle* by whose light
> All things I see,
> And in the heart of Earth, and night
> Find Heaven, and thee.

Such lines as the concluding couplet of sonnet 30,

> But if the while I think on thee, dear friend,
> All losses are restor'd and sorrows end,

are lines which Herbert certainly, and Vaughan possibly, might have addressed to Christ. To a Christian willing to consider them carefully, and to refrain from reading into them implications which he might wish to be there but which are not recognisably there, many of Shakespeare's more 'hyperbolical' sonnets must seem in the strict sense idolatrous, for in them the supreme object of the poet's contemplation is a human life, regarded, not as the symbol or incarnation of something that transcends it, but as in itself transcendent: all-supplying, all-restoring, all-sufficing. Shakespeare might almost be saying, blasphemously parodying St. Paul: 'I live; yet not I, but my friend liveth in me.'

In several of his poems George Herbert has dwelt on the possibility and desirability of writing a kind of religious love-poetry and has declared that, while other poets address love-poems to their mistresses, he will address 'approaches' and 'window-songs' to Christ.[1] The fact cannot be demonstrated, but I find it hard not to suppose that Herbert's stylistic models for his so intimate and colloquial religious love-poems were some of the more serious of Donne's *Songs and Sonets*,[2] the only secular love-poems (the term seems necessary in order to distinguish them from Herbert's religious love-poems) of which Shakespeare's more 'religious' sonnets occasionally remind me. I am not thinking so much of such things as the probably deliberate and, for a true Platonist, blasphemous anti-Platonism of

> If ever any beauty I did see,
> Which I desir'd, and got, 'twas but a dreame of thee

in *The good-morrow*, which might be compared with Shakespeare's declarations (never, like Donne's, with any suggestion of deliberate flouting or parody) that all other beauties are but shadows of his friend's substance, or of such things as Donne's provocatively blasphemous attribution to his mistress, in *The Dreame*, of the power to read thoughts directly, or of the blasphemously hyperbolical compliments to various noble patronesses in some of his presumably later poems, for of this kind of learned and elaborate fooling there is no trace in Shakespeare. I am thinking rather of those poems where Donne declares that he and his beloved are a whole world in themselves, that 'nothing else is', that princes do but play them, and that

[1] See especially the poem *Dulnesse*.
[2] Herbert could have known them only in manuscript, since Donne's poems were not printed until the year of Herbert's death. Herbert's mother, though, had been for many years an intimate friend of Donne's.

> All other things to their destruction draw
> Only our love hath no decay.

Elsewhere[1] I have attempted to analyse what seemed to me the dis-
tinguishing characteristics of these poems, which, I insisted, were not
poems of courtship but poems about the oneness and all-sufficingness of
two lovers' unalterably established love, and I suggested that perhaps
what had puzzled many critics was, as it were, the enclosedness both
of the poems and of the experience they expressed—the fact that Donne
never allowed himself to be deflected from his concentration upon the
thisness of this experience into either descriptions of visual beauty or
into any kind of transcendentalism, into any reflections upon the possibility of sublimating this experience into anything other than itself.
There is a 'religiousness' (or an idolatrousness) about these poems of
Donne's, a concentration upon the actual, as distinct from the possible,
meaningfulness, or all-meaningfulness, of the relationship, together
with a passionately hyperbolical vehemence and sweepingness, which
seems to me more comparable than anything else in any other love-
poetry with the 'religiousness' of Shakespeare's sonnets. Here too appears
that theme of 'compensation' which plays so great a part in Shakespeare's
sonnets, for I find it impossible not to feel that Donne, whose prospects
of worldly advancement seemed at the time, and long continued to
seem, irreparably blighted by the consequences of his clandestine marriage, is trying to persuade himself, or at least defiantly proclaiming,
that, in return for the private world which he and his wife have been
able to create, the public world has been 'well lost'.

Consider *The Canonization*, in the first stanza of which, although
he does not positively declare, as Shakespeare might have done, that the
various activities and professions he mentions are nothing to him in
comparison with his love, Donne nevertheless alludes to them in such
a manner and in such a tone of impatient contempt as to imply that this
is so:

> For Godsake hold your tongue, and let me love,
>   Or chide my palsie, or my gout,
> My five gray haires, or ruin'd fortune flout,
>   With wealth your state, your minde with Arts improve,
>   Take you a course, get you a place,

---

[1] *The Monarch of Wit: an analytical and comparative Study of the Poetry of John Donne*, 6th ed.,
1962, pp. 213 ff.

> Observe his honour, or his grace,
> Or the Kings reall, or his stamped face[1]
> Contemplate, what you will, approve,
> So you will let me love.

Then, after asking who has been injured by their love and again alluding to various preoccupations and professions with the same impatient contempt, Donne devotes a stanza to the old *double-entendre* of 'dying' for love, which he wittily associates with the fable of the Phoenix, declaring that 'we two being one, are it'; and in the next stanza, returning to the unmetaphorical sense of 'dying', declares that, if they cannot live by love, they can at least die by it and be buried in poems that will lead future ages to regard them as love's saints:

> And thus invoke us: You whom reverend love
>   Made one anothers hermitage;
> You, to whom love was peace, that now is rage;
> Who did the whole worlds soule contract, and drove
>   Into the glasses of your eyes
>   (So made such mirrors, and such spies,

[1] This must have been written after James I's accession in 1603 and therefore some considerable time after Donne's marriage in December 1601. There is every reason to believe that all the poems I am considering were partly inspired by Donne's experience of married love, or—to put the matter in another way—that the kind of love they celebrate was one which Donne had not experienced before his marriage; whether, though, they were actually addressed to his wife is another matter. The second stanza of *The Anniversarie*, a poem from which I have quoted two lines on p. 218, begins:

> Two graves must hide thine and my coarse,
> If one might, death were no divorce.

Now although it is true that when Donne's wife died in 1617 he then intended, as his Latin epitaph upon her reveals, to be buried beside her in St. Clement Danes, that he eventually requested in his will that he should be buried in St. Paul's, and that this change of mind might be taken to suggest that he did not regard as absolutely binding the custom of burying a husband in his predeceased wife's grave and a wife in her predeceased husband's, it is hard not to suppose that in the lines quoted he means, *not* 'If we could die at the same moment, and be buried in the same grave, death would be no divorce', but 'If we were married, we could be buried in one grave, but, since we are not, we shall have to be buried separately'. In other words, he imagines the person addressed as *not* being his wife. His wife is both in this poem and not in it; or she may be said to share it with a creature of Donne's imagination, a creature she herself has enabled Donne's imagination to create. Similarly, she is both in and not in *The Canonization*, a poem which she shares with an imaginary mistress suggested partly by herself and partly by recollections of Ovid's *Amores*. The person to whom all these poems are addressed is always imagined as a mistress, never as a wife—except in so far as Donne is able to feel as assured of the equality and permanence of her love for him as if she were his wife. While his clandestine courtship and marriage were 'romantic', his married life, as many letters from 'my hospital at Mitcham' abundantly reveal, was not, and it may be that the imagined mistress of these poems was in some sort a compensation. Relevant, perhaps, are certain passages in his sermons (*e.g.* ed. Potter and Simpson, Vols. I, 194, VIII, 251) where he speaks of his and other men's 'sinfull memory of old sins' and 'sinfull sorrow' that they could not continue in those sins.

> That they did all to you epitomize),
> Countries, Townes, Courts: Beg from above
> A patterne of your love!

The Canonization is full of Donne's characteristic energy, and its expressed conviction that the world has been well lost for love at least produces 'that willing suspension of disbelief for the moment which constitutes poetic faith'. What, though, keeps recurring to me after 'the moment', and suggests to me some deep difference between this poem and Shakespeare's sonnets on the theme of 'compensation', is a strong suspicion that the germ of the whole poem was a passage in Ovid's *Amores*, which Donne has brilliantly transposed, transformed and extended. There are similar 'variations on a theme in Ovid's *Amores*' in some other of the *Songs and Sonets* and in several of the *Elegies*.[1] In the *Amores* the young Ovid, like Propertius, seems to be continually mocking at Augustus's campaign to purify Roman morals, and in the first line of this passage, which concludes the tenth elegy of his Second Book,

> Felix, quem Veneris certamina mutua rumpunt!

the phrase *Felix, quem* has the appearance of being a deliberate parody of those verses and sentences in which various poets and philosophers had declared who was the truly happy man: 'Happy he' who knows the causes of things, who has achieved the Golden Mean, who knows the rustic gods, who dies for his country, and so forth.

> Felix, quem Veneris certamina mutua rumpunt!
>   di faciant leti causa sit ista mei!
> induat adversis contraria pectora telis
>   miles et aeternum sanguine nomen emat:
> quaerat avarus opes et, quae lassarit arando,
>   aequora periuro naufragus ore bibat;
> at mihi contingat Veneris languescere motu,
>   cum moriar,[2] medium solvar et inter opus,

[1] See my *The Monarch of Wit*, pp. 55–66, 74–7 (the *Elegies*), p. 149 (*The Indifferent*) and pp. 188–90 (*The Sunne Rising*).

[2] The position of *cum moriar* is harsh and unusual. In the ninth-century Puteaneus manuscript at Paris, on which most texts are based, a later (eleventh-century) hand has given these two lines as:

> At mihi, cum moriar, Veneris languescere motu
>   eveniat . . .

which, though easier and clearer, should perhaps be regarded either as an interpretation or as an unauthentic emendation.

atque aliquis nostro lacrimans in funere dicat
'conveniens vitae mors fuit ista tuae'.

('Happy he whom Venus's mutual contests bring to his end! May the
gods make that the cause of my decease! Let the soldier present his breast
to opposing darts and purchase an eternal name with his blood; let the
miser go in search of riches and, shipwrecked, drink with his perjured
mouth the waves his ploughing vessel has left behind: may it be mine,
though, when I die, to be enfeebled by the motions of love, and may I
collapse in mid-act! And may some weeper at my funeral declare:
"Suitable to your life was that death of yours".') It is true that the 'love'
which Donne celebrates in *The Canonization* is something more than
Ovid's *Veneris certamina mutua* and *Veneris motus*, and that his transformation of Ovid's epigrammatic mourner at the funeral into the 'all'
who shall invoke Donne and his partner as love's saints is a variation
very remote from the original theme; nevertheless, whatever element
of real conviction may have co-operated or supervened, it is hard not
to suppose that the initial inspiration of Donne's poem was 'literary' in
a sense in which that of Shakespeare's sonnets on the theme of 'compensation' was not.

The first stanza of *The Sunne Rising*,[1] beginning 'Busie old Foole,
unruly Sunne', is another brilliant transformation of a passage in Ovid's
Amores,[2] although, after declaring that the sun only goes further to fare
worse, Donne then proceeds to elaborate the defiant and original hyperbole that he and his partner compose a world more complete and perfect
than the great globe itself:

> She is all States, and all Princes, I,
>   Nothing else is.
> Princes do but play us; compar'd to this,
> All honor's mimique; All wealth alchimie.
>   Thou sunne art halfe as happy 'as wee,
>   In that the world's contracted thus;
>   Thine age askes ease, and since thy duties bee
>   To warme the world, that's done in warming us.
> Shine here to us, and thou art every where;
> This bed thy center is, these walls, thy spheare.

[1] The line in this first stanza,

> Goe tell Court-huntsmen, that the King will ride,

proves that this poem also was written after King James's accession.

[2] I, xiii: see *The Monarch of Wit*, pp. 188–90.

The same hyperbole appears in the second and third stanzas of *The good-morrow*:

> And now good morrow to our waking soules,
> Which watch not one another out of feare;
> For love, all love of other sights controules,
> And makes one little roome, an every where.
> Let sea-discoverers to new worlds have gone,
> Let Maps to other, worlds on worlds have showne,
> Let us possesse one world, each hath one, and is one.
>
> My face in thine eye, thine in mine appeares,
> And true plaine hearts doe in the faces rest,
> Where can we finde two better hemispheares
> Without sharpe North, without declining West?

In these poems there is some approximation to Shakespeare's character-istic theme of 'compensation', to his sweepingness, and to what I have called his 'religiousness', although even here one has the impression that Donne, in comparison with Shakespeare, is not being, what the youthful Mrs. Humphry Ward is reported to have wished that her Uncle Matthew would more often be, 'wholly serious'. Many, if not most, of Shakes-peare's contemporaries would perhaps have regarded the term 'witty' as a sufficiently complimentary description of even his most moving sonnets, but Shakespeare, when expressing what means most to him, is never witty in Donne's manner. One is reminded of that temptation from which Donne, in *The Litanie*, a more orthodoxly 'religious' poem, characteristically prayed to be delivered:

> When we are mov'd to seeme religious
> Only to vent wit, Lord deliver us.

To 'vent wit' was always one of Donne's keenest pleasures and most besetting temptations, and even in the poems I have mentioned I am not sure whether this rather than, as with Shakespeare, a profound conviction, was not the main source of his inspiration. In their defiance and their sweepingness there is something Shakespearean, but, on the other hand, splendid as they are, do they not convey some impression of bravado, theatricality, and even attitudinising, such as we never find in Shakes-peare's sonnets—something of the bravado and contemptuous defiance of one who has, or who is pleased for the moment to regard himself as having, in modern phraseology, 'contracted out'? Did this paradoxical antithesis between the lovers' world and the great world arise in Donne as the spontaneous expression of a profound and permanent way of thinking and feeling, or did it suddenly present itself to him as a wonderful subject for the venting of wit and metamorphosing of Ovid? I have said that these poems, like Shakespeare's sonnets, have a 'passionately hyperbolical vehemence', but I must confess that I have never felt quite happy about the common attribution of 'passionateness' to Donne's love-poetry. It certainly communicates a tremendous energy, but, if we are to describe this as 'passionateness', is it not perhaps more akin to the passionateness of an actor than to the passionateness of Shakespeare?

Let us have before us three sonnets which I have not previously quoted and which, both in their likeness and their unlikeness, it is especially illuminating to compare with these poems of Donne's.

57

Being your slave, what should I do but tend
Upon the hours and times of your desire?
I have no precious time at all to spend,
Nor services to do, till you require.
Nor dare I chide the world-without-end hour
Whilst I, my sovereign, watch the clock for you,
Nor think the bitterness of absence sour
When you have bid your servant once adieu;
Nor dare I question with my jealous thought
Where you may be, or your affairs suppose,
But, like a sad slave, stay and think of nought
Save, where you are how happy you make those.
　　So true a fool is love that in your will,
　　Though you do any thing, he thinks no ill.

Although here, as in Donne's poems, there is a complete absence of the theologising, philosophising and 'transcendentalism' which we often (though by no means always) find in Petrarch, and although Shakespeare's desire, like Donne's, terminates—to employ scholastic terminology—upon its object, there emerges a profound difference, which may, it is true, be related to the fact that Donne's poems are not about friendship but about perfect love between man and woman—the difference that, while Shakespeare insists upon the nothingness of his own life, and of all that the world can offer him, apart from his share in the life of his friend, Donne insists on the nothingness of the world in comparison with their mutual love, and that, while Shakespeare habitually speaks of a 'you' and a 'me', Donne, in these poems, habitually speaks of an 'us'. Except perhaps for *A nocturnall upon S. Lucies day* and *Twicknam garden*, that curious, not very serious, and characteristically Donnish variation on the Petrarchan theme of the lover surrounded by beautiful sights which are no compensation for the absence, loss or unresponsiveness of the beloved, except for these, I can recall no passage in Donne's secular, as distinct from his divine, poems where he speaks, in a manner at all approaching that in which Shakespeare so continually does, of the nothingness of his own life apart from that of his beloved. In sonnet 109 Shakespeare comes perhaps as close as anywhere else to Donne's declaration that 'nothing else is', yet how different is his accent!

> O, never say that I was false of heart,
> Though absence seem'd my flame to qualify.
> As easy might I from myself depart
> As from my soul, which in thy breast doth lie:
> That is my home of love: if I have ranged,
> Like him that travels I return again,
> Just to the time, not with the time exchanged,
> So that myself bring water for my stain.
> Never believe, though in my nature reign'd
> All frailties that besiege all kinds of blood,
> That it could so preposterously be stain'd,
> To leave for nothing all thy sum of good;
>   For nothing this wide universe I call,
>   Save thou, my rose; in it thou art my all.

So too in 112:

> Your love and pity doth the impression fill
> Which vulgar scandal stamp'd upon my brow;
> For what care I who calls me well or ill,
> So you o'er-green my bad, my good allow?
> You are my all-the-world, and I must strive
> To know my shames and praises from your tongue;
> None else to me, nor I to none alive,

That my steel'd sense or changes right or wrong.[1]
In so profound abysm I throw all care
Of others' voices, that my adder's sense
To critic and to flatterer stopped are.
Mark how with my neglect I do dispense:[2]
      You are so strongly in my purpose bred
      That all the world besides methinks are dead.

(In this sonnet it is impossible not to regret that the force of the characteristically Shakespearean personifications and metaphors is to some extent
weakened by clumsy inversions and expletives: 'doth the impression fill',
'stoppèd are', 'do dispense'. Donne would probably have boggled at
'stoppèd are', although he often permits himself similar inversions,
incompatible though they are with his predominantly colloquial style:
for example, in *The Dreame*:

That love is weake, where fear's as strong as hee;
'Tis not all spirit, pure, and brave,
If mixture it of *Feare*, *Shame*, *Honor*, have.)

   In sonnet after sonnet and in one universalising and, as it were,
annihilating metaphor after another Shakespeare has conveyed the
impression that there is nothing either in this world or above it that
can compare with the meaningfulness to him of his friend. 'A lover,'
one might say, adapting Fabian's confirmatory words to Sir Andrew
Aguecheek about the 'cowardice' of the disguised Viola, 'a most devout
lover, religious in it': far more literally, unmetaphorically, unpretendingly
'religious' than Donne in those poems which, of all other love-poems,
seem to me most comparable with some of Shakespeare's sonnets, far
closer to the all-else-annihilatingness, all-else-resigningness of the 'religious love-poetry' of George Herbert. At first glance Shakespeare's
sonnets may well seem far more traditional, far less surprisingly and
excitingly original than Donne's *Songs and Sonets*, with all their 'new-
found methods' and 'compounds strange'; and yet, when we attempt,
as I have been doing in this study, to compare Shakespeare with other
poets in poems where there is at least some apparent similarity of topic,

[1] 'No one else by whom my inflexible mind can be either rightly or wrongly changed
being either alive to my perception or I to his praise or blame.'
[2] 'Compound with, obtain a dispensation from', a common Shakespearean usage and
construction: 'Mark how I excuse my (apparent) neglect of you.'

we soon reach a point where difference begins to seem greater than resemblance, where differences in degree swell into differences in kind, and where Shakespeare seems comparable only with himself.

So far, in my attempt to illuminate the *thisness* of certain of Shakespeare's sonnets by dwelling on some of the profound differences between them and even those of Donne's poems which, of all other love-poetry, they most resemble, I may have conveyed the impression that my intention has been to exalt Shakespeare at the expense of Donne. Something still remains to be said about the difference between the relationships which the two poets are celebrating. When I remarked that *A nocturnall upon S. Lucies day* was the only deeply serious poem where Donne speaks, as Shakespeare so continually does, of the nothingness of his own life apart from that of his beloved, I might have added that this poem is about the actual or imagined death of the beloved, and that in other poems Donne is celebrating a oneness with his beloved such as Shakespeare seems seldom, if ever, to have experienced in his relations with his friend. The difference here is more than the difference between married love and what Chaucer called 'love of friendship'; it is the difference between love perfectly and love all too imperfectly returned. Nowhere in those poems which we may safely assume to have been inspired, or partly inspired, by Donne's experience of marriage is there any suggestion of those haunting doubts ('Thou may'st be false, and yet I know it not', 92), of that recurring sense of insecurity ('Wretched in this alone, that thou may'st take All this away and me most wretched make', 91), and of those faults and wrongs which, though the poet is ready to forgive them, have deeply pained him, which move like a dark undertone through Shakespeare's sonnets. Nowhere in these poems of Donne's is there less than perfect assurance that her love for him is equal to his love for her; nowhere, one might almost say, in Shakespeare's sonnets is there unmistakable evidence that Shakespeare really believed that his friend, in any deep and meaningful sense of the word, loved him at all. At most, perhaps, his friend 'quite liked him'. Saddest of all, I think, are those sonnets where Shakespeare speaks of their difference in rank, and sometimes of his own profession, as an insuperable barrier between them, for they suggest that he may actually have had to endure (and to forgive) just such slights and insults as Beethoven was always so groundlessly (and, I fear one must add, so ignobly) suspecting in his aristocratic friends and patrons—in, for example, that great and generous spirit the Archduke Rudolf, a friend not merely aristocratic but royal, who, when Beethoven was living in his palace, quietly gave orders that, when

their two bells rang simultaneously, Beethoven's was to be answered
first, lest he should feel himself slighted.

> Let me confess that we two must be twain,
> Although our undivided loves are one:
> So shall those blots that do with me remain
> Without thy help by me be borne alone.
> In our two loves there is but one respect,[1]
> Though in our lives a separable[2] spite,
> Which, though it alter not love's sole effect,
> Yet doth it steal sweet hours from love's delight.
> I may not evermore acknowledge thee,
> Lest my bewailed guilt should do thee shame,
> Nor thou with public kindness honour me,
> Unless thou take that honour from thy name:[3]
> >   But do not so; I love thee in such sort
> >   As, thou being mine, mine is thy good report.
>
> >   (36)

What was Shakespeare's 'bewailed guilt'? The guilt, I fear, of not being
quite a gentleman and of not merely having been associated but, even
after his friend had 'taken him up', of continuing to be associated with
what Mrs. Quickly called 'these harlotry players'—a 'blot', a perpetual
cause of social embarrassment, which the coat of arms he had successfully
applied for had not even begun to remove.

> O, for my sake do you with Fortune chide,
> The guilty goddess of my harmful deeds,
> That did not better for my life provide
> Than public means which public manners breeds.
> Thence comes it that my name receives a brand;
> And almost thence my nature is subdu'd
> To what it works in, like the dyer's hand:
> Pity me then and wish I were renew'd.
>
> >   (111)

---

[1] Regard, affection.
[2] Separating.
[3] How it could ever have been supposed (by Samuel Butler and others) that Shakespeare's
friend was other than a man of exalted rank I have never been able to understand: is it conceivable that Shakespeare could have spoken of a social equal's 'honouring him with public
kindness'?

Sonnet 117 reads almost like an apology for having spent time in writing plays for the 'unknown' public instead of in writing something, or performing some other services, for his 'private friend':

> Accuse me thus: that I have scanted all
> Wherein I should your great deserts repay;
> Forgot upon your dearest love to call,
> Whereto all bonds do tie me day by day;
> That I have frequent been with unknown minds,
> And given to time your own dear-purchas'd right;
> That I have hoisted sail to all the winds
> Which should transport me farthest from your sight.
> Book both my wilfulness and errors down,
> And on just proof surmise accumulate;
> Bring me within the level of your frown,
> But shoot not at me in your waken'd hate:
>   Since my appeal says, I did strive to prove
>   The constancy and virtue of your love.

And sonnet 87 seems to declare 'You have made me feel that in every way I am too much your inferior, too much beneath your notice'. That it was Shakespeare who had been made to feel like this rouses a disgust with aristocratic pretension which it requires remembrance of such a friend and patron as Beethoven's Archduke Rudolf to counter-balance.

> Farewell! thou art too dear for my possessing,
> And like enough thou know'st thy estimate:
> The charter of thy worth gives thee releasing;
> My bonds in thee are all determinate.
> For how do I hold thee but by thy granting?
> And for that riches where is my deserving?
> The cause of this fair gift in me is wanting,
> And so my patent back again is swerving.
> Thyself thou gav'st, thy own worth then not knowing,
> Or me, to whom thou gav'st it, else mistaking;
> So thy great gift, upon misprision growing,[1]

---

[1] Resulting from a mistake or misunderstanding; perhaps 'growing, like a fruit, upon a stalk, or on a tree, or in a soil, of misunderstanding'.

Comes home again, on better judgment making.
Thus have I had thee, as a dream doth flatter,
In sleep a king, but, waking, no such matter.

And yet, despite all this, Shakespeare continued to love his friend and to
write those sonnets on the theme of what I have called 'compensation'.
Rilke used to maintain (it was, apparently, just one of those things which
he, like some other poets, somehow found it necessary to believe) that
no man was capable of loving as a woman could, and he assembled a
kind of private pantheon of great unrequited women lovers, *die grossen
Liebenden*, who had been content with *die besitzlose Liebe*, possessionless
love. He had never, it would seem (if he knew them at all), made any
profound study of Shakespeare's sonnets, where the most wonderful
expression of 'possessionless love' in all literature is to be found. I have
spoken of the 'religiousness' of so many of them, and have insisted that
with these the only real parallels are in certain kinds of religious poetry:
is not this, perhaps, another way of saying that they are expressions, not
of fulfilment or of full knowledge, but of faith—faith which the author
of the *Epistle to the Hebrews* (xi, 1) defined as 'the substance of things
hoped for, the evidence of things not seen'? For although Shakespeare
never employs Platonic or transcendental language, one cannot but feel
that his love immeasurably transcends its immediate object, even though
he himself may have been unaware of this, or, at least, unwilling to admit
it. Behind many, perhaps behind all, of his great affirmations one is
aware of an immense weight of conquered negation, but who can say
precisely what it was that he had to overcome? Evidence, sometimes
too strong to be disregarded, of his friend's unworthiness and all too
limited capacity to return his love? Or his own inclination, his own
temptation, to attend to such evidence, to dwell upon it, to interpret it
to his friend's, instead of to his own, discredit, the discredit of not having
loved strongly enough and singly enough to elicit a stronger love from
his friend?

Is it not because of this element of faith and conquered negation
that Shakespeare's finest sonnets communicate an intensity of inner
vibration such as we do not receive from Donne's love-poems? Those
poems are unique of their kind, and no one who can fully appreciate
them would wish them otherwise, but they are superficial in comparison with Shakespeare's sonnets, and, although it would be inadequate,
it would not be wholly inappropriate to describe them as glorious
fun. For a profundity, a plangency, an intensity of inner vibration more

comparable with that which some of Shakespeare's sonnets communicate
we must turn to some of Donne's religious poems:

> Seale then this bill of my Divorce to All,
> On whom those fainter beames of love did fall;
> Marry those loves, which in youth scattered bee
> On Fame, Wit, Hopes (false mistresses) to thee.
> Churches are best for Prayer, that have least light:
> To see God only, I goe out of sight:
>   And to scape stormy dayes, I chuse
>   An Everlasting night.[1]

As one contemplates in religious poetry such as Donne's and George
Herbert's and then in Shakespeare's sonnets the great resemblances and
the great differences in these expressions of what can best be described
as the life of faith, one seems to be standing at a place where two paths
diverge and to become aware of a distinction, not merely between
religion and what may be called religiousness, but also between religion
and the tragic view of life, in one or other of which man's profoundest
attempts to make sense of living have always ended and, it may be, will
always end. The adoration of Donne and Herbert is directed towards a
divine and invisible beloved, of whom their knowledge is imperfect but
in whom their faith is perfect, and the element of doubt and conflict in
their poetry concerns themselves and their own unworthiness. They
can never doubt that, if they themselves love worthily, their love will
be worthily returned. Shakespeare's adoration is directed towards a
mortal and visible beloved, whose worthiness and responsiveness he is
sometimes compelled to doubt, and one can never feel quite certain,
and perhaps Shakespeare himself could never feel quite certain, whether
what he is celebrating is the beloved or the love which the beloved has
inspired. This continual oscillation between doubt at the heart of assurance and assurance at the heart of doubt is the dramatically tragic and
tragically dramatic element in Shakespeare's sonnets, and it may well
be that it was in it and out of it that some of the greatest moments in
his tragedies arose.

> Had it pleas'd Heaven
> To try me with affliction; had they rain'd
> All kind of sores and shames on my bare head,

---

[1] *A Hymne to Christ, at the Authors last going into Germany.*

Steep'd me in poverty to the very lips,
Given to captivity me and my utmost hopes,
I should have found in some place of my soul
A drop of patience; but, alas, to make me
The fixed figure for the time of scorn
To point his slow and moving finger at!
Yet could I bear that too, well, very well;
But there, where I have garner'd up my heart,
Where either I must live, or bear no life;
The fountain from the which my current runs,
Or else dries up; to be discarded thence!
Or keep it as a cistern for foul toads
To knot and gender in![1]

Whether it was a beloved's actual unworthiness or the machinations of an Iago that could lead one to feel like this, to experience this, it was the perpetual possibility, 'in this vile world', of such 'strange mutations' that made Shakespeare not unwilling to 'yield to age'.

[1] *Othello*, IV, ii, 47–62.

First-line index of Sonnets
quoted or mentioned

(Note: Those of Shakespeare's Sonnets which have been merely referred to by number and without quotation are here marked with an asterisk. The Petrarch index includes canzoni as well as sonnets, and the Ronsard index includes a few odes and elegies.)

SHAKESPEARE

Other English Sonneteers

DANIEL

DRAYTON

DRUMMOND

SIDNEY

SPENSER

SURREY

Italian Sonneteers

MICHELANGELO

PETRARCH

TASSO

French Sonneteers

DESPORTES

DU BELLAY

RONSARD

General index

(Note: This index is intended to be useful: no attempt has been made to record every appearance of every proper name.)

2. General:
the first Roman poet to declare that lyrical poetry could confer immortality, 28; compared with Shakespeare on this topic, 31-2, 37-8; his metaphorical personifications compared with Shakespeare's, 31-2, 34-5; probably suggested the topic of poetic immortality to the Roman elegiac poets; 38, 40, 41, who, in their love-poetry, seldom approach his *gravitas*, 43-4; echoes of his Censorinus and Lollius odes in Petrarch's sonnets, 45, 47, 49; Petrarch's use of the word *carte* perhaps imitated from him, 45, note 2; kinds of self-dramatisation which Ronsard may have learnt from his Odes, 60; only once inserts his own name in the Odes, 63, note 1; the great master of the topic *carpe diem*, which he sometimes combines with that of *carpe florem*, 95-7; attempt to imagine Shakespeare writing sonnets on these topics, 99-100; Petrarch's imitation of the last two stanzas of *Inter vitae*, 105, 301, 208; the first Roman poet to use the metaphor of ploughing with wrinkles, 137; personifications of Time and Age, 138-9; his debt to the Greek lyric poets more demonstrable than that to his training in rhetoric, 152; a panegyrical topic which may have influenced some elaborations of the 'pastoral hyperbole' by English poets, 166; contrast between his procession of the seasons in *Diffugere nives* and that in one of Shakespeare's sonnets, 192; possible influence of a passage in his Epodes on one of Shakespeare's sonnets, 161, note 1.

Housman, A. E., regarded *Diffugere nives* as the most beautiful of all Latin poems, 30.

Huxley, Aldous, on George Herbert's 'inner weather', 13; on 'Tragedy and the whole Truth', 144-5.

hyperbole, literal and metaphorical meanings of the word, of which the use as a rhetorical term was suggested to treatise-writers by poets, not *vice versa*, 151-7; 'the pastoral hyperbole', 165-7.

JAGGARD, William, publisher of *The Passionate Pilgrim*, 14.

James I, King, allusion to his accesion in the 'mortal moon' sonnet, 14.

Johnson, Francis R., on 'Shakespearian Imagery and Senecan Imitation', 37, note.

Johnson, Samuel, impossible to dissociate the man from his work, 129; his strange remark that we had no poetic diction before Dryden, 136; on the importance of little things, 143; on the variety of *Hamlet*, 145; on Shakespeare's willingness to comprise an 'unwieldy sentiment' in 'words such as occur', 190.

Jonson, Ben, un-Shakespeareanness of some of his disciples, 50; his remark that Shakespeare 'needed braking', 193.

KASSNER, Rudolf, on the new depth-dimension given to the human consciousness by Christianity, 52, 106; on the 'world of the spirit', and the 'world of the soul', 125-6; on surrealism, 128; on the mythical and improbable life of Mozart, who 'might have had any face', 130.

Keats, John, the beginning, in his Odes, of a tendency to accept transience as the price of uniqueness, 118; passages in his letters where he seems to be groping towards a distinction similar to Kassner's between *Geist* and *Seele* (126-9):

declare that his mistress's reputation for beauty is an illusion created by himself, 43; on the topic *carpe florem*, 99; has the nearest approach in ancient poetry to the Shakespearean topic of Love as the defier of Time, 107; declares that Helen's beauty has reappeared in Cynthia, 164–5; the most 'romantic' of the Roman poets and the only one who has thoroughly exploited the situation of the unrequited lover concealing his distress in romantic solitude, 178–9.

Puttenham, George (or whoever was the author of *The Arte of English Poesie*), on hyperbole, 153–4, 176.

Pythagoras, Ovid's summary of his philosophy in the last book of the *Metamorphoses*, 39.

RILKE, Rainer Maria, culmination in his *Duino Elegies* of a tendency to accept transience as the price of uniqueness, 118; Kassner on his un-Platonicness, 125–6; comparison of his metaphor of one sitting before the stage of his heart with Shakespeare's metaphor of a summoning to the sessions of thought, 204, note 4; his ideal of 'possessionless love', of which he might have found in Shakespeare's Sonnets the most wonderful expression in all literature, 229.

Ronsard (*for sonnets and poems quoted, see separate index*), on poetry as immortalisation (57–69): presumptuous and sometimes absurd imitations of the classical poets on this topic in his odes, 57–8, 63; un-Petrarchan and un-Shakespearean self-exaltation even in his love-sonnets and poems, 58 ff.; adapts to his own glorification some of Petrarch's professions of poetic insufficiency, 59–60, 64; two imitations of the Ovidian phrase which inspired Shakespeare's 'the better part of me', 61; possible influence on Shakespeare, 61–2, 169–70; pieces of self-dramatisation which he may have learnt from some of Horace's odes, 60, 67; Hélène de Surgères merely the occasion for the erection of further monuments to his own glory, 64; comes near to saying that her beauty is an illusion created by himself, 65; imitation and originality in *Quand vous serez bien vieille*, 66–9; on the Petrarchan topic that in his beloved God and Nature have shown once for all what they can achieve, 169–70; various Petrarchan presentations of himself as the solitary lover: hiding his distress among forests and rocks, 180–1, being reminded of her by all he sees, 184–5, being surrounded by delights which are no compensation for her absence, 187–9; less essentially Christian than Shakespeare, and perhaps not without a certain superficiality, 58, note 2; less widely read in England that Du Bellay and Desportes, 61; influence on Spenser, 71–2, 73, 75; possible influence on Daniel, 81; further from Petrarch than Tasso, 78–9, whose two most famous sonnets he seems to have imitated, 54, 66, 68; an anti-hyperbolical sonnet concluding with a Petrarchan compliment, 117; imitated what poets did rather than what rhetoricians described, 152; regrettable that Elizabethan sonneteers did not more often follow his admirable use of rhetorical patterns, instead of trying to translate their conceptions into metaphors, 187–9; often, unlike Shakespeare, at his best when most traditional and imitable, 201.

Rudolf, Archduke, Beethoven's patron, 226–7.

Rufinus, his epigram on the garland sent to Rhodocleia, 98, on Melite, 164.

SAPPHO, may sometimes have promised immortality to her friends and lovers, 30; Horace's lines about her in the Lollius ode imitated by Petrarch, 47, 49; what she considered 'the finest thing on black earth', 209–10, 213.

Seneca, Shakespeare transformed what he borrowed from him to a greater extent than any other Elizabethan dramatist, 36–7.

SHAKESPEARE, WILLIAM,

   1. Sonnets:

      (a) *Chronology and order:* period of composition probably 1597–1607, 14–15; order in the Quarto substantially Shakespeare's own, 13; need not be suspected merely because of variations of style within groups, 15, note, 196, note, 201, note 2; sonnets urging the friend to marry probably the earliest and the result of some external suggestion, 16, 101; sonnets on Love as the defier of Time probably later than those on poetry as its defier, 101; vocabulary, 113, notes 1 and 3, and syntax, 103, note 2, sometimes that of the later plays.

      (b) *Allusions to persons and events:* external facts about 'Mr. W. H.' and the 'Dark Lady', 11–12 (*see also:* 'W. H., Mr.', 'Dark Lady', The, Pembroke, William, third Earl of); death of Queen Elizabeth and accession of James I, 14, 111; disgrace of the Earl of Essex in 1599, 14, 110–11; Jesuit conspiracies and Gunpowder Plot, 14–15, 109; 'Sidney's sister, Pembroke's mother', 18.

      (c) *Topics and attitudes:* preliminary list of large general topics treated in the Sonnets, 21–3; treatment of the topic of poetry as immortalisation compared with Horace, 31–2, 37–8, with Ovid, 33–4, with Propertius, 42, with Petrarch, 49–52, with Ronsard, 58, 75, with Spenser, 75–6, 78, with Daniel, 79, 82, 84–5, with Drayton, 86–91; Shakespeare the only English poet to achieve Horatian and Ovidian resonance on this theme, and never with self-exaltation, 75–6, 78; contrast with Tasso on the topic of 'eternity in love protested', 56–7; sometimes declares, and perhaps always implies, that his friend has been the sole inspirer of his verse, 50, 84; in comparison with the 'realistic' ancients appears as an uncompromising idealist in his habitual defiance of Time, 100–1; sonnets on Love as the defier of Time (102–18): ought they to influence our interpretation of the presumably earlier sonnets on poetry as the Defier of Time?, 102; a statement apparently inconsistent with Shakespeare's habitual defiances of Time, 104; nothing really comparable in other poets with Shakespeare's defiances of Time, 105–8; contrast between the stability of his love and the instability of the political scene a topic peculiar to Shakespeare and Drayton, 109–10; passages in presumably earlier sonnets apparently inconsistent with Shakespeare's declaration that he has been celebrating in his friend only what is beyond the reach of Time, 113–15: solution of this problem—nowhere has he particularised what he has been celebrating, 115–18; a pervading idealism and spirituality, but no specifically philosophical or theological conceptions, distinctions, or terms (119–33): only one sonnet at all like those of Michelangelo and Donne, 119–20; contrast between Michelangelo's sonnets to Vittoria Colonna and Shakespeare's to his friend, 121–4, and attempt to distinguish between their different kinds of 'spirituality', 124–9; desire to escape from the 'strange mutations' of 'this vile world' a link between the sonnets and the tragedies, 132-3, 146, 231; Shakespeare's personifications of Time, Age, and Youth compared with those of Ovid (134-8) and of Horace (138-40): age as hateful to him as to the ancients and to Leopardi, 138, 140, 142; Shakespeare's 'un-Platonic hyperbole' or inverted Platonism defined, exemplified and contrasted with various kinds of poetic *encomia* from ancient times until the Renaissance (149-77): praises his friend's transcendence in a completely untranscendental way, 151; his friend is the incarnation of all past and all possible beauty, etc., 161-3, but not the reminder of a Platonic pattern or idea 'laid up in heaven', 163; resemblances and differences between the kinds of hyperbole and comparison in 'What is your substance, whereof are you made' and those in various poetical *encomia* from ancient times until the Renaissance, 164-71; Shakespeare perhaps not aware that his inverted Platonism was exceptional, 177; significant differences between some of Shakespeare's sonnets written during absence and various appearances of the Solitary Lover in poems from ancient times until the Renaissance (178-202): two situations significantly absent in Shakespeare, 178-83; Petrarch and Ronsard nearest to him when they employ the 'catalogue of uncompensating delights', 185 ff., but they do not declare that these delights are but shadows of the beloved's substance, 195, or suggest, as Shakespeare sometimes does, that there is an element of recognised but love illusion in their love, 199-200; Shakespeare's sonnets on the theme that his friend's love is a compensation for all his own deficiencies, losses, misfortunes and sorrows, 202-6; hard to find even the topic itself in previous European poetry, let alone anything like Shakespeare's treatment of it, 206-9; something more like precedent for his declarations that nothing could be a compensation for the loss of his friend, 209-10, but even here there is nothing really comparable with Shakespeare's passionate vehemence, 211-13; the 'religiousness' of Shakespeare's love (214-31): the only real parallels with his many variations on the theme of 'compensation' are in religious poetry such as Herbert's and Vaughan's, 216-17, although some of Donne's *Songs and Sonets* have a certain affinity with them, despite great differences, 217-26; but while Donne never doubts that he is loved as unalterably as he loves, Shakespeare is haunted by uncertainty and often writes as one who has been deeply wounded and has been made to feel that he is a player, not a gentleman, 226-9; he is celebrating a 'possessionless love', 229; his Sonnets, like the religious poetry of Donne and Herbert, mirror a life of faith, but this faith, unlike theirs, is ultimately not religious but tragic, 229-31.

(*d*) *Absence of certain topics and attitudes:* 'ingrateful beauty threatened', 43, 55; *carpe diem*, 99-100; *carpe florem*, 100-1; pleading and courtship, 79, 181, 216; self-pity, 181; languishing adoration, 183, 216; self-dramatisation, 69, 90; no remarks about the mellowness of age and inexperience of youth, 142; nothing that evokes the creator of the great comic characters and comic scenes, 143; no implicit recognition of 'other kinds of experience which are possible', 143.

(*e*) *Style:* Shakespeare's metaphorical personifications compared with

Horace's, 31-2, 34-5, 138-40, 192, and with Ovid's, 134-8; Dantesquely periphrastic nature of his few allusions to external events, 111-12; abundance of metaphor, but almost no detailed or direct description, 112, 183, 189-90, 194; his impressionistic metaphors: nothing like them except in Pindar and the choruses of Greek tragedy, 190, 202, sometimes incoherent, 191-3; element of 'tragicke Pageant' and allegory perhaps suggested by the example of Spenser, 71; unsatisfactory hovering between metaphor and allegory, 112-13, 197-9, 200-2; hyperbole: the most characteristic feature of Shakespeare's style both in the sonnets and in the tragedies, 116, 155-7, 159, 167; why he only has two anti-hyperbolical sonnets, 116-17; Donne's use of hyperbole sometimes utterly different from Shakespeare's, 171-5, sometimes rather similar, 218; what may have begun as hyperbole in something like the Puttenham sense ended as the only possible means of expression, 175-6; anything like Shakespeare's passionately hyperbolical vehemence not to be found in ancient love-poetry, but only in passages in epic and tragedy expressing hatred or defiance, 213; concentrated generalisation, 194; when most like his contemporaries nearly always below his best, 165, 195, 201, 210; catalogues and repeated pattern very rare, 188, 194; 'poeticisms', 136, 176; slovenly craftsmanship, 69, 161, 165, 196, 225.

2. Poems and Plays:
Venus and Adonis and *The Rape of Lucrece*, two poems dedicated to an earlier friend, 20; *A Lover's Complaint*, l. 250 ('religious love'), 214; *Antony and Cleopatra*: I, i, 33-8 ('Let Rome in Tiber melt'), 215; III, iii, 44 ('This creature's no such thing'), 64; V, ii, 1-8 ('Tis paltry to be Caesar'), 212; V, ii, 86-8 ('For his bounty, there was no winter in't'), 167; V, ii, 198-200 ('Which my love makes religion to obey'), 215; V, ii, 314-21. ('In this vile world?'), 133, 231; *Cymbeline*: IV, iv, 11 ('drive us to a render'), V, iv, 17 ('No stricter render of me than my all'), 113, note 3; *Hamlet*: its variety achieved at the cost of sacrificing intensity, 145; III, i, 59, 70 ('a sea of troubles', 'the whips and scorns of Time'), 205-6; III, iv, 45-8 ('and sweet religion makes A rhapsody of words'), 215; V, ii, 347 ('that fell serjeant Death'), 196, note; V, ii, 358-60 ('And in this harsh world draw thy breath in pain'), 133; *1 Henry IV*: II, iv, 435 ('these harlotry players'), 227; *2 Henry IV*: V, iii, 2 ('a last year's pippin of mine own graffing'), 100; *2 Henry VI*: V, ii, 40 ('let the vile world end'), 132; *King Lear*: IV, i, 3-6 ('The lamentable change is from the best'), 211; IV, i, 10-12 ('strange mutations'), 133, 231; V, ii, 9-11 ('Men must endure Their going hence'), 111, note; V, iii, 314 ('the rack of this tough world'), 133; *Love's Labour's Lost*, V, ii, 413 ('russet yeas and honest kersey noes'), 117; *Macbeth*: I, vii, 21-3 ('Pity, like a naked new-born babe Striding the blast'), 35-6; II, ii, 15-16 ('the crickets cry'), 112, note 2; II, ii, 60-4 ('Will all great Neptune's ocean wash this blood'), 36; *Othello*: I, i, 63 ('in compliment extern'), 113, note; II, i, 186 ff. ('If after every tempest come such calms'), 156; III, iii, 368 ff. ('On horror's head horrors accumulate'), 156; IV, ii, 47 ff. ('Had it pleas'd Heaven'), 230-31; V, ii, 362 ('More fell than anguish, hunger, or the sea'), 159; *Richard II*: I, iii, 229 ('help Time to furrow me with age'), 138; *Romeo and Juliet*: I, ii,

Magistrates, 215; original, like Chaucer and Milton, within, not, like Donne, outside of, the main tradition of European poetry, 177.

Shaw, Bernard, his *Dark Lady of the Sonnets*, 17; his contempt for Shakespeare's 'beglamouring' and 'heroics', 157, 159.

Sidney, Sir Philip (*for sonnets quoted or mentioned, see separate index*), a kind of self-dramatisation he may have learnt from Ronsard, 60, 90; four anti-hyperbolical sonnets, perhaps suggested by Du Bellay and Ronsard, 116–17; possible reminiscence of the pseudo-Virgilian *Lydia* in his sonnet to the moon, 182, note.

Skinner, Cyriack, Milton's sonnet to him, 96, 99.

Sophocles, never felt so old as Shakespeare did, 141; the last speech of his Ajax compared with Othello's, 158.

Spenser, Edmund (*for sonnets quoted, see separate index*), 'Cuddies Embleme' suggests that he is more likely to have derived the notion of the divine inspiration of poets from Ovid than from Plato, 41, note; review of the contents of his *Complaints*, 70; in *The Ruines of Time* was the first English poet to treat memorably the topic of poetic immortality, 70–1; 'E.K.'s commentary on *The Shepheardes Calender* perhaps suggested by the example of Ronsard, whom Spenser is often emulating, 71–2; the topic of poetic immortality in the *Amoretti* (72–8): incongruous combinations of Petrarchan 'keepings' and Ronsardian bragging, 72–5; contrast between the mortality of the verse and the immortality it promises, 76–7; only one really memorable sonnet on this topic, 78; imitation in the *F.Q.* of Tasso's song about gathering the rose of love, 99.

Statius, the phrase 'better half' possibly suggested by him, 33, note.

Strato, epigram quoted, 56, note 2.

Surrey, Henry Howard, Earl of, his imitation of a sonnet of Petrarch's (*see also separate index*), 105, 201, 209.

Swift, Jonathan, on happiness as 'a perpetual possession of being well deceived', 199, 213.

Sylvester, Joshua, his translation of Du Bartas one of the great sources of a certain kind of poetic diction, 136; Shakespeare's 'that fell serjeant Death' and 'that fell arrest' almost certainly suggested by him, 196–7, note.

TASSO, Torquato (*for sonnets quoted, see separate index*), on the eternalising power of poetry, 53–4; two sonnets combining the topics 'ingrateful beauty threatened', 'immortality promised', 'eternity in love protested', 54–6, 81: these imitated by Ronsard (?), 54, 66, 68, Desportes, 54, 79–81, Daniel, 54, 78–82, Drayton (?), 86, note 1: un-Petrarchanness and un-Shakespeareanness of these topics, 55–7, though treated with Petrarchan and Shakespearean absence of self-exaltation, 79; imitated by Spenser in the *Amoretti*, 75, and in the *F.Q.* (gathering the rose of love), 99; his stanzas *Against Beauty*, 208.

Terence, possible influence of a passage in his *Eunuchus* on one in *Othello*, 156, note.

Theocritus, promises immortality to Hieron of Syracuse in his sixteenth Idyll, 28; tenth and twelfth Idylls imitated by Ronsard, 60–1, 189, note; the 'pastoral hyperbole' in his eighth Idyll imitated by Virgil, 165–6; the topic of lamenting Nature, which first appears in his first Idyll, easily lent itself to rhetorical exaggeration, 180.

Theognis, declares that he has made Kyrnos immortal, 29–30.
Thorpe, Thomas, publisher of the Sonnets, 15, 20.
Tibullus,
  1. Passages quoted:
     I, iii, 83 ff., p. 67, iv, 61 ff., p. 42; III, xix, 9–12, pp. 207–8.
  2. General:
     Ovid's funeral elegy upon him, 40–1; on the immortalising power of
     poetry, 42; Homeric passage about Delia spinning by lamplight imitated
     by Ronsard, 67; passage in one of the elegies falsely ascribed to him on
     the general topic that love is enough, 207–8.
Tyler, Thomas, his attempt to identify Mary Fitton with the 'Dark Lady', 17.

VAGANAY, Hugues, his edition of Ronsard, 57, note, 59, note.
Vaughan, Henry, affinity between some things in his poetry and Shakespeare's
  sonnets on the theme of 'compensation', 216–17.
Verdi, Giuseppe, never felt so old as Shakespeare did, 141.
Virgil, a reminiscence of him (Eclogues, II, 17–18) in Tasso's sonnet to Alfonso II,
  54; 'signs' his own name at the end of the Georgics, 63, note 1; metaphor of
  ploughing with wrinkles (Aen. VII, 417), 137; his debt to Homer and Theocritus more demonstrable than that to his rhetorical training, 152; in his
  seventh Eclogue imitates Theocritus's use of the 'pastoral hyperbole', 166; the
  pseudo-Virgilian Lydia quoted, 181–2.

'W. H., MR.' external facts about him in the sonnets, 11–12; William Herbert,
  third Earl of Pembroke, the likeliest candidate for his position, 15–21.
Ward, Mrs. Humphry, wished her Uncle Matthew would more often be 'wholly
  serious', 222.
Warton, Thomas, on Shakespeare as 'the universal and accurate observer of real
  Nature' and on a line in Il Penseroso, 112.
Wilson, F. P., on 'Shakespeare's Reading', 37, note.
Wordsworth, William, his declaration that with the Sonnets 'Shakespeare un-
  locked his heart', 131; influence of Chaucer's Physician's Tales on 'Nature's
  Lady', 171; his lines about 'the bare trees and mountains bare' compared with
  two lines of Shakespeare as an example of concentrated generalisation, 194.

YEATS, W. B., 'When you are old and grey and full of sleep', and The Folly of
  being comforted, their likeness and unlikeness to Ronsard's Quand vous serez bien
  vieille, 69; in his poems about Maud Gonne greatness and particularity advance
  together, 118; on 'the conviction that the commonplace shall inherit the earth',
  158; his assertion that 'Shakespeare cared little for the State', 215.